VOICES for the EARTH

VITAL IDEAS FROM AMERICA'S BEST ENVIRONMENTAL BOOKS

DANIEL D. CHIRAS
editor
and the Sustainable Futures
Society

JOHNSON BOOKS: BOULDER

The titles selected for inclusion in *Voices for the Earth* were nominated by a national committee. The views expressed by the authors in their summaries or excerpts do not necessarily represent the views of the Sustainable Futures Society.

All author royalties will be paid to the Sustainable Futures Society.

Cover design by Bob Schram/Bookends

Cover photograph by Bill Ross/Westlight

Library of Congress Cataloging-in-Publication Data

Chiras, Daniel D.
    Voices for the earth : vital ideas from America's best
environmental writers / Daniel D. Chiras and the Sustainable Futures
Society.
        p.   cm.
    Includes bibliographical references.
    ISBN 1-55566-146-7 (alk. paper)
    1. Environmental degradation.   2. Environmental protection.
3. Sustainable development.   I. Sustainable Futures Society.
II. Title.
GE140.C482   1995
363.7—dc20   95-11887
                                                           CIP

Printed in the United States by
Johnson Printing
1880 South 57th Court
Boulder, Colorado 80301

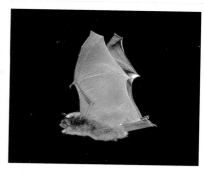

VOICES
for the EARTH

*To my dear friend
Lynn Vanatta, a bright
star in the nighttime
sky.*

TABLE OF CONTENTS

INTRODUCTION

Humorist Ogden Nash once quipped, "There has been lots of progress during my lifetime, but I'm afraid it's heading in the wrong direction." Except for those individuals who live with blinders on, most people would agree with this view. Most would concur that although our lives may be getting better, our long-term prospects are eroding. Dirty air, crowded cities, lost species, and vanishing open space seem unsustainable. Economist Herman Daly put it best when he wrote: "Most nations are treating the Earth as a corporation in liquidation."

Many of us wonder, often out loud, if society can find a path that provides for our needs—allowing people to reach their full potential, permitting us to live comfortably, and permitting our culture to flourish —without creating deserts and toxic waste dumps in our footsteps or without turning our skies into grimy smears across the horizon.

We at the Sustainable Futures Society think that the people of the world can meet our needs without bankrupting the only habitable piece of real estate in the solar system. In fact, we believe that humankind can go further. That is, we can meet our needs while improving on our future, creating a better world for all Earth's inhabitants.

Protecting and restoring the Earth's ecological life support systems, however, will require profound changes in our economy and our way of life. But that is not all.

To live sustainably on the Earth will necessitate a dramatic shift in the way we think. No longer can we view the world in mechanistic ways. We must learn to think in terms of systems. We must also shift our time frame for decision-making. Many proponents of change also call for a shift in our ethical realm to create a new, Earth-friendly belief system that mutually benefits people, the economy, and the planet.

To help stimulate the necessary shifts in the ways we think and act, we at the Sustainable Futures Society invited a distinguished group of authors, educators, scholars, and activists to nominate books that they felt offered the clearest analyses of contemporary social, economic, and environmental problems and the best solutions for restructuring our world for sustainability.

The authors whose books were nominated for inclusion in this, our inaugural edition of *Voices for the Earth*, were then asked to pen summaries of their books—succinct accounts that showcased their main ideas and insights. Our intent was to provide overviews of what some of the world's leading thinkers have to offer. Our fondest hope in launching this project was to create a vehicle that would help disseminate vital ideas to a global audience and, in so doing, to help foster the growing synergy between environment and development that has emerged since the Earth Summit in 1992. We also hope that these cutting-edge ideas will stimulate action that's badly needed to steer human society onto a sustainable course.

This book provides an opportunity to scan the landscape of contemporary thought. It also provides a chance to explore new ideas. You may find in it familiar titles that you have already read. In such cases, *Voices for the Earth* will provide an opportunity to refresh your memory or to reacquaint yourself with some of the information that may have gotten misfiled in your gray matter.

Voices for the Earth is a forum for what we hope will be an exciting and challenging discourse on the future of human civilization. In assembling this work, we found that some of the ideas presented here contradict others. This is not unexpected, and we think it adds to the depth of the book and the openness of debate that must occur as we chart and experiment with a new future. Ralph Waldo Emerson once reminded us that "life is a perpetual instruction in cause and effect." In any event, we encourage all readers to explore the authors' conclusions and to debate these ideas so that ultimately we can all find a path to a mutually satisfying, humane, and sustainable future.

Daniel D. Chiras, Editor
Evergreen, Colorado

Nomination Committee Members*

Ann Causey, Faculty Member, Auburn University
Barbara Dean, Senior Editor, Island Press
Hazel Henderson, Author, Futurist
Gary Huber, Director, Sustainable Futures Society
Amory and Hunter Lovins, Rocky Mountain Institute
Rod Nash, Professor, University of California, Santa Barbara
Charles Olmstead, Professor, University of Northern Colorado
Sandra Postel, Vice President, Worldwatch Institute
David Wann, Author, EPA policy analyst, Denver
Dale Whitney, Instructor, Metro State College
David Williams, Special Assistant, Bureau Land Management

*Committee members were asked to nominate two to three titles for inclusion in the first edition of *Voices for the Earth*. Because many committee members are also authors or are associated with publishers, we asked them not to nominate their own books, a request all participants honored ungrudgingly.

Acknowledgments

The Sustainable Futures Society and I would like to thank all of the extraordinary authors who contributed essays to this collection. Their hard work and dedication to this project has been heartening. We greatly appreciate their timely submission of articles and willingness to respond to editorial comments. We would also like to thank the publishing companies that permitted us to publish excerpts and adapted material for this work. A world of thanks to authors and publishers alike for helping make this dream—and this vehicle for the dissemination of vital ideas—a reality!

Many thanks also to Debbie Browne who helped develop an effective marketing plan for the Sustainable Futures Society and to Carole Newman of the Sustainable Futures Society who helped with many of the day-to-day chores associated with a project of this magnitude and also helped promote the book. Thanks also to Wendy Luck, board member of the Sustainable Futures Society, for her efforts to help promote this book.

Three talented authors, Charles Fletcher, Patricia Wafer, and Lloyd Timberlake, also deserve many thanks for excerpting and writing Dave Foreman's, Garrett Hardin's, and Stephan Schmidheiny's chapters, respectively. I would also like to thank all of the members of the Sustainable Futures Society for their moral and financial support.

Finally, a special thanks to my generous parents, my dear friends, and my two delightful sons, Skyler and Forrest, for providing a much-needed counterbalance to the hectic and tumultuous pace of my life.

A Word about the Sustainable Futures Society

Offering creative solutions to society's most pressing problems . . .

Mission: To foster a transition to a global sustainable society.

Goals: To promote a broader understanding of the principles, policies, and practices of sustainability and to encourage their adoption.

Audience: Our programs address a high-impact audience consisting of influential local, state, and national policymakers, journalists, business leaders, environmentalists, educators, and citizens—that is, people whose decisions and actions can help shape a sustainable future.

What is a Sustainable Society? A sustainable society is one that meets the needs of present generations while ensuring future generations the ability to meet theirs. It enables people to reach their full potential, yet protects the planet's rich biodiversity.

Sustainable development requires root-level solutions to the problems of our times. Most experts agree that in order for a solution to be sustainable, it must make sense simultaneously from at least three perspectives: social, economic, and environmental.

How do we get there? The Sustainable Futures Society believes that human civilization can steer onto a sustainable course by using the resources we need and using them efficiently, by recycling all materials to the maximum extent possible, by tapping into the generous supplies of clean, economical renewable energy, by restoring damaged ecosystems, and by stabilizing population. We also firmly believe that to create an enduring human presence we need changes in our ethics and fundamental changes in the systems that provide for human needs, for instance, transportation, housing, waste management, energy, and so on.

Sustainable Futures Society Programs

• Sustainable Development Program. Our sustainable development program helps communities, states, and nations understand the need for and adopt sustainable development strategies. We're currently focusing on rural communities in the United States and have developed a one-day workshop to assist communities in understanding the principles and practices of sustainability.

• Policy Analysis Program. This program offers in-depth analysis of public policies in a variety of areas, including economics, energy, environment, transportation, housing, waste management, and a host of other areas. Our organization analyzes policies and suggests revisions, or proposes new policies, if necessary, to promote sustainable development goals and objectives.

• National Indicators Project. We have developed a set of social, economic, and environmental indicators for the state of Colorado and have assembled a team that can provide similar service for other states and communities. We are also preparing an alternative set of indicators of progress for the United States, which will be published in our book *State of the Nation*.

• The *Voices for the Earth* series offers in-depth summaries of the best environmental books of the 1980s and 1990s written by the authors themselves and nominated by a panel of leading environmental thinkers.

• Conferences, workshops, and seminars on sustainability with high-impact policymakers, business people, journalists, and educators.

Basic Benefits Package

As a member you receive:

• Three issues per year of our newsletter, *Sustainable Futures*

• Free copies of *Voices for the Earth* and other books published by the Sustainable Futures Society.

• 20-percent discounts on all conferences, workshops, publications, slide shows, and other products

- The opportunity to actively participate in our programs

- The satisfaction that you're part of a positive, creative movement to create a sustainable society

For more information or to join, contact us at our national headquarters at 5947 Brook Forest Road (before July 1, 1995) or 9124 Armadillo Trail (after July 1, 1995), Evergreen, Colorado 80439, or call (303) 674-9688.

PART I

SIGNS OF DESPAIR/SIGNS OF HOPE:
CREATING A NEW SYNTHESIS

Anne LaBastille

MAMA POC
AN ECOLOGIST'S ACCOUNT OF AN
EXTRAORDINARY EXTINCTION

Anne LaBastille made her book writing debut in 1978 with the publication of
Woodswoman. *A riveting tale of life on the shores of a remote wilderness lake in the
Adirondack Mountains,* Woodswoman *recounts the hardships the author endured
living in solitude close to the land as well as the many joys of a simple existence. It
details her love of nature that has inspired a stellar career. Whether fighting to protect the wilderness lake she writes about in* Woodswoman *or speaking out against
careless development in the Adirondacks, this tireless ally to all who love the Earth
graces us with her vision, passion, and dedication.*

In her summary of Mama Poc, *Anne LaBastille recounts an ecological horror story,
the tale of the giant grebe, a charming Guatemalan bird that over a brief period of
twenty-five years slid into oblivion right before her eyes. Subject to natural forces beyond
human control as well as countless ecologically careless human activities, the giant grebe
is now officially listed as extinct. Although this account may engender great sadness in
a world filled with despair, it reminds us that extinction at the hands of human beings
is a frightening, almost inexorable phenomenon. It also serves as a warning to us. As
we pollute our air and water and tear apart the biological infrastructure of our lives,
we too may be on an ecological slide edging ever closer to extinction.*

Adapted with permission from Anne LaBastille, Mama Poc: An Ecologist's
Account of an Extraordinary Extinction, *W. W. Norton Co., New York, 1991.
A version of this story also appeared in* International Wildlife.

What can I say as I skim my binoculars along the shoreline of Lake Atitlán (Ah-tít-lon) these days, knowing my beloved giant grebes are gone? How do I feel when I gaze over one of the loveliest lakes on Earth, seeing it daily grow more murky, polluted, and crowded each day?

My brain shrugs cynically—twenty-four years of research, commitment, and conservation efforts wasted. My heart rallies hopefully—perhaps the grebes were martyrs to the larger cause of saving the lake and its watershed. But my soul reels from witnessing the swift, brutal extinction of a species.

I didn't know what kind of bird swam by me in 1960 at Lake Atitlán in the Guatemalan highlands. Roughly the size of a wood duck, it was charcoal black with a massive head, black throat, and broad white beak circled with a black mark. Its crisp white eye ring and tuft of a tail gave the waterbird an alert, jaunty appearance. Yet, existing field guides showed no such species. Local Indians told me it was a "funny duck," or the "poc" ("Poc" is the Maya Indian name for giant grebes).

Full of curiosity, I visited Guatemala City's Museum of Natural History. The director, Jorge Ibarra, proudly showed me his only museum specimen and pronounced it a giant piedbilled grebe.

"This bird lives *only* at Lake Atitlán," Dr. Ibarra said solemnly, "and is *very* rare. It can't fly and barely walks. Dr. Ludlow Griscom, your famous American ornithologist, named and described it in 1929 and counted over two hundred. Then, Dr. Alexander Wetmore, head of the Smithsonian Institution, visited in 1936, censused the same number, and confirmed that *Podilymbus gigas* was a 'truly huge' distinct species. That's about all we know."

How amazing, I thought, to find an animal on which there was so little known. The challenge of writing a popular article about the pocs grew in my mind. I flew to Central America the winter of 1964–65, intending to spend four to eight *weeks* at Lake Atitlán. I never realized it would be the start of twenty-four *years* trying to save the grebes and the lake, or that this would lead to a doctoral thesis, several articles, scientific papers, and my book, *Mama Poc* (New York: W.W. Norton Co., 1990). As far as can be determined, I'm the first ecologist to have carefully documented an animal from a healthy balanced population to zero; and its habitat from a sound ecosystem to a badly decimated one within two decades.

At twilight shortly before Christmas, I disembarked from a clattering old bus in the Indian town of Panajachel and walked to the shores of Lake Atitlán. Immense thunderheads of pewter, their tops tinged with peach, towered above the three volcanoes that backdrop the lake. Flashes of lightning lit up their bowels and thunder rumbled over the distant Pacific coast. Gray wavelets with highlights of electric blue lapped restlessly on the beach. I caught my breath at the majestic scene.

Atitlán! "Big water!" How aptly named. The lake is a mile high and 1,200 feet deep, with volcanoes towering 11,300 feet above it and 75 miles of precipitous shoreline surrounding it. Crossroads of turbulent winds collide over the lake each afternoon, producing the dreaded "chocomil" (fury of the demons). At other times, cold northers whip up four-foot waves making travel by boat dangerous.

Next morning I was innocently exploring the reed beds, determined to find all the pocs and pick the best ones for photos and observations. With my bare feet, blond pigtails, khaki field clothes, and binoculars, I was soon recognized at the "crazy gringa bird lady." That term of endearment, "Mama Poc," came later.

Over the next month, I covered every foot of shoreline and censused each poc, coot, gallinule, and duck. I even counted thirty-two weekend chalets that shared the lakefront with twelve colorful Indian villages. Something was wrong, though. Instead of the two-hundred-plus giant grebes found in 1960, only eighty existed.

Troubled, I consulted Armando, the blue-eyed, burly, kindly Guatemalan who rented me his motorboat and assisted me in his spare time. "You may have missed some birds," he counseled. "They are so wary and dive so far. You should try counting at night with a full moon. No wind. Use your tape recorder. I'll help you."

But after three nights of cruising that quick-silvered lake past pitch-black reeds, we found only eighty birds! How could the world's entire population of these flightless grebes be cut by more than one-half in five years?

I stayed on during the six-month dry season and discovered many things. Hunting and poaching were *not* major problems. Natives seldom ate these fish-eating birds. Indians harvested reeds and had for centuries. They weave bed mats and little seats for their huts since they don't use modern furniture. This fragile fringe of wetland vegetation—fifteen miles out of the seventy-five—was the only roosting, hiding, and nesting habitat for waterbirds, small fishes, and young crabs. Although this cottage industry did diminish available habitat, it didn't seem a sufficient reason for the sudden decline of the grebes.

I also unearthed a law passed in 1959 that prohibited killing or molesting pocs and other waterbirds at Lake Atitlán. Another, passed in 1955, declared Atitlán and its watershed a national park. No one knew about them, however, and there was no enforcement by game wardens or park rangers in Guatemala then.

My biggest discovery was that Pan American Airlines and the Panajachel Tourist Board had introduced two thousand largemouth bass fingerlings into Atitlán in 1960 to improve sport fishing and attract tourists. No thought was given to possible environmental impacts in those early days.

Largemouth bass are notorious carnivores. By surveying fifty-six local fishermen and crabmen, I confirmed that the numbers of tiny native fishes and freshwater crabs, which they depended upon for food, had dropped dramatically. Because Indians earned about $100 to $300 annually, they could not afford fishing tackle or spear guns to catch bass. They used small hooks and lines or underwater wicker traps baited with corn. Coincidentally, an on-going medical anthropological study by Stanford University confirmed that many Indians were suffering from protein deficiency.

The largest bass caught weighed twenty-five pounds. Such fish could easily swallow frogs, water snakes, and young waterbirds. I hypothesized that bass were competing directly with both the pocs *and* the Indians for food, and probably preying on the chicks of giant grebes. No wonder the poc population had plummeted. Whereas it had taken ten thousand or more years of evolution to turn this once-migratory species into a flightless species, an Ice Age relic, it could be wiped out in a split second of geologic time by this unwise exotic introduction. I simply *had* to save the giant grebes.

Accordingly, I increased my time on the lake, recording poc behavior, calls, food habits, and reproductive displays. I verified that pocs could not fly, being aerodynamically incapable with their small wings and chunky bodies. They had "traded" flight for diving and swimming over the centuries. So have two other grebe species on Lakes Titicaca and Junin in Peru. I also collected four adult specimens and shipped them to Cornell and Yale universities.

In March, after days of struggling through some of the densest, tallest reeds on Earth, I found my first nest. It was a monstrous cone of soggy reeds that weighed close to one hundred pounds! Here, I glimpsed my first chick. The precocious puffball was striped like a little zebra. It stared at me boldly before scrambling over the nest edge, diving a few inches, and popping to the surface like a tiny cork. One parent waited nearby, calling "poc-poc-poc." The baby climbed onto its back and nestled safely into the feathers. Only two hours old. Imagine!

One day near the nest site, I met Edgar Bauer, a young, courteous coffee farmer. He offered to let me work along his shore where many pocs lived. During my hours sitting in the boat, I conceived of a conservation plan called "Operation Protection Poc." It combined enforcement, conservation education, habitat management, arts and crafts, and a small sanctuary. *If* I could get grant money, maybe this campaign could stop the giant grebes' downward slide and return them to former numbers.

Back in the States that summer, I received funding, applied for a Ph.D. program at Cornell, and interested *National Geographic* in a possible article. On return to Guatemala, I contacted the minister of agriculture. He promised to match my modest funds, appoint a game warden, supply gas for the boat and building supplies for the refuge. While Edgar, my coffee farmer friend, and I sat sipping espresso under his giant avocados, I asked if he would become the part-time game warden. To my delight he agreed. Best of all, the minister appointed Armando, my Guatemalan assistant, and me as honorary ones. All my life I'd wished to work in this field, but no women wardens were allowed in those days. As far as I knew, in 1966, I was the only female conservation officer in the Western Hemisphere, albeit a foreign and honorary one!

My second dry season was full of activity. Jorge Ibarra, the museum director, lectured in the elementary schools. He told the kids how the birds only lived here and were 100 percent Guatemalan. Armando started laying out a stone wall and visitors center at the reed-lined cove we'd chosen for a sanctuary. Edgar patiently oversaw the workmen and delivered building supplies with his boat. He also patrolled and put up poc posters in every Maya village. Local painters and weavers began using the poc motif and selling these crafts in local markets. Fortunately, I'd hit upon two points most persuasive to Latin and Indian mentalities—national pride in the birds and local economics.

Next we held a meeting with the Mayan reed cutters and hammered out a compromise between cutting reeds and saving habitat. This became a presidential decree in 1968 and did much to help the pocs.

Suddenly, David G. Allen, an American bird photographer, was sent down by *National Geographic*. Armando and I abandoned everything to assist him for a month while he obtained superb photos.

Then, two more successes took place. World Wildlife Fund, International, sent money for a new motorboat for Edgar. And, the Guatemalan National Postal Service took my suggestion to print beautiful postage stamps of grebes. Besides the First Day Cover (a philatelist's term for the special combination of stamps sold only on the first day a new stamp series is issued and is usually on one sheet of paper), there were a four-cent (local), a nine-cent (Central America), and a twenty-one-cent (air mail). At last my giant grebes could fly!

Within two-and-a-half years, the series sold out and grossed $123,000. How I wished I'd gotten my hands on that money for Operation Protection Poc. We completed the refuge during the winter of 1967 and had removed the bass and restocked the lake with six thousand native fishes. Now it was time to catch and transfer pocs. This last job proved hardest of all. We tried traps, decoys, mirrors, night-lighting with nets, scuba, canoes, and Indians but *nothing* worked. Finally, using a time-consuming snare method, I caught two pairs and put them in the small refuge. Within two years, they produced chicks. Celebrating with a gala inauguration under a rainbow sky, the Guatemalan government declared this its first national wildlife refuge.

Before I left for Cornell, Armando and I checked *every* lake in Guatemala to see if another place might serve to raise pocs. Afterwards, I could truthfully say that only Lake Atitlán contained the unique set of ecological and geological conditions that allowed giant grebes to survive.

By spring 1968, wild pocs had increased to more than 125 birds—a remarkable rise from a low of eighty. My estimate of carrying capacity for Atitlán was 280 grebes. Our modest conservation campaign (especially habitat protection), it appeared, had reversed the trend towards extinction and nudged the pocs back to their historical numbers. Things were in safe, capable hands with my two friends and the government, or so I thought. It was time to earn my Ph.D. With tearful farewells, I left Armando, Edgar, and the grebes, promising to come back often.

On a hot June day at Cornell, I opened a letter from Edgar and read that the National Institute for Electrification had proposed a hydroelectric project for Lake Atitlán. Underwater tunnels would drain water down to Pacific slope turbines. Four rivers would be diverted into the lake. The lake would drop twenty-three feet in ten years. That would be the end of the reeds and pocs.

I was a "prisoner" to the university. So I rounded up several professors to get advice. One scientist predicted that in only seventy-seven years the sapphire-blue, crystal-clear lake water would be replaced with dirty brown river water. We wrote to key conservation figures, including Prince Bernhard, Prince Phillip, and Sir Peter Scott. Our thrust was *not* to stop energy development, but to urge *alternative sources* and save this magnificent lake, the Indians' fish and reeds, and a growing tourist economy.

Months later, Edgar wrote that the project had been halted and other solutions sought. By now I was a freelance writer and consultant, so could only visit Atitlán for short periods. The government continued Operation Protection Poc, and the World Wildlife Fund provided Edgar with another patrol boat. The poc population had increased to 232.

Then came the devastating earthquake of 1976. Twenty-three thousand people were killed in Guatemala and deep fissures opened on Lake Atitlán's floor. The water level started falling. When only two feet of water were left in the refuge, we *had* to release the grebes. Setting them free filled us with despair. I cried, looking over the empty refuge. Two years later it was bone dry and planted with corn and beans. The lake gives, and the lake takes away . . .

Edgar, an expert agronomist, watched the reeds yellow and die. One day he said calmly, "Anna, if I can grow coffee, I can grow reeds." Calling sixty Mayan reed cutters together, he and Pedro, his assistant, asked for volunteers. In two-and-a-half years, they transplanted seventy-five thousand clumps of reeds from shallower to deeper water. Edgar estimated a 75-percent survival rate.

Nevertheless, when I spent three weeks there in 1980, the ecological picture looked grim. The lake had dropped twelve feet in four years. Half the habitat was gone (only 6½ miles left). Moreover, people had "discovered" Lake Atitlán. I now counted 308 chalets with another forty-five more under construction. Owners were pulling out reeds to make beaches, docks, and terraces. There was no law to control this activity. A three-tower, sixteen-story condominium loomed near Panajachel—an intrusion on that tranquil landscape. Worst of all, Edgar and I counted only 130 grebes. That meant one hundred had vanished in five years! Why?

Following my visit I had no word from Edgar for months. News was full of the political unrest in Central America. The U.S. State Department issued a travel advisory for Guatemala, so I canceled plans to return. Finally, Pedro wrote. I learned that on May 7, 1982, Edgar was killed by unknown assailants at night on his farm. His buildings were burned down and the WWF boat disappeared. Not only was Operation Protection Poc over, but I had lost a loyal friend and colleague. The giant grebes were now listed in I.U.C.N.'s *Red Data Books* as highly endangered and threatened with extinction.

A year later, Pedro wrote me again. He was now a government game warden. The WWF boat had been found inside a reed bed, faded and corroded, but still serviceable.

The civil war eased. In 1984, I found myself in an old boat with seven other biologists crossing Lake Atitlán. In a cooperative international effort, the Guatemalan government, U.S. Fish and Wildlife Service, and International Council for Bird Preservation had arranged for us to make a new census and consider captive breeding pocs. It was a last-ditch attempt, for the birds were down to fifty-five. When a population reaches fifty or less, its chances of survival become minimal and genetic viability and variability are lost.

A private zoological park offered their facilities and a young graduate student, Susan McVean, flew down. But, because so little is known about raising grebes of any kind—there are only twenty-one species worldwide—we decided to begin our work with common piedbills. They are close relatives of giants which are abundant and can fly. However, I'd seen very few at Atitlán. Susan raised two clutches and next planned to try giants. Unfortunately, she never got the chance.

Our team found that the water level in Atitlán had dropped sixteen feet and fishermen were using gill nets that could easily have drown the pocs. The human population had more than doubled since 1964 and villagers needed more food. Saddest of all was the old refuge. Apparently the visitors center had been used as a military outpost with machine guns and sandbags replacing cameras and binoculars. After all the love and commitment lavished here, it was a bitter lesson for me: nobody cares about wildlife during war.

The U.S. Fish and Wildlife Service sent Dr. Laurie Hunter to the lake in 1986–87 to investigate *why* grebe numbers were still slipping. I flew down to help her with a new census. In the first fifteen miles of shoreline, we saw no birds and scarcely any reeds. Then, a very skittish, very brownish grebe swam by. "I *think* it's a poc," I said, "but . . . something's different."

"I've seen this one fly," replied Laurie soberly. "And others are nesting throughout the year instead of only in March, April, and May. I think Common [grebes] have pushed out giants, or hybridized with them."

We counted only thirty-two grebes that week. Later Laurie live-trapped, weighed, and measured twelve of these. They were all commons, not giants, not hybrids. No more than twenty pocs could exist, if that. In June 1987, Dr. Hunter, announced to the international scientific community that the poc, *as a species,* was extinct.

I grieved all summer. Questions plagued me. How long should a person, or a country, keep fighting to save an endangered species? How much should be spent? I realized that Guatemala was just recovering from severe political problems and could hardly afford a program like that underway in the United States to save the California condor. Finally, I admitted the no-win combination of food loss (bass), habitat destruction by natural events and human actions, and competition by common grebes had been too much for the pocs.

Gradually, I directed my sorrow into preparing an educational exhibit about the pocs and donating it to the Museum of Natural History and the Guatemalan public.

Jorge Ibarra, the Guatemalan Institute of Tourism, and I inaugurated this exhibit in November 1987. It was a gala affair with over 350 guests. That evening we started "Amigos de Lago Atitlán," a volunteer citizens group pledged to protect the lake and prevent pollution. Lastly, the late Edgar Bauer received the credit he so richly deserved.

During a trip to Atitlán in 1993, Pedro and I found the lake was dying. It had dropped twenty-four feet and now 501 luxurious weekend homes ringed the shores. The fragile band of shoreline reeds and cattails upon which all aquatic life and water quality depends was 83 percent gone. Raw sewage and storm water was running directly into the lake from four villages. Plastic litter floated everywhere and brilliant green strands of algae edged some villages. Indian women still washed dirty clothing with non-biodegradable soaps in the lake, adding to the lake's pollution. On any given morning, over four hundred women can be seen doing their families' laundry in Atitlán. Pedro and I saw what looked like four giant grebes, but we didn't even bother with them now.

So what did it all amount to? Certainly I honed my skills as an ecologist, made wonderful friends, educated people about conservation, and helped both Maya Indians and pocs for a while. I was a good Mama Poc; and I think that Operation Protection Poc served as a good model for Guatemala at a time when no other existed.

On the other hand, Edgar was murdered, pocs are extinct, and the lake's tranquil shores are crowded and soiled. The birds were surely biological indicators of a larger disaster to this ecosystem. They were the "keystone species" which, once gone, started the rest of the chain crumbling. How much is repairable? How much is irreversible? It's hard to know.

What happened to my grebe and Lake Atitlán is not unique. It is occurring all over the world. This single true story of an incredible extinction in one microcosm is being repeated every day, every year. By various estimates, between forty to one hundred species become extinct every day. While some may seem unimportant—like ants or grass or a flightless bird—we can never know the true value of a species until its gone. Sometimes the smallest creature can be highly significant in the web of life.

For me, the plight of the poc is a parable to warn us to take much, much better care of our planet and the many species that share it with us.

Dave Foreman

CONFESSIONS OF AN ECO-WARRIOR

Why do we continue to destroy the wilderness in the name of social and economic progress? Do citizens have a right to defend our vanishing wilderness through ecotage—or monkey wrenching? Is ecotage a legitimate means of social expression or a subversive attack on progress? In this summary of his stirring book, Confessions of an Eco-Warrior, *Dave Foreman unabashedly stands firmly on the side of wilderness, outlining what is wrong with our current thinking and our way of life. Foreman offers more than criticism, however. His book presents a wide array of solutions that many may find threatening—for example, the establishment of large environmental reserves to protect species diversity. Are his ideas radical? Yes, but especially so if you ignore or deny the primal importance of Earth to human life and to the survival of the millions of species that share this planet with us. Are his ideas necessary and important? Only time will tell.*

The ecologist Raymond Dasmann says that World War III has already begun, and that it is the war of industrial humans against the Earth. He is correct. All of us are warriors on one side or another in this war; there are no sidelines, there are no civilians. Ours is the last generation that will have the choice of wilderness, clean air, abundant wildlife, and expansive forests. The crisis *is* that severe.

We are living now in the most critical moment of the three-and-a-half-billion-year history of life on Earth. For this unimaginably long time, life has been developing, expanding, blossoming, and diversifying, filling every available niche with different manifestations of itself, intertwined in complex, globe-girdling relationships. But today this diversity of perhaps 30 million species faces radical and unprecedented change. Never before—not even 65 million years ago during the mass extinctions of the dinosaurs at the end of the Cretaceous era—has there been such a high rate of extinction as we are now witnessing, such a drastic reduction of the planet's biological diversity.

Not only is this blitzkrieg against the natural world destroying ecosystems and their associated species, but our activities are now beginning to have fundamental, systemic effects upon the entire life-supporting apparatus of the planet: upsetting the world's climate; poisoning the oceans; destroying the atmospheric ozone layer that protects us from excessive ultraviolet radiation; changing the CO_2 ratio in the atmosphere and causing the "greenhouse effect"; and spreading acid rain, radioactive fallout, pesticides, and industrial contamination throughout the biosphere. Clearly, in such a time of crisis, the conservation battle is not one of merely protecting outdoor recreation opportunities or a matter of aesthetics or "wise management and use" of natural resources. It is a battle for life itself, for the continued flow of evolution.

The crisis we now face calls for *passion*. When I worked as a conservation lobbyist in Washington, D.C., I was told to put my heart in a safe deposit box and replace my brain with a pocket calculator. I was told to be rational, not emotional, to use facts and figures, to quote economists and scientists. I would lose credibility, I was told, if I let my emotions show. But, damn it, I am an animal. A living being of flesh and blood, storm and fury. The oceans of the Earth course through my veins, the winds of the sky fill my lungs, the very bedrock of the planet makes my bones. I am alive! I am not a machine, a mindless automaton, a cog in the industrial world, some New Age android. When a chain saw slices into the heartwood of a two-thousand-year-old coast redwood, it's slicing into my guts. When a bulldozer rips through the Amazon rain forest, it's ripping into my side. When a Japanese whaler fires an exploding harpoon into a great whale, my heart is blown to smithereens. I am the land, the land is me. Why shouldn't I be emotional, angry, and passionate? Madmen and madwomen are wrecking this beautiful, blue-green, living Earth. Fiends who hold nothing of value but a greasy dollar bill are tearing down the pillars of evolution abuilding for nearly four thousand million years.

Along with passion, we need *vision*. We must envision and propose the restoration of biological wildernesses of several million acres in all of America's ecosystems, with corridors between them for the transmission of genetic variability. Wilderness is the arena for evolution, and there must be enough of it for natural forces to have free rein.

Passion and vision are essential, but without *action* they are empty. The Earth is crying. Do we hear it? Martin Luther King Jr. once said that "if one has nothing worth dying for, one has nothing worth living for." In 1848, Henry David Thoreau went to jail for refusing, as a protest against the Mexican War, to pay his poll tax. When Ralph Waldo Emerson came to bail him out, Emerson said, "Henry, what are you doing in there?" Thoreau quietly replied, "Ralph, what are you doing out there?"

Earth First!

The early conservation movement in the United States was a child—and no bastard child—of the establishment. They were an elite band, sportsmen of the Teddy Roosevelt variety, naturalists like John Borroughs, outdoorsmen in the mold of John Muir, pioneer foresters and ecologists on the order of Aldo Leopold, and wealthy social reformers like Gifford Pinchot and Robert Marshall. It was not until Earth Day in 1970 that the environmental movement received its first real influx of the antiestablishment radicals, as Vietnam War protesters found a new cause, the environment.

As a conservation lobbyist, I learned that extremists were ignored in the councils of government. We tried to demonstrate that preserving wilderness did not conflict all that much with the gross national product, and that clean air actually helped the economy. During the Carter Years, editorials proclaimed that environmentalism had been enshrined in the establishment, that conservation was here to stay. But we had lost to timber, mining, and cattle interests on every point. Of 80 million acres still roadless and undeveloped in the 190 million acres of national forests, the Department of Agriculture recommended that only 15 million receive protection from road building and timber cutting. Moreover, damn it, we, the conservationists, had been moderate. The antienvironmental side had been extreme, radical, and emotional, their arguments full of holes. We had been factual, rational. We had provided more—and better—serious public comment. But we lost.

We lost in part because wilderness, after all, is the most radical notion in human thought. Wilderness says: Human beings are not paramount, Earth is not for *Homo sapiens* alone, human life is but one life form on the planet and has no right to take exclusive possession. Yes, wilderness for its own sake, without any need to justify it for human benefit. Wilderness for wilderness. Because it is the laboratory of human evolution, and because it is home.

So it was only proper that on March 21, 1981, at the spring equinox, the traditional time of rebirth, Earth First! held its first national gathering at Glen Canyon Dam. The five of us on the dam attached rope to a grill, shouted out "Earth First!" and let three hundred feet of black plastic unfurl down the side of the dam, creating the impression of a growing crack. Those on the bridge returned the cheer. Then Edward Abbey told the protesters of the "green and living wilderness" that was Glen Canyon. "And they took it away from us. The politicians, in cahoots with the developers, stole this treasure from us in order to pursue and promote their crackpot ideology of growth, profit, and power—growth for the sake of power, power for the sake of growth. Oppose. And if opposition is not enough, we must resist. And if resistance is not enough, then subvert."

Earth First! was founded on the following principles:

- *A placing of Earth first in all decisions, even ahead of human welfare if necessary.* The primary consideration should be for the long-term health and biological diversity of Earth.
- *A refusal to use human beings as the measure by which to value others.* An individual human life has no more intrinsic value than does an individual grizzly bear life.
- *An enthusiastic embracing of the philosophy of Deep Ecology or biocentrism.* All living creatures and communities possess intrinsic value, inherent worth.
- *A realization that wilderness is the real world.* Remember that only a tiny portion of the history of the human species has occurred outside of wilderness.
- *A recognition that there are far too many human beings on Earth.* Even if inequitable distribution could be solved, 6 billion human beings

converting the natural world to material goods and human food would devastate natural diversity.

- *A deep questioning of, and even an antipathy to, "progress" and "technology."* For every material achievement of progress, there are a dozen losses of things of profound and ineffable value.
- *A refusal to accept rationality as the only way of thinking.* We can become more cognizant of ultimate truths by sitting quietly in the wild than by studying in a library.
- *A lack of desire to gain credibility of "legitimacy" with the gang of thugs running human civilization.* The American system is very effective at co-opting and moderating dissidents by giving them attention and then encouraging them to be "reasonable" so their ideas will be taken seriously.
- *An effort to go beyond the tired, worn-out dogmas of left, right, and middle-of-the-road.* These doctrines, whether blaming capitalism, communism, or the devil for all the problems in the world, merely represent internecine squabbles between different factions of humanism.
- *An unwillingness to set any ethnic, class, or political group of humans on a pedestal and make them immune from questioning.* Workers are victims of an unjust economic system, but that does not absolve them of what they do.
- *A willingness to let our actions set the finer points of our philosophy and a recognition that we must act.* We will never figure it all out, we will never be able to plan any campaign in complete detail, none of us will ever entirely transcend a polluting lifestyle, but we can act. We can act with courage, with determination, with love for things wild and free.
- *An acknowledgment that we must change our personal lifestyles to make them more harmonious with natural diversity.* Arne Naess, the Norwegian philosopher and originator of the term "Deep Ecology," points out that we are not able to achieve a true Deep Ecology lifestyle, but it is the responsibility of each of us to move in that direction.
- *A commitment to maintain a sense of humor and a joy of living.* We're fighting for beauty, for life, for joy. We kick up our heels in delight in the wilderness, we smile at a flower and a hummingbird. We laugh. We laugh at our opponents and, more important, we laugh at ourselves.

- *An awareness that we are animals.* Human beings are primates, mammals, vertebrates. We reject the New Age eco-la-la that says that we must transcend our base animal nature and take charge of our evolution in order to become higher, moral beings.
- *An acceptance of monkey wrenching as a legitimate tool for the preservation of natural diversity.* The monkey wrench itself is a symbol of resistance.
- *Earth First! is a warrior society.* We are characterized by our willingness to defend Earth's abundance and diversity of life, even if that defense requires sacrifices of comfort, freedom, safety, or, ultimately, our lives.

Threats to Wilderness

Road building is one of the major threats facing wilderness. Twenty-one miles is the farthest point from a road in the lower forty-eight states; there are few places ten miles or more from a road. The National Forest System contains a large share of the wilderness in the lower forty-eight states, but is also boasts 375,000 miles of road—the largest road network managed by any single entity in the world. During the next half-century, the forest service plans to build an additional 350,000 to 580,000 miles of road, mostly for logging. At least 100,000 miles of that will be in currently roadless areas. This road construction costs the American taxpayer half a billion dollars a year. Reducing or, better yet, eliminating the bloated forest service road building budget in the congressional appropriations process in one of the best ways to defend wilderness.

Logging is another serious threat to wilderness. Not until after World War II did the marketing of national forest timber attract interest as the stocks on corporate lands became depleted. In the last forty years, the annual cut on the national forests has increased steadily, until today the forest service brags that it is logging (i.e., destroying) a million acres of wilderness a year. It is important to keep in mind that "harvesting" 10 to 12 billion board feet of timber a year from national forests (about a fifth of the nation's total timber production) exceeds sustained yield, but also that most timber sales in remaining roadless areas on the national forests are below cost sales. It costs the forest service (and thus the taxpayer) more to offer and prepare these sales for cutting than timber companies pay for them.

Mining and energy extraction, even though they have affected a smaller acreage than have logging or grazing, where they have occurred, their impact has been momentous. Mining on the national forest and BLM lands is sanctioned by the 1872 Mining Act. This allows any individual or corporation to claim minerals on federal lands. Dozens of square miles of public land become an industrial complex, and elk, bear, and other animals are displaced. Like logging and grazing, mining and energy extraction on the public lands is a gigantic rip-off.

Grazing and the livestock industry have probably done more basic ecological damage to the western United States than has any other single agent. Streams and riparian vegetation have been degraded almost to the point of no return throughout much of the West. Less than 3 percent of the original riparian community remains in Arizona. In arid and semiarid lands, soils are often bound together and capped by cryptogamic soil-lichen association. Trampling by cattle destroys this delicate layer and opens the soil to massive erosion from rainfall. Some of the worst desertification in the world is occurring on land managed by the United States Forest Service and BLM; 225 million acres of land in the lower forty-eight are undergoing severe or very severe desertification. The Wilderness Act specifically permits livestock grazing if it had occurred established prior to designation of the area as Wilderness. The 1980 Colorado Wilderness Bill extended the rights of commercial graziers in Wilderness Areas, permitting them even to use motorized vehicles to manage their herds.

Experts estimate that the forest service and the BLM lose over $100 million a year on their grazing programs. When erosion, lowered recreational values, loss of biodiversity, and numerous other hidden costs are factored in, the subsidy to the livestock industry grows to gargantuan proportions, very roughly $2 billion annually or $66,666 per public-lands rancher. The proud, independent public-lands rancher as the paragon of the free-enterprise system? Forget it. He is a welfare bum.

Finally, we must recognize that *all* of us are destroying wilderness because of the alienation of our society from nature; because of human arrogance; and because of the gross overpopulation of our species combined with the wasteful lifestyle of modern humans, which converts 30 percent of Earth's photosynthetic production to human purposes.

In Defense of Monkey Wrenching

Monkey wrenching includes such acts as pulling up survey stakes, putting sand in the crankcases of bulldozers, rendering dirt roads in wild areas impassable to vehicles, cutting down billboards, and removing and destroying trap lines. Monkey wrenching is nonviolent and is aimed only at inanimate objects, *never* toward physically hurting people.

The goals of monkey wrenching are to block environmentally destructive projects, to increase the costs of such projects and thereby make them economically unattractive, and to raise public awareness of the taxpayer-subsidized devastation of biological diversity occurring throughout the world.

Monkey wrenching, contrary to public opinion, is not a recent fad resulting from Edward Abbey's 1975 novel *The Monkeywrench Gang*. It has a long and distinguished history in the United States, going all the way back to the Boston Tea Party in 1773. If those who object to breaking the law under all circumstances were consistent, they would condemn the farmers of Lexington and Concord in 1775, as well as the demonstrators in Tiananmen Square in Beijing. Let us also remember that all of the resistance movements operating against the Nazis in Europe during World War II were acting illegally. Conversely, the Nazi atrocities were completely legal.

We are not talking about a football game or a high-school debate here; we are discussing the continuation of three-and-a-half billion years of evolution. We are talking about what the ecologist Raymond Dasmann refers to as "World War Three"—the war between humans and the Earth. A preservation victory by conservationists is always temporary: a "saved" river can be later dammed, a "saved" forest can be later cut, but a dammed river or a clearcut forest is irretrievably lost (at least in a human time scale).

Contrary to the demagogues' claims, no one has been injured in any monkey wrenching operation carried out by preservationists. The true ecoterrorists are the planet-despoilers: those in the Forest Service and the timber industry who are annihilating thousand-year-old forests for paper bags and picnic tables. The list of ecoterrorists is endless, but it does not include the brave and conscientious individuals who are defending threatened wild areas by placing a monkey wrench into the gear of the machine. Putting grinding compound into the crankshaft of a logging yarder may not be civil, but crucifying three-and-a-half billion years of evolution on a cross of gold is far more uncivil. Eco-saboteurs have taken off the white gloves and are getting their fingernails dirty. It's a nasty job, but somebody's got to do it.

Dreaming of Big Wilderness

It was Bob Marshall (the person responsible for originally organizing and funding the Wilderness Society in 1935) who instituted a *system* for protecting wildlands on the national forests, designating about 14 million acres as "Primitive Areas" and setting up a process to study them more formally and establish firm boundaries. In 1951, Howard Zahniser, executive secretary of the Wilderness Society, called for congressional designation of Wilderness Areas. In 1955, Senator Hubert Humphrey introduced the first version of the Wilderness Act. After eight years of hearings, the Wilderness Act was signed into law on September 3, 1964, by President Lyndon Johnson.

The Wilderness Act established a National Wilderness Preservation System initially composed of the pre-existing Wilderness and Wild Areas on the National Forests. It directed the Forest Service to study and make recommendations on the remaining Primitive Areas, and directed the National Park Service and U.S. Fish and Wildlife Service to do likewise for roadless areas on the lands they managed. Congress reserved for itself the power to add or delete areas to or from the system. Construction of roads, use of motorized vehicles or equipment, and commercial cutting of timber were all prohibited in Wilderness Areas.

Nine million acres of wilderness were established by the Wilderness Act in 1964. Thanks to wilderness-minded citizens, 90 million are protected today. I have no desire to be the skunk at the garden party. Nonetheless, let us not fool ourselves. Of the 90 million acres in the National Wilderness Preservation System, only 34 million are outside of Alaska. If the Wilderness System is to be anything more than a museum offering a tantalizing glimpse of a bygone North America, if it is to be more than an outdoor gymnasium and art gallery, if it is to preserve representative samples of dynamically evolving natural ecosystems, we must have an inspirational objective. Conservationists must lead, instead of politely responding.

We must ask deeper questions of our nation: Is 2 percent of the acreage of the forty-eight states adequate for our Wilderness Preservation System? When you say you only want worthless lands, you get worthless lands. Monumental, yes. Scenic, indeed. Even breathtaking. But not the rich, virile areas needed by sensitive species. Yellowstone National Park, as spellbinding as it is, cannot stand on its own as an ecosystem. Its boundaries were drawn not by nature but by politicians who kowtowed to the dollar. Bison cannot eat scenery or geysers. The unspectacular private lands north of Yellowstone, now used as cattle ranches, are their necessary winter range, as they have been for millennia. Designated Wilderness Areas and National Parks cannot survive as effective sanctuaries if they remain island ecosystems. Outside impacts such as acid precipitation, other forms of air pollution, and toxic and radioactive contamination can devastate the natural integrity of protected areas.

It is time to draw the line on what is now wild. In many cases, all that is necessary to recover native ecosystems, to reintroduce extirpated wildlife, and to repair damaged landscapes is to close roads, cease damaging activities, and leave the land alone. These areas should be designated Wilderness Recovery Areas.

We must restore large ecological wilderness preserves. These core areas and smaller Wilderness Areas and Wilderness Recovery Areas should be linked to one another by undeveloped corridors. Such corridors are vital for the transmission of genetic diversity between core preserves. We must discard the notion of static landscape preservation. What is being preserved in Wilderness Areas is the process of evolution, of speciation, of seral changes in the ecosystem.

Finally, we must preserve wilderness for its own sake. Conservationists must develop a new reason for wilderness, a new understanding of the place of humans in the natural world, a new appreciation for the other nations of life inhabiting this beautiful blue-green living planet. We should recognize that the true reason we favor wilderness preservation is because it's right. Because it is the real world, the arena of evolution; because it is our home. Not only should conservationists recognize that it is the inherent value of natural diversity that argues for its preservation in our hearts, *but it is also the most effective argument for preservation.* Unless we challenge our fellow humans to practice self-restraint, to share Earth voluntarily with our wild fellows, the wilderness crusade is pissing in the wind.

Whither Earth First!?

I am a reluctant radical. I have always been a little embarrassed carrying a sign at a demonstration. I have never felt entirely comfortable sitting in front of a bulldozer or chaining myself to the doors of a National Park visitor center. I regret the need to damage private property of any sort. I do not like to take an uncompromising stand; I much prefer to sit down and work out our differences respectfully and rationally. I feel more at home in the guise of a peacemaker than that of a rabble-rouser.

Earth First! was not conceived in an attitude of revolution for the hell of it, radicalism for its own sake, or antiestablishment rebellion. We do not engage in radical action because we are primarily motivated by opposition to authority, but because we are *for* something—the beauty, wisdom, and abundance of this living planet.

Since 1980, Earth First! has led the effort to reframe the question of wilderness preservation from an aesthetic and utilitarian one to an ecological one, from a focus on scenery and recreation to a focus on biological diversity. Similarly, we have gone beyond the limited agenda of mainstream conservation groups to protect a *portion* of the remaining wilderness by calling for the reintroduction of extirpated species and the restoration of vast wilderness tracts. We have brought the discussion of biocentric philosophy—Deep Ecology—out of dusty academic journals. We have effectively introduced nonviolent civil disobedience into the repertoire of wildland preservation activism. We have also helped to jolt the conservation movement out of its middle-age lethargy and reinspire it with passion, joy, and humor. In doing all of this, Earth First! has restructured the conservation spectrum and redefined the parameters of debate on ecological matters.

I am not an anarchist or a "Yippie." I am a conservationist. I believe that human overpopulation is the fundamental problem on Earth today. Although I will continue to applaud the courageous actions of those operating with the Earth First! name, it is time for me to build a campfire elsewhere. In other words, I am no longer part of the Earth First! movement. I no longer represent it and I am no longer represented by it.

There are a variety of scenarios of what may happen to Earth First! under the triple pressures of external harassment from the FBI, encouragement to moderate from the establishment, and internal divisiveness. No matter what happens, the hot green chilies from the original Earth First! will remain a permanent part of the conservation movement. Neither feral adolescents, the co-opting whirlpool of the American mainstream, nor even the FBI can stop us.

Donella Meadows, Dennis Meadows, and Jørgen Randers

BEYOND THE LIMITS

In 1972, Donella Meadows and three of her colleagues at MIT stunned the world with a rather alarming assessment of the fate of human society that predicted limits to economic and population growth. The conclusions, based on a complex computer model of human society that allowed them to predict the future of humankind under different sets of assumptions, was published in the best-selling book, Limits to Growth. *In this book, the authors stated that if present growth trends in world population, industrialization, pollution output, food production, and resource depletion continued unchanged, human society would exceed planetary limits within the next hundred years. Since its publication, at least seventeen computer studies have corroborated the findings of the Meadows's team.*

Several years ago, however, three members of the original team convened to update the model, to consider new data, and to subject it to computer analysis. This time, though, their predictions are even more dire. They assert that, in many cases, resource demand and pollution output have already exceeded sustainable rates. In other words, human societies have transcended critical ecological boundaries. In short, the authors contend that we humans are living beyond the limits and that to continue along this path only risks further collapse.

Beyond the Limits *is more than another gloom-and-doom book. It offers considerable insight into the systems that comprise our world. It fosters systems thinking. Equally important, this book outlines solutions essential to steer human civilization onto a sustainable course. The authors remind us that the world faces not a preordained future, but a choice. One path, the current one, assumes that the Earth is an unlimited supply of resources and, accordingly, pursues a course of unbridled growth. The other recognizes that limits are very real and very close and prescribes actions that can help us live within those limits. It is the path most experts agree that leads us to a sustainable future.*

Twenty years ago, after working with global data and with a computer model called World3, we came to the following conclusions in a book titled *The Limits to Growth*:

1. If present growth trends in world population, industrialization, pollution, food production, and resource depletion continue unchanged, the limits to growth on this planet will be reached sometime within the next hundred years. The most probable result will be a sudden and uncontrollable decline in both population and industrial capacity.
2. It is possible to alter these growth trends and to establish a condition of ecological and economic stability that is sustainable far into the future. The state of global equilibrium could be designed so that the basic material needs of each person on earth are satisfied and each person has an equal opportunity to realize his or her individual human potential.
3. If the world's people decide to strive for this second outcome rather than the first, the sooner they begin working to attain it, the greater will be their chances of success.

Now with an updated model, with more extensive data, and after twenty years of growth and change in the world, we believe that our original conclusions are still valid, but they need to be strengthened:

1. Human use of many essential resources and generation of many kinds of pollutants have already surpassed rates that are physically sustainable. Without significant reductions in material and energy flows, there will be in the coming decades an uncontrolled decline in per capita food output, energy use, and industrial production.
2. This decline is not inevitable. To avoid it two changes are necessary. The first is a comprehensive revision of policies and practices that perpetuate growth in material consumption and in population. The second is a rapid, drastic increase in the efficiency with which materials and energy are used.

3. A sustainable society is technically and economically possible. It could be much more desirable than a society that tries to solve its problems by constant expansion. The transition to a sustainable society requires a careful balance between long-term and short-term goals and an emphasis on sufficiency, equity, and quality of life rather than on quantity of output. It requires more than productivity and more than technology; it also requires maturity, compassion, and wisdom.

These conclusions constitute a conditional warning, not a dire prediction. They offer a living choice, not a death sentence. The choice isn't a gloomy one. It does not mean that the poor must be frozen in their poverty or that the rich must become poor. It could mean the solution of problems such as poverty and unemployment that humanity has been working at inefficiently or fruitlessly by trying to maintain physical growth.

We hope that the world will make the choice for sustainability. We think that a better world is possible and that the acceptance of physical limits is the first step toward getting there. We see "easing down" not as a sacrifice, but as an opportunity to stop battering against the earth's limits and to start transcending self-imposed and unnecessary limits within human institutions, minds, and hearts.

Overshoot

The following are characteristics of a society that has grown *beyond its limits*—a society that is drawing upon the earth's resources faster than they can be restored, and that is releasing wastes and pollutants faster than the earth can absorb them or render them harmless.

- Falling stocks of groundwaters, forests, fish, soils.
- Rising accumulations of wastes and pollutants.
- Capital, energy, materials, and labor devoted to exploitation of more distant, deeper, or more dilute resources.
- Capital, energy, materials, and labor compensating for what were once free natural services (sewage treatment, flood control, air purification, pest control, restoring soil nutrients, preserving species).
- Capital, energy, materials, and labor diverted to defend or gain access to resources that are concentrated in a few remaining places (such as oil in the Middle East).

Population and Capital in the Global Ecosystem

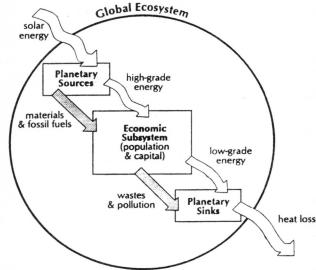

Population and capital are sustained by flows of fuels and nonrenewable resources from the planet, and they produce outflows of heat and waste, which contaminate the air, waters, and soils of the planet. (Source: R. Goodland et al.)

- Deterioration in physical capital, especially in long-lived infrastructure.
- Reduced investment in human resources (education, health care, shelter) in order to meet consumption needs or to pay debts.
- Increasing conflict over resources or pollution emission rights. Less social solidarity, more hoarding, greater gaps between haves and have-nots.

A society like this is in a state of *overshoot*. To overshoot means to go too far, to grow so large so quickly that limits are exceeded. When an overshoot occurs, it induces stresses—in this case in both natural and social processes—that begin to work to slow and stop growth.

If humanity does not correct its condition of overshoot, problems like the ones listed above will worsen until human productive capacity, ingenuity, adaptability, and attention are overwhelmed. At that point overshoot will turn into collapse.

However, collapse is not the only possible outcome. The human society can ease down from beyond the limits. That need not mean reducing population or capital or living standards, though it certainly means reducing their growth. What must go down, and quickly, are *throughputs*—flows of material and energy from the supporting environment, through the economy, and back to the environment.

Fortunately, in a perverse way, the current global economy is so wasteful, inefficient, and inequitable that it has tremendous potential for reducing throughputs while raising the quality of life for everyone. While that is happening, other measures—nontechnical measures, evolutionary human measures—can restructure the social system so that overshoot never happens again.

Looking into the Future with Worlds

To understand how the human economy and the environment may unfold in the future, we use a computer model called World3. World3 is, like all models, much, much simpler than the real world. It is, however, more dynamically sophisticated than many computer models. It is a nonlinear feedback model, one that tries to capture the forces behind population and capital growth, the layers of changing, interlinked environmental limits, and the delays in the physical and economic processes through which human society interacts with its environment.

World3 shows, in no uncertain terms, that if the world system continues to evolve with no significant changes, the most likely result is not only overshoot, but collapse, and within another few decades. One possible future, by no means the only one, is shown in Scenario 1.

In this scenario the world society proceeds along its historical path as long as possible without major policy change. Technology advances in agriculture, industry, and social services according to established patterns. The simulated world tries to bring all people into an industrial and then post-industrial economy.

The global population in this scenario rises from 1.6 billion in 1900 to over 5 billion in 1990 and over 6 billion in the year 2000. Total industrial output expands by a factor of 20 between 1900 and 1990, and it does so while using only 20 percent of the earth's total stock of non-renewable resources. In 1990, 80 percent of these resources remain. Pollution in that year has just begun to rise significantly. Life expectancy is increasing, services and goods per capita are increasing, food production is increasing. But major changes are just ahead.

Just after the simulated year 2000 pollution rises high enough to begin to affect the fertility of the land. At the same time land erosion

Scenario 1

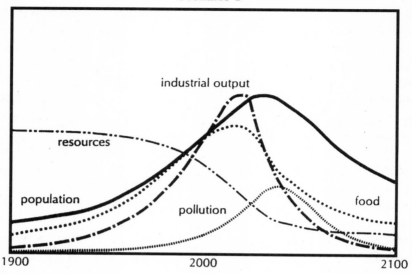

increases. Total food production begins to fall after 2015. That causes the economy to shift more investment into the agriculture sector. But agriculture has to compete for investment with a resource sector that is also beginning to sense some limits.

Between 1990 and 2020 in this scenario, population increases by 50 percent and industrial output by 85 percent. Therefore the nonrenewable resource use rate doubles. What was a 110-year supply of nonrenewable resources in 1990 is only a 30-year supply in 2020. So many resources have been used that much more capital and energy are required to find, extract, and refine what remains.

As both food and nonrenewable resources become harder to obtain in this simulated world, capital is diverted to producing more of them. That leaves less output to be invested in capital growth. Finally the industrial capital plant begins to decline, taking with it the service and agricultural sectors. For a short time the situation is especially serious, as population keeps rising, because of lags inherent in the age structure and in the process of social adjustment. Finally population too begins to decrease, as the death rate is driven upward by lack of food and health services.

This scenario is *not a prediction*, but we believe it is a possibility, one among many. Another very different possibility is shown in Scenario 10. To produce it we introduce technical, social, and economic measures quite different from those that are currently being pursued in the world. That is the purpose of a model, not to predict, but to test the "what if" possibilities.

In Scenario 10 people in the simulated world decide on an average family size of two starting in 1995, and they have available effective birth control technologies. They also set themselves a consumption limit. When every family attains roughly the material standard of living of present-day Europe, it says "enough" and turns its attention to achieving other, nonmaterial goals. Furthermore, starting in 1995, this world puts a high priority on developing and implementing technologies that increase the efficiency of resource use, decrease pollution emissions, control land erosion, and increase land yields.

We assume in Scenario 10 that these technologies come on only when needed and only after a development delay of twenty years, and that they have a capital cost. The capital is available for them, however, because in this restrained society, capital does not have to support rapid growth or to ameliorate a spiraling set of problems caused by growth. By the end of the twenty-first century in this scenario, the new technologies reduce nonrenewable resource use per unit of industrial output by 80 percent and pollution production per unit of output by 90 percent. Land yield declines slightly in the early twenty-first century as pollution rises (a delayed effect of pollution emissions around the end of the twentieth century), but by 2040 pollution begins to go down again. Land yield recovers and rises slowly for the rest of the century.

The population in Scenario 10 levels off at just under 8 billion and lives at its desired material standard of living for at least a century. Average life expectancy stays at just over eighty years, services per capita rise 210 percent above their 1990 levels, and there is sufficient food for everyone. Pollution peaks and falls before it causes irreversible damage. Nonrenewable resources deplete so slowly that half the original endowment is still present in the simulated year 2100.

We believe that the world could attain a sustainable state similar to that shown in Scenario 10. We think it is a picture not only of a feasible world, but of a desirable one, certainly more desirable than a world that keeps on growing until it is stopped by multiple crises.

Scenario 10 is not the only sustainable outcome the World3 model can produce. There are tradeoffs and choices. There could be more food and less industrial output or vice versa, more people living with a smaller

Scenario 10

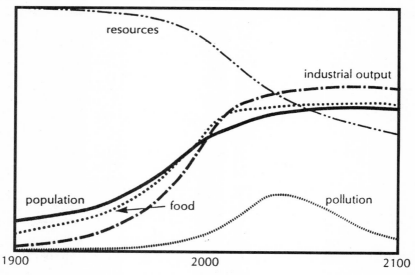

stream of industrial goods or fewer people living with more. The world society could take more time to make the transition to equilibrium—but it cannot delay forever, or even very long. When we postpone for twenty years the policies that brought about the sustainable world of Scenario 10, the population grows too large, pollution builds too high, resources are drained too much, and a collapse is no longer avoidable.

Beyond the Limits and Still Growing

Physical expansion is still the dominant behavior of human society, though the resource base is declining. In 1991 the human population was 5.4 billion. In that year the population grew by over 90 million people, a one-year addition equivalent to the total populations of Mexico plus Honduras, or to eight Calcuttas. World population is still growing exponentially. Under the most favorable circumstances, the World Bank projects that the population will not level off until late in the next century, at 12.5 billion people.

Industrial production is also growing, even more rapidly than the population. It has doubled over the past twenty years. Along with it have doubled, or more than doubled, the number of cars, the consumption of coal and natural gas, the electric generating capacity, the production of grain, the generation of garbage, the emissions of greenhouse gases.

World Population

Billions of people

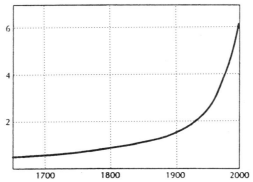

In 1991 world population growth rate was estimated to be 1.7%, corresponding to a doubling time of 40 years. (Sources: United Nations; D.J. Bogue)

If the economy were to support 12.5 billion people, all living the way present North Americans live, it would have to expand at least twenty-fold—twenty more industrial worlds added to the existing one!

The industrial world that already exists is using the earth's resources unsustainably. It is not meeting the basic needs of all the world's people, and yet, given current knowledge and technology, all needs could be met without exceeding the earth's limits.

Fact: Of the more than 5 billion people on earth, over 1 billion at any time are eating less food than their bodies require. Every day an average of 35,000 people die of hunger-related causes, most of them children.

Possibility: If the food grown each year on earth were equitably distributed, and if less of it were lost to spoilage and waste, there would easily be enough to give all people an adequate, varied diet.

Fact: During the past twenty years deserts expanded by 288 million acres, nearly the size of France. Each year 16 to 17 million acres of cultivated land are made unproductive because of erosion, and another 3.6 million acres because of salination and waterlogging. Soil erosion exceeds soil formation on a third of U.S. cropland and on 1,300 million acres in Asia, Africa, and Latin America. Fertilizers and pesticides acidify and alter soils and run off to contaminate ground and surface waters.

Possibility: Farming methods that conserve and enhance soils are known and used by some farmers on every continent. In both temperate and tropic zones, some farms are obtaining high yields consistently

World Industrial Production
Index (1963 = 100)

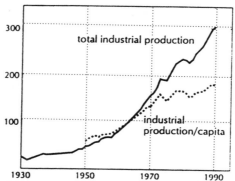

World industrial production also shows clear exponential increase, despite fluctuations due to oil price shocks. The 1970 to 1990 growth rate in total production has averaged 3.3% per year. The per capita growth rate has been 1.5% per year. (Sources: United Nations; Population Reference Bureau)

without high rates of application of fertilizers and pesticides. More food could be grown, and it could be done in ways that are ecologically, economically, and socially sustainable.

Fact: Before the industrial revolution there were 14 billion acres of forest on the earth. Now there are 10 billion acres, only 3.6 billion of which are undisturbed primary forest. Half of the world's forest loss has occurred between 1950 and 1990. China has lost three-fourths of its forests. Europe has no primary forests left. The United States has lost one-third of its forested cover, and 85 percent of its primary forest. Half of the tropical forest is gone; half of what remains has been logged and degraded. At current logging rates the rest will be gone within fifty years and with it perhaps half the species of life on earth.

Possibility: Forest cutting could be greatly reduced while demand for wood products is still fulfilled. Half of U.S. wood consumption could be saved by increasing the efficiency of sawmills and construction, by doubling the rate of paper recycling, and by reducing the use of disposable paper products. Logging could be conducted so as to reduce its negative impact on soils, streams, and unharvested trees. Fast-growing forests could be replanted on already logged lands. High-yield agriculture could reduce the need to clear forests for food, and more efficient stoves could reduce the need for firewood.

Fact: The average North American uses forty times as much energy as the average person in a developing country. The energy use of the human economy grew sixtyfold between 1860 and 1985, and it is projected to grow by another 75 percent by the year 2020. At present, 88 percent of the commercial energy used in the world comes from the fossil fuels—coal, oil, and gas.

Fact: Fossil fuels are limited both by their sources (the deposits in the earth) and by their sinks (the atmosphere, waters, and soils to which their combustion products and refinery by-products go). The primary product of fossil fuel combustion is carbon dioxide, a greenhouse gas, which is rapidly increasing in the atmosphere. Its atmospheric concentration is now higher than it has been for the past 160,000 years, and it is still growing exponentially.

Possibility: Through efficiency measures alone the world could maintain its total energy use at or below the current level with no reduction in productivity, comfort, or convenience in the rich countries and with steady economic improvement in the poor countries. Efficiencies of that magnitude would make it possible to supply most or all the world's energy needs from solar-based renewables, whose costs are dropping steadily.

Fact: As inputs of energy and materials to the human economy increase, outputs of waste and pollution also increase. Some forms of

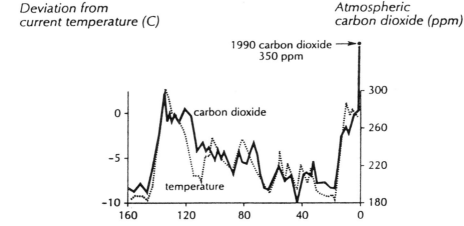

Carbon Dioxide and Global Temperature Over the Past 160 Thousand Years

Deviation from current temperature (C)

Atmospheric carbon dioxide (ppm)

pollution, such as lead in gasoline and DDT, have been greatly reduced, primarily by outright bans. In rich countries some widespread pollutants, such as nitrogen oxides in air and phosphates in streams, have been reduced or held constant, at considerable expense. Other kinds of pollutants, particularly nuclear wastes, hazardous wastes, and greenhouse gases, continue to grow unabated.

Fact: Knowledge about the environment and concern for it has grown enormously all over the world. In twenty years the number of environmental ministries in the world's governments has risen from ten to over one hundred. Global monitoring systems now exist, and global conferences, information networks, and agreements have been put into place.

Possibility: The reorganization of manufacturing and farming practices to reduce pollution outputs has barely begun. Increased efficiencies of fuel and material use and more complete material recycling will reduce both depletion of sources and pollution of sinks. Great reductions in pollution will be a natural result of pricing products to include their environmental costs, and of the adoption of the idea of sufficiency—simply reducing unnecessary, wasteful consumption.

All over the earth soils, forests, surface waters, groundwaters, wetlands, and the diversity of nature are being degraded. Even in places where renewable resources appear to be stable, such as the forests of North America or the soils of Europe, the quality or health of the resource is in question. Deposits of fossil fuels and high-grade ores are being drawn down. There is no plan and no sufficient investment program to power the industrial economy after nonrenewable resources are gone. Pollutants are accumulating; their sinks are overflowing. The chemical composition of the entire atmosphere is being changed.

If only one or a few resource stocks were falling while others were stable or rising, one might argue that growth could continue by the substitution of one resource for another. But when many stocks are eroding and many sinks are filling, there can be no doubt that human withdrawals of material and energy have grown too far. They have overshot their sustainable limits.

The Dynamics of Overshoot and Collapse

A growing population and economy can approach the limits to its physical carrying capacity in one of four ways:

1. It can keep growing without interruption, as long as its limits are far away or growing faster than it is.

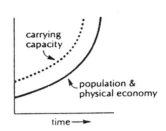

2. It can level off smoothly, slowing and then stopping in a smooth accommodation with its limits, if and only if it receives accurate, prompt signals telling it where it is with respect to its limits, and only if it can respond to those signals quickly and accurately—or if the population and economy limit themselves well below external limits.

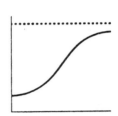

3. It may overshoot its limit for awhile, make a correction, and undershoot, then overshoot again, in a series of oscillations, if the warning signal from the limits to the growing entity is delayed, or if the response is delayed, and if the supporting environment is not erodable when overstressed, or if it is able to recover quickly from erosion.

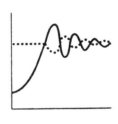

4. If the signal or response from the limit is delayed and if the environment is irreversibly eroded when overstressed, then the growing economy will overshoot its carrying capacity, degrade its resource base, and collapse. The result of this overshoot and collapse is a permanently impoverished environment and a material standard of living much lower than what could have been possible had the environment never been overstressed.

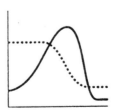

We submit that the human population and economy, drawing resources from a large but finite planet, forms a system that is structured, unless altered by human intelligence and human self-restraint, for overshoot and collapse. The prevailing industrial ethic is one of continuous growth. The resource base is both limited and erodable. The response of biological and geochemical systems to human abuse comes only after long delays. The human population acts only after further delay. And physical processes, from human population growth to forest growth to global climate change, operate with considerable momentum.

A population-economy-environment system that contains feedback delays and slow physical responses, thresholds, and erosion is literally *unmanageable*. No matter how brilliant its technologies, no matter how efficient its economy, no matter how wise its decision makers, it can't steer itself away from hazards, unless it does its best to look far forward and to test its limits very, very slowly. If it keeps its focus only on the short term and if it constantly tries to accelerate, it will overshoot.

The advent of new technologies and the flexibility of the market system are no antidotes to overshoot, and they cannot by themselves prevent collapse. In fact they themselves operate with delays that *enhance* the economy's tendency to overshoot. Technology and markets serve the values of society. If the primary goal is growth, they will produce growth, overshoot, and collapse. If the primary goals are equity and sustainability, then technology and markets can also help bring about those goals.

Overshoot is a condition in which the delayed signals from the environment aren't yet strong enough to force an end to growth. That means that a society in overshoot still has a chance, if it acts quickly, to bring itself below its limits and avoid collapse.

There even may be a recent example of the human world doing just that in its response to the destruction of the ozone layer.

The Ozone Layer: Back from Beyond the Limits?

The ozone story illustrates all the ingredients of an overshoot and collapse system: exponential growth, an erodable environmental limit, and long response delays, both physical and political.

- *The growth*: Chlorofluorocarbons, or CFCs, are some of the most useful compounds ever invented by human beings. They were originally sold as refrigerants under the trade name Freon. Then they were found to be useful in insulation, as propellants in aerosol cans, as solvents for cleaning metals. By the early 1970s, the world was making a million tons of CFCs per year and discarding them safely into the atmosphere, or so everyone thought.

- *The limit*: High in the atmosphere, twice as high as Mount Everest, is the gossamer ozone layer that screens out a particularly harmful wavelength from the sun's incoming light—W-B, a stream of energy of just the right frequency to destroy the organic molecules that make up all life. If the ozone layer thins and more W-B light reaches the earth's surface, the results will include human skin cancers, blindness in many kinds of animals, decreased growth of green plants, and disruption of oceanic food chains. Each one percent decrease in the ozone layer is expected to produce a one percent decrease in soybean yield and a 3 percent to 6 percent increase in human skin cancer.

- *Signals*: The first scientific papers postulating that CFCs could destroy the ozone layer were published in 1974. The first measurements of a precipitous drop in ozone concentration over Antarctica were taken in the late 1970s and finally published in 1985. Since then, scientists have come up with an explanation of the "ozone hole" and have uncovered the disquieting fact that each atom of chlorine released into the stratosphere from the decay of a CFC molecule can destroy about 100,000 ozone molecules.

- *Delays*: After its manufacture, a CFC molecule may be released quickly into the atmosphere from an aerosol can, or it may remain for years in a refrigerator or air conditioner. Upon its release, it takes about fifteen years to rise up to the stratosphere. Its residence time there may vary, depending on the type of CFC, from sixty-five to five hundred years.

- *The human response*: The first official international meeting to discuss the ozone layer was convened by the United Nations Environment Program in 1985. It produced no agreement. But by 1987 the "Montreal Protocol" was signed by thirty-six nations, agreeing to cut their production of CFCs in half by 1998. Continuing ozone deterioration then spurred the world to toughen that agreement: ninety-two nations agreed in London in 1990 to phase out all CFC production by 2000. In 1991, in response to further ozone depletion, several nations unilaterally moved up their deadlines for eliminating CFCs.

It took thirteen years from the first scientific papers to the signing of the Montreal Protocol. It will take thirteen more years until the protocol, as strengthened in London, is fully implemented. The chlorine already in the stratosphere will remain there for more than a century. In fall 1991 the Antarctic ozone hole was the deepest ever measured, and in winter 1992 chlorine concentrations in the stratosphere over the Northern Hemisphere were the highest ever measured.

This is a story of overshoot and of a remarkable, worldwide human response. Whether or not it will be a story of collapse depends on how erodable or self-repairable the ozone layer is, on whether future atmospheric surprises appear, and on whether humanity has acted, and will continue to act, in time.

Six Steps to Avoid Collapse

Six broad measures lead to the avoidance of collapse in the World3 model and, we believe, in the world. Each of them is described here in general terms. Each can be worked out in hundreds of specific ways at all levels, from households to communities to nations to the world as a whole. Any step in any of these directions is a step toward sustainability.

- *Improve the signals.* Learn more about and monitor both the welfare of the human population and the conditions of local and planetary sources and sinks. Inform governments and the public as continuously and promptly about environmental conditions as about economic conditions. Include real environmental costs in economic prices; recast economic indicators like the GNP so that they do not confuse costs with benefits, or throughput with welfare, or the depreciation of natural capital with income.

- *Speed up response times.* Look actively for signals that indicate when the environment is stressed. Decide in advance what to do if problems appear (if possible, forecast them before they appear) and have in place the institutional and technical arrangements necessary to act effectively. Educate for flexibility and creativity, for critical thinking and for systems understanding.

- *Minimize the use of nonrenewable resources.* Fossil fuels, fossil groundwaters, and minerals should be used only with the greatest possible efficiency, recycled when possible (fuels can't be recycled, but minerals and water can), and consumed only as part of a deliberate transition to renewable resources.

- *Prevent the erosion of renewable resources.* The productivity of soils, surface waters, rechargeable groundwaters, and all living things, including forests, fish, game, should be protected and, as far as possible, restored and enhanced. These resources should only be harvested at the rate they can regenerate themselves. That requires information about their regeneration rates, and strong social sanctions or economic inducements against their overuse.
- *Use all resources with maximum efficiency.* The more human welfare can be obtained with the less throughput, the better the quality of life can be while remaining below the limits. Great efficiency gains are both technically possible and economically favorable. Higher efficiency will be essential if current and future world populations are to be supported without inducing a collapse.
- *Slow and eventually stop exponential growth of population and physical capital.* There are real limits to the extent that the first five items on this list can be pursued. Therefore this last step is the most essential. It involves institutional and philosophical change and social innovation. It requires defining desirable, sustainable levels of population and industrial output. It calls for goals defined around the idea of "enough" rather than "more." It asks, simply but profoundly, for a vision of the purpose of human existence that does not entail constant physical expansion.

This last and most daunting step toward sustainability requires solutions to the pressing problems that underlie much of the psychological and cultural commitment to growth: the problems of poverty, unemployment, and unmet nonmaterial needs. Growth as presently structured is in fact not solving those problems or is solving them only slowly and inefficiently. But until better solutions are in sight, society will never let go of its addiction to growth. Therefore there are three problems for which completely new thinking is urgently needed.

- *Poverty.* "Sharing" is a forbidden word in political discourse, probably because of the deep fear that real equity would mean not enough for anyone. "Sufficiency" and "Solidarity" are concepts that can help structure new approaches to ending poverty. Everyone needs assurance that sufficiency is possible for everyone and that there is a high social commitment to ensure it. And everyone needs to understand that the world is tied together both ecologically and economically.

There is enough to go around, if we manage well. If we don't manage well, no one will escape the consequences.

- *Employment.* Human beings need to work, to have the satisfaction of personal productivity, and to be accepted as responsible members of their society. That need should not be left unfulfilled, and it should not be filled by degrading or harmful work. At the same time, employment should not be a requirement for the ability to subsist. An economic system is needed that uses and supports the contributions that all people are able and willing to make, that shares work and leisure equitably, and that does not abandon people who for reasons temporary or permanent cannot work.

- *Nonmaterial needs.* People don't need enormous cars; they need respect. They don't need closetsful of clothes; they need to feel attractive and they need excitement, variety, and beauty. People need identity, community, challenge, acknowledgment, love, joy. To try to fill these needs with material things is to set up an unquenchable appetite for false solutions to real and never-satisfied problems. The resulting psychological emptiness is one of the major forces behind the desire for material growth. A society that can admit and articulate its nonmaterial needs and find nonmaterial ways to satisfy them would require much lower material and energy throughputs and would provide much higher levels of human fulfillment.

The Sustainable Society

A sustainable society is one that can persist over generations, one that is far-seeing enough, flexible enough, and wise enough not to undermine either its physical or its social systems of support. It is, in the words of the World Commission on Environment and Development, a society that "meets the needs of the present without compromising the ability of future generations to meet their own needs."

In a sustainable society population, capital and technology would be balanced so that the per capita material living standard is adequate and so that the society's material and energy throughputs meet three conditions:

1. Its rates of use of renewable resources do not exceed their rates of regeneration.
2. Its rates of use of nonrenewable resources do not exceed the rate at which sustainable renewable substitutes are developed.

3. Its rates of pollution emission do not exceed the assimilative capacity of the environment.

A sustainable society is not necessarily a "zero growth" society. That concept is as primitive as is the concept of "perpetual growth." Rather a sustainable society would discriminate among kinds of growth and purposes for growth. It would ask what growth is for, who would benefit, what it would cost, how long it would last, and whether it could be accommodated by the sources and sinks of the earth.

That is to say, a sustainable society would be less interested in *growth* than in *development*. As a recent World Bank report says: "Following the dictionary distinction . . . To 'grow' means to increase in size by the assimilation or accretion of materials. To 'develop' means to expand or realize the potentialities of; to bring to a fuller, greater, or better state. When something grows it gets quantitatively bigger; when it develops it gets qualitatively better."

A sustainable society would not paralyze the poor in their poverty. To do so would not be sustainable for two reasons. First, the poor would not and should not stand for it. Second, keeping any part of the population in poverty would not, except under dire coercive measures, allow the population to be stabilized. For both practical and moral reasons any sustainable society would have to be just, fair, and equitable.

A sustainable society would not experience the despondency and stagnancy, high unemployment and bankruptcy that current market systems undergo when their growth is interrupted. The difference between the transition to a sustainable society and a present-day economic recession is like the difference between stopping an automobile with the brakes and stopping it by crashing into a brick wall. A deliberate transition to sustainability would take place slowly enough so that people and businesses could find their proper places in the new society.

There is no reason why a sustainable society need be technically or culturally primitive. Freed from both material anxiety and material greed, human society could have enormous possibilities for the expansion of creativity.

A sustainable world need not be a rigid one, or a centrally controlled one. It would need rules, laws, standards, boundaries, and social agreements, of course, as does every human culture. Rules for sustainability, like every workable social rule, would be put into place not to remove freedoms but to create them or to protect them against those who would destroy them. *They could permit many more freedoms than would ever be possible in a world that continues to crowd against its limits.*

Diversity is both a cause of and a result of sustainability in nature, and therefore a sustainable human society would be diverse in both nature and culture.

A sustainable society could and should be democratic, evolving, technically advanced, and challenging. It would have plenty of problems to solve and plenty of ways for people to prove themselves, to serve each other, to realize their abilities, and to live good lives—perhaps more satisfying lives than any available today.

The Next Revolution

We don't underestimate the gravity of the changes that will take the present world down from overshoot and into sustainability. We think a transition to a sustainable world is technically and economically possible, but we know it is psychologically and politically daunting. The necessary changes would constitute a revolution, not in the sense of the American or French political revolutions, but in the much more profound sense of the Agricultural and Industrial Revolutions.

Like those revolutions, a sustainability revolution would change the face of the land and the foundations of human self-definitions, institutions, and cultures. It is not a revolution that can be planned or dictated. It won't follow a list of fiats from a government or from computer models. The sustainability revolution, if it happens, will be organic and evolutionary. It will arise from the visions, insights, experiments, and actions of billions of people. It will require every human quality and skill, from technical ingenuity, economic entrepreneurism, and political leadership to honesty, compassion, and love.

Are any of the necessary changes, from resource efficiency to human compassion, really possible? Can the world actually ease down below the limits and avoid collapse? Is there time? Is there enough money, technology, freedom, vision, community, responsibility, foresight, discipline, and love on a global scale?

The general cynicism of the day would say there is not a chance. That cynicism, of course, is a mental model. The truth is that no one knows. The world faces not a preordained future, but a choice. The choice is between models. One model says that this finite world for all practical purposes has no limits. Choosing that model will take us even further beyond the limits and, we believe, to collapse within the next half century.

Another model says that the limits are real and close, and that there is not enough time and that people cannot be moderate or responsible or compassionate. That model is self-fulfilling. If we choose to believe it, we will get to be right.

A third model says that the limits are real and close, and there is just exactly enough time, with no time to waste. There is just exactly enough energy, enough material, enough money, enough environmental resilience, and enough human virtue to bring about a revolution to a better world.

That model might be wrong. All the evidence we have seen, from the world data to the global computer models, suggests that it might be right. There is no way of knowing for sure, other than to try it.

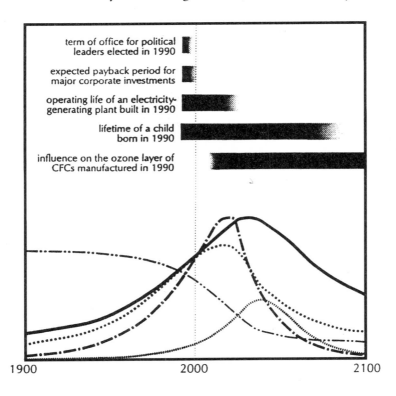

Donella H. Meadows

THE GLOBAL CITIZEN

Are the world's environmental problems really as serious as experts think? What is expo-
nential growth and why is it important to understand its powerful influence? Can we
feed the world's people without pesticides? Should we be glad when the GNP goes up?
These and dozens of other essential questions are addressed in Donella Meadow's The
Global Citizen, *a delightful collection of essays from her syndicated weekly column*
bearing the same title. The column and the book attempt to present an environmental
perspective—and more importantly—a systems view of the issues facing the global com-
munity in a medium that is prone to ignore the deeper issues of the environment.

For this anthology, Donella Meadows submitted two columns from The Global
Citizen *to give the reader a small taste of what her book has to offer. The first selection*
is on the nature of exponential growth and its relevance to you and me. The second pre-
sents an often told tale of a great deed of Elzeard Bouffier, a Frenchman who purportedly
replanted the denuded hillsides near his home, bringing the land back to life. The first
column inspires urgency and deeper understand; the second inspires hope and reminds us
all of the importance of individual action and lifelong dedication to the cause.

Reprinted with permission from Donella Meadows from her syndicated column,
The Global Citizen, *and collected in book form in* The Global Citizen, *Island*
Press, Washington, D.C., 1991.

Nothing Is So Powerful As an
Exponential Whose Time Has Come

The reason environmentalists are so often gloomy is that they know
what the word "exponential" means.

"A lack of appreciation for what exponential increase really means leads society to be disastrously sluggish in acting on critical issues," said Dr. Thomas Lovejoy of the Smithsonian Institution in a speech that has been reverberating through the environmental community. "I am utterly convinced that most of the great environmental struggles will be either won or lost in the 1990s, and that by the next century it will be too late."

What is he talking about? What does "exponential increase" mean?

It means growing like this: 1, 2, 4, 8, 16, 32. Doubling and then doubling again and then doubling again. Everyone understands that, right?

Not really, not at a gut level. For example, suppose you agree to eat one peanut on the first day of the month, two peanuts on the second, four peanuts on the third, eight peanuts on the fourth, and keep doubling every day. How long do you think you can keep going? How long will a pound can of shelled peanuts last you?

The first pound of peanuts will be gone on the ninth day; you'll eat half the can that day and feel pretty queasy. On the tenth you'll eat a whole pound, if you can, which I doubt. By the fifteenth you'll be scheduled to eat thirty-two pounds of peanuts. You'll have to eat roughly your own weight in peanuts by the seventeenth; on the twenty-first day the total will have risen to one ton; and by the end of the month, assuming a thirty-day month, it will be five hundred tons.

Just a few doublings add up ferociously fast—that's what Lovejoy was saying.

Mexico, with a population of 84 million and a doubling time of twenty-nine years, will, if it keeps that up, grow to 168 million in twenty-nine years and to 672 million within the lifetime of a child born today. That's nothing compared with Kenya, which has a doubling time of seventeen years. If it keeps growing at that rate, in seventy years there will be ten Kenyans for every one today.

Until the 1970s world oil consumption was growing at 7 percent per year. That means doubling every ten years. (The doubling time of anything growing exponentially is seventy divided by its annual growth rate—seventy divided by 7 percent is a ten-year doubling time.) Every ten years we used as much oil as we had used in all previous history. Every ten years we had to go out and discover as much oil as we had ever discovered before—and then, to keep going, discover twice that much in the next ten years.

We didn't keep going. We couldn't have. Exponential growth makes the cupboard bare very fast. Even if the entire earth were filled with nothing but high-grade crude oil, if we used it with an annual growth rate of 7 percent, it would be gone in 342 years. There's still plenty of oil around now, but we've been burning it faster than we've been discovering it for twenty years.

You may have heard that we have one thousand years' worth of coal. If we burn 7 percent more of it each year than the year before (which we may well do, substituting it for the disappearing oil), it will last just sixty-one years, and it will bring on a global climate change much faster than even the worst pessimists are now expecting.

Said Lovejoy in 1988, "I find to my personal horror that I have not been immune to naiveté about exponential functions. While I have been aware that the . . . loss of biological diversity, tropical deforestation, forest dieback in the northern hemisphere, and climate change are growing exponentially, it is only this very year that I think I have truly internalized how rapid their accelerating threat really is."

You don't get much reaction time when your problems grow exponentially. My favorite story to illustrate that point is an old French riddle.

Suppose you own a pond on which a water lily is growing. The lily doubles in size each day. If the lily were allowed to grow unchecked, it would completely cover the pond in thirty days, choking off other forms of life in the water. For a long time the plant is almost invisible, and so you decide not to worry about cutting it back until it covers half the pond. On what day will that be?

On the twenty-ninth day.

We are emitting carbon dioxide and several other greenhouse gases into the atmosphere exponentially. We are clearing tropical forest at an exponential rate. The human population is growing exponentially. Human energy use, human production of synthetic chemicals, deserts, and trash are growing exponentially. Our economy is growing exponentially, and we cheer it on, although an economic growth rate of, say, 3.5 percent per year means another whole industrial world plopped down on top of this one in just two decades.

We can't keep it up. If we understood the consequences of exponential growth, we wouldn't even want to try.

The Man Who Planted Trees and Grew Happiness

I belong to a twenty-nation network of environmentalists and resource managers, which has taken as its guiding document a beautiful story about a single Frenchman. Our network consists of East and West Europeans, Russians, North and Latin Americans, Asians, and Africans. The story goes to all our hearts. Here it is.

In 1914 Jean Giono was hiking through the barren hills of Provence in southern France. Charcoal burners had deforested the land, the streams had dried up, the villages were deserted. Desperately in need of water, Giono finally found a lone shepherd who gave him a drink from his well and invited him to spend the night in his cottage.

The shepherd's name was Elzeard Bouffier. He was fifty-five years old. His wife and son were dead; he lived with his sheep and his dog.

That night Giono watched Bouffier sort out one hundred perfect acorns from a bag. The next day, up in the hills, Giono accompanied Bouffier as he planted them. Bouffier also tended seedlings of birch and beech that he had planted in dried-up watercourses. He told Giono that he planted one hundred acorns every day. He supposed he had planted one hundred thousand of them, twenty thousand of which had sprouted, one-half of which would live and grow.

"It was his opinion," Giono notes, "that this land was dying for want of trees. He added that, having no very pressing business of his own, he had resolved to remedy this state of affairs. I asked him if the land belonged to him. He answered no. Did he know whose it was? He did not. . . . He was not interested in finding out. He planted his hundred acorns with the greatest care."

Giono went off to fight in World War I and did not return for five years. When he came back, he saw that "a sort of grayish mist covered the mountaintops like a carpet." The oldest oaks were now ten years old, and trees covered an area two miles by five miles. Bouffier had given up his sheep because they threatened the young trees. Now he was keeping bees and still planting one hundred acorns a day.

The trees were starting a chain reaction of nature restoring itself. "I saw that water flowing in brooks that had been dry since the memory of man. As the water reappeared, so there reappeared willows, rushes, . . . and a certain purpose in being alive."

In 1935 the French Forest Service came by to protect this "natural forest" from charcoal burning. By that time Bouffier was ten miles away at the leading edge of the forest, still planting.

The last time Giono saw Bouffier was in 1945. Bouffier was then eighty-seven, still at work. "Peaceful, regular toil, the vigorous mountain air, frugality, and above all serenity of spirit had endowed this old man with awe-inspiring health. He was one of God's athletes."

The entire region had been transformed. When Giono had first visited in 1914, the few residents "had been savage creatures, hating one another, living by trapping game, little removed, both physically and morally, from the conditions of prehistoric man. All about them nettles were feeding upon the remains of abandoned houses."

By 1945, "Hope had returned. Ruins had been cleared away, dilapidated walls torn down and houses restored. People . . . had settled here, bringing youth, motion, the spirit of adventure. The new houses, freshly plastered, were surrounded by gardens where vegetables and flowers grew in orderly confusion. On the lower slopes of the mountain I saw little fields of barley and rye."

According to Giono, Elzeard Bouffier died peacefully in 1947 at the hospice in Banon.

A member of my international network from Switzerland showed me this story in German. It was originally written in French and first published in English in *Vogue* in 1954. It has been reprinted many times and in many languages. The German edition I first saw ends with an interview with Giono, in which the interviewer points out that there is no record of Bouffier's death at Banon and asks exactly where Bouffier's forest is.

Giono replies, "If you go to Vergons, Banon, or Le Larne, you will see nothing. Since that time everything has been changed so that silos for atom bombs, shooting ranges, and various oil reservoirs could be placed there. Only a few groves remain. Be content with the story and the spirit of the deed."

I asked the European members of the network to check the authenticity of Elzeard Bouffier. They could find no information. Stewart Brand, reprinting it in the *Whole Earth Catalog* in 1980, asked, "Is the story true? I've heard vociferous denials and confident affirmations." Brand then listed stories of other undoubtedly real tree planters: the Hoedads of California and Wendy Campbell-Purdy, who has planted 130,000 trees in the desert of Algeria. In these cases the same phenomenon followed the tree plantings—streams were restored, soil was improved, wildlife, villages, gardens, and grains returned.

Recently, Chelsea Green Publishing Company issued a new edition of Giono's story with an afterword by Norma L. Goodrich, a scholar of French literature. She states that the story of Elzeard Bouffier is fiction—loving, hopeful, heartfelt fiction.

It is fiction that has inspired thousands of real people to carry out every day their own particular equivalent of planting one hundred acorns. "The Man Who Planted Trees" is beloved by my colleagues in twenty countries. It is my own favorite story. Real or unreal, it doesn't matter, it still strengthens me.

"Be content with the story and the spirit of the deed."

Garrett Hardin

LIVING WITHIN LIMITS
ECOLOGY, ECONOMICS, AND
POPULATION TABOOS

The debate over limits to growth is often confused by inaccuracies and erroneous assumptions. Few assumptions are as dangerous as the notions of a limitless world and infinite human capabilities to meet our needs. These two beliefs, so deeply ingrained in our psyches, spawn environmentally and socially reckless economic activity.

In Living Within Limits, *Garrett Hardin teases the arguments out of the population-environment debate and presents a coherent treatise on the existence of limits and the importance of learning to live within them. Very much a book on obeying the laws of nature,* Living Within Limits *sets the framework for a revolution in informed opinion by illustrating the fundamental relationship between quantity and quality—numbers of people and quality of life.*

Hardin argues for local actions and warns against promiscuous altruism—aid to those developing nations that cannot be saved by foreign aid. He points out the insanity of generous immigration policies that spread misery globally. Hardin also describes the counterproductive nature of the concept of individualism—how it affects our thinking and how it subordinates the interests of humankind to the interests of the self.

Adapted from Garrett Hardin, Living Within Limits: Ecology, Economics, and Population Taboos, *Oxford University Press, New York, 1993. Summarized by Patricia Wafer.*

Earth Day 1970 was the first in a long series of celebrations of our reverence for the planet and our responsibility to its stewardship. Earth Day 1970 came about in large part because of a rash of books on the population explosion, many of which predicted an apocalyptic future if the human population continued to grow at present rates. Swayed by such proclamations, United Nations Secretary General U Thant declared that the world had little more than a score of years to solve the population problem or be overwhelmed by it.

In the years that followed, an avalanche of discouraging reports on population and the environment appeared in various media. On Earth Day's twentieth anniversary, though, the topic of population was virtually ignored. Was that because population had stopped growing?

Hardly. The previous two decades had witnessed a stunning 47-percent increase in world population. During that period, 1.7 billion people had been added to the human population, bringing the global total to 5.3 billion.

In the decade of the 1980s, though, activists who warned of the continuing dangers of population growth were voices in the wilderness. Talk of limits to growth had fallen out of vogue. New developments such as the high-yield crops of the Green Revolution had spurred an unquenchable technological optimism. Stirred by new technologies, some futurists proclaimed that science could create a bold new world of perpetual frontiers with unlimited potential for humans. Other scientists talked of feeding the masses by harvesting the sea. Still others envisioned colonies in outer space as a remedy to Earth's most pressing problems.

The view of the world as a limitless supply of materials for human welfare is not a new idea by any stretch of the imagination. It finds its most recent roots in the Industrial Revolution, an era in which science and technology seemed to dispel the notion of limits. In more recent times, the limitless world view has nourished the public's craving for optimism.

The resistance to limits and measures to control population size has emerged in part from both liberal and conservative factions in many nations. Marxists, for instance, assert that the advance of technology coupled with distributional justice (an equitable sharing of resources) will automatically solve all problems mistakenly labeled "population." A similar conclusion springs from conservative capitalists who invoke the spirit of laissez-faire economics to generate a theory of automatic population regulation—by letting business generate wealth we will all prosper and, in the process, reduce our family size.

Five centuries before Christ, Buddha stated, "I teach only two things; the cause of human sorrow and the way to become free of it." Restated in the scientific language of today, Buddha's statement translates accordingly: one must carefully look for causes before prescribing remedies. This, in fact, is the obligation of science.

The present work proceeds along the Buddhist path—first to reveal that overpopulation is a root cause of human sorrow and then to uncover ways to free ourselves of the sorrow by returning to a limited world view.

Four centuries of sedation by the delusion of limitlessness have left humanity floundering in a wilderness of rhetoric and wishful thinking. Hucksters would have us believe that to accept the reality of limits is to become a pessimist. Most scientists agree with an aphorism attributed to Hagel: "Freedom is the recognition of necessity." Until we abandon the limitless world view and learn again to live contentedly within limits, we cannot free ourselves.

Balancing Supply and Demand

Robert Malthus (the economist who set the stage in the early 1800s for population panic) was considered by many to be a gloomy and heartless man. Yet his theories were based soundly in the laws of supply and demand and the need that the two be balanced. He complained to his critics that it was "an utter misconception of my argument to infer that I am an enemy to population . . . I am only an enemy to vice and misery, and consequently to that unfavorable proportion between population and food which produces those evils."

We might, in fact, look upon Malthus as a provisionally cheerful fellow if we interpret his theories not as a prediction for inevitable catastrophe, but rather as precautionary words. While Malthus warned that disaster is a natural outcome of perpetual population growth, he implied that disaster can be forestalled if society can find the will to end population growth. Today even China, which twenty years ago refuted all Malthusian notions, has capitulated to his logic. Third World nations have begun to recognize that any step forward—increased food production, construction of houses, roads, and schools, or creation of jobs—soon becomes two steps back if soaring numbers of needy new members of society outstrip its capacity to provide.

Does population growth necessarily create suffering and pain? Overpopulation often can be visibly tied to disturbing consequences: hunger, disease, deforestation, and loss of soil. But, to be fair, we must admit that there is another side to the coin. A larger population sometimes does open up desirable new opportunities. Economies of scale are also an economic fact of life. A small country cannot manufacture an automobile at a reasonable price; and only a very large nation can afford the extensive infrastructure required to send men and women to the moon. Where is the happy medium between the good and bad resulting from population growth? It is a delicate question of balance.

Cowboy Economics

In the fifth century B.C., Herodotus generalized, "Man stalks across the landscape and deserts follow in his footsteps." Throughout history, human exploitation of the Earth has followed a certain progression: colonize; destroy; move on. The restless "moving on" of the human species has depended, of course, on always having fresh land to move to. Today, our territorial expansion is coming to an end, and humans soon will be, consciously or forcibly, reduced to living within the limited resources of our Earth.

For the past two hundred years, the idea of unlimited progress has been the ruling paradigm of western society, penetrating every corner of our lives. But today, increasing anxiety about the depletion of resources and the increase in waste and pollution makes some of us wonder whether we are not at last approaching the "limits of perfectibility" of our materialistic world. Problems of the allocation of scarce resources have, at last and inevitably, become central in human affairs.

Economist Kenneth Boulding coined the term "cowboy economics" to characterize an economic system that seeks only to economize human effort. Hungry Kit Carson would shoot a buffalo and eat only the tongue, leaving the rest of the carcass to spoil. Had he dismembered the animal and smoked the meat to preserve it, he would have been worse off for having wasted precious time. This type of system worked in the Wild West only because the land was rich in resources and human population was scarce. For a time, wasteful behavior was affordable. But times have changed. We can no longer afford to live on the subsidies of nature. In our heavily populated world, we are finding that resources are finite and the wide open frontier is no more.

Leading science fiction writer Robert Heinlein once said, "We have just about used up this planet; time to go find another one." While it is possible that we may some day be able to send an inoculum of our species to some distant planet, it is beyond belief that we will be able to export human bodies as fast as we can produce babies. As of 1991, more than a quarter of a million people would have had to be shot off the Earth each day just to keep Earth's population constant. Clearly, we must make our behavior fit the reality of a limited Earth. Continued population growth will only produce a more crowded, degraded world.

Coinciding Views of Liberals and Conservatives on Limits to Growth

In an 1879 publication entitled *Progress and Poverty*, Henry George defiantly proclaimed "that the injustice of society, not the niggardliness of nature, is the cause of the want and misery which the current theory attributes to overpopulation." Blaming poverty on inequitable political systems, while ignoring the changing ratio of population to resources, has continued to be the practice of political liberals from George's time to the present. It has been a favorite practice of Third World leaders, along with denial and scapegoating, as exemplified at the first United Nations conference on population, held in Bucharest in 1974. Here, the head of China's delegation stated, "Population is not a problem under socialism. The primary way of solving the population problem lies in combating the aggression and plunder of the imperialists." The intellectual descendants of George, along with other delegates from the Third World, warmly welcomed his analysis. Indeed, in the years that followed, any talk of reducing the population of minorities or Third World nations was construed, among most liberals, as something akin to racism.

At the Bucharest conference, India's delegate added the most memorable phrase: "Development is the best contraceptive." This slogan was repeated by the United States ten years later at the second U.N. conference on population in Mexico City.

The common and unconsciously shared ideology of these very different nations was (and is) a deep faith in technological progress. Conservatives in political matters do not often speak of inequities—in fact, they are eager to conserve the wealth and power of the present generation of the rich. In this quest, however, they concur with political liberals in downgrading the importance of the population-to-resources ratio. Ever ardent in their defense of time-honored customs, no matter how pathological the consequences, conservatives have remained indifferent to the needs of generations to come.

Ecological conservatives, on the other hand, remain true to the principles of the Stoic philosopher, Epicurus, who said, "Nothing is created out of that which does not exist." This may be interpreted as a statement of economics: there is little or no true production in the world, merely alternations of various sorts among the different forms of matter and energy. But many economists seem to twist this fact on their balance sheets.

It is surprising how many hard-headed business people live in a world of illusion created by deceptive words. The financial world habitually speaks of yearly "production" of oil. But the unvarnished truth is this: we human beings have never produced so much as a single barrel of petroleum. Only nature produces oil—and at a very slow rate. Creative accountants and journalists looking for positive headlines would have us believe that world oil reserves have risen. But, in fact, petroleum is being destroyed a million times faster than it is being synthesized by today's geological processes.

The Myth of Exponential Growth

A second intellectual revolution in "informed opinion" is demanded if economics is to reflect reality. For centuries, we have assumed that material wealth can grow endlessly. Perpetual growth has become the religion of the most powerful actors in our commercial society. However, in the long-term, infinite growth—whether of bank accounts, populations, or national economies—is not consistent with the boundaries of the world we live in. Graphs aptly illustrate that consequences of growth curves that soar off the page are *out of this world*.

Malthus was correct in assuming that the human species has the potential to increase exponentially (or, as he said, "geometrically"). Darwin expanded upon this thought twenty-five years after Malthus's death, stating, "There is no exception to the rule that every organic being naturally increases at so high a rate, that, if not destroyed (controlled), the Earth would soon be covered by the progeny of a single pair." Malthus predicted that human fertility would be limited by an increase in "food production," which could grow only arithmetically. However, since his time, significant improvements in agricultural production have occurred. The scientific-industrial evolution has permitted us to extract sustenance from the environment more efficiently, allowing population to equilibrate about a new set point.

However, the central notion of Malthus's theory—that exponential growth is kept under control by "misery"—is sound. Ecologists have found that potentially exponential biological reproduction is kept in check by counterbalancing forces. That is, exponential reproduction moves each species to its optimum point, the carrying capacity of the environment. However, the actions of other species—predators, competitors, disease germs—carving out their own living, tend to stabilize growth at that point.

For most of history, humans have followed the rules. The average rate of population growth has been very slow—only .02 percent a year, yielding a doubling every 3,500 years. When human population moved beyond the optimum point, other balancing forces such as famine, epidemics, and war, pruned the growth of the human race. At times, humankind itself has acted as a regulator, adjusting to the population/subsistence gap, as demonstrated by the Irish who chose during the potato plight to marry at a much later age.

Today, however, we are far from zero population growth. Although the growth rate of the world's population has slowly declined from 2 percent in the early 1960s to 1.7 percent in the late 1980s, 93 million more people are born each year than die during the same time. Europe is cited as a region in which population growth has leveled off, yet at its 1988 growth rate of .3 percent per year, Europeans will find their numbers to have doubled in 233 years. In Africa, fertility is approaching a high never reached before. Tragically, this occurrence is taking place in areas that are already experiencing immense environmental destruction because of overpopulation.

For a time, it seemed that Malthus was wrong in predicting that population growth multiplies misery because the Industrial Revolution had changed the population set point. Today, we see that we cannot continue to move the set point upwards without limit. With each improvement in agricultural production, we see diminishing returns. Fertilizer application, for example, increases productivity for a while. However, at some point adding more fertilizer becomes counterproductive. In our push to increase productivity without limit, we are toying with the balance of nature's system.

Carrying Capacity

The Earth, and each part of it, have a limited carrying capacity that applies to all populations—human and nonhuman. Before we tackle the complicated question of what the human carrying capacity of the Earth might be, the much simpler question of the meaning of carrying capacity for nonhuman species should be studied.

For the simplest case, we imagine a pasture of fixed dimensions in a mild climate; in this are pastured a constant number of cows that have no other source of food year-round. The carrying capacity of the pasture is the maximum number of animals that can be sustained by this food source year after year, without diminishing the quality of the pasture. Because photosynthesis is less in winter than in summer, a stable carrying capacity must be tied to the least favorable conditions (winter). Moreover, we must allow for the variability of the climate by tying carrying capacity to the least favorable years.

The wise pastoralist is careful not to exceed carrying capacity because of consequences first for the pasture (diminished growth of grass and soil erosion) and secondly for the animals themselves. Exceeding the carrying capacity in one year diminishes the carrying capacity in subsequent years, until scarcely any animals at all can be supported on what was initially a rich resource. Many, perhaps most, of the deserts of the world have been produced by biological populations that exceeded the carrying capacity. Sadly, if restoration does occur it takes much, much longer than destruction.

On the American scale of living, the carrying capacity of the Earth is only about one-hundredth as great as it would be if people would be content with the barest minimum of goods. The average American, in fact, draws upon the resources of nine acres. Most urbanites "occupy" what agricultural geographer Georg Bourgstrom called "ghost acreage," which is out of sight and out of mind. Human carrying capacity thus must be determined by values and lifestyle and is therefore less precise.

At a sustainable population size, the quality of life and the quantity of it are inversely related. We might say that the population size and the amount of luxury—not only goods but such sensible measures as "safety factors"—are tradeoffs. Those who would opt for the maximum number of human lives are, whether they realize it or not, opting for maximizing human misery as well. On the other hand, opting to equilibrate the set point of population at a smaller number will mean that the good things of life are present in greater abundance.

Clearly, choices must be made. Equally clearly, such choices cannot be made intelligently until we recognize that clinging to the presumption of perpetual growth is both foolish and irresponsible. We are ultimately governed by the "Laws of Nature," and the words of Francis Bacon should be our guides: "Nature to be commanded must be obeyed."

Trying to Escape Malthus

Our contemporary anthropocentric bias is rooted in most surviving religions' view of our place in nature. The belief that only humans were made in God's image fostered a certainty that people are different from all other creatures over which we have dominion. This view places people as masters of their destiny. The world is seen as vast with limitless opportunities for humankind, and human history is linked with progress, which need never cease. Many believe that we can interfere with nature and make our own rules. They base their actions on hopes, for example, that saving infants will reduce the birthrate or that feeding the work force will make everyone more productive.

As "humanitarians," we continue to send foreign aid that addresses "death control" while ignoring birth control—to which it should be tied. Bluntly put, we are not showing respect for life if we do not show equal respect for the functions and necessity of death. Ultimately, it must be asked if, in pursuing aid policies that focus on suffering today, we are not compounding suffering tomorrow. Giving death control priority ultimately increases the death rate because it ensures further increase in human numbers. Survival of infants in poor countries has not resulted in a decrease in fertility. Today, almost without exception, these nations find their population has grown far beyond the human carrying capacity of the land.

Further growth of population in an already overstrained environment ensures the further destruction of that environment through loss of soil, forests, wild species, and productivity. Logic would have it that if we fail to bring about a benign transition to zero population growth by conscious human intervention, nature may, of its own accord, bring about a malignant transition by increasing the death rate to meet the birth rate.

Every act of charity should be followed by a post-audit to determine both the good and harm it has done. This is difficult enough to do well in our own community; it is very difficult to do from a distance of thousands of miles. Adam Smith recognized the difficulty of minding the business of others in 1759 when he stated: "The administration of the great system of the universe . . . is the business of God, and not man. To man is allotted a much humbler department, but one much more suitable to the weakness of his powers, and to the narrowness of his comprehension—the care of his own happiness, and that of his family, his friends, his country."

Biting the Bullet

Our world itself is in the dilemma of the lifeboat; it can only hold so many before it sinks. Not everyone can be saved. There are no easy answers, but the solution is clear. Because the production of human beings is the result of very localized actions, corrective actions must be local, or incentive dissolves. Nations with rapidly rising populations must suffer the consequences alone. Jean Pierre Proudhon, a nineteenth-century thinker, challenged universalism by stating, "If all the world is my brother, then I have no brother." We must choose our loyalties carefully and be wary of "promiscuous" altruism lest it destroy all.

Insane economics result when a few reap profits at the cost of all. But often today, we see the principle of shared costs matched with private profits in effect. William Lloyd's 1833 treatise on the tragedy of the village commons aptly illustrates the principle's faultiness. Common pastures inevitably suffer from overgrazing as each villager seeks to maximize his own profits at the cost of all. Freedom in a commons brings ruin to all. Just as surely, letting the world suffer the consequences of the unrestrained population growth of individual nations will only ensure that it ends in a suicidal commons.

The wisdom is very old: Don't put all your eggs in one basket. Given sovereign nations with closed borders, it is possible for humanity to carry out many experiments with population control. Each nation can observe the successes and failures of others. However, learning by trial and error is perilous if unrestricted migration converts the globe into a single huge experiment. As long as the intelligence of the human species is less than perfect—which will forever be the case—parochialism is superior to the cosmopolitan approach.

Generous immigration policies work against the resolution of population problems in a another way. Of all the problems facing a multicultural nation, none is more resistant to solution than population control. Every method proposed in a multiethnic society elicits a knee-jerk cry of genocide! Difficulty in achieving unanimity of purpose increases in proportion to ethnic diversity in the population, particularly when it comes to population issues.

Unless immigration can be strictly controlled, no country can succeed in controlling its population size. To best nurture both unity and progress, a double policy should be embraced: great diversity worldwide and limited diversity within each nation.

Individualism, Population, and Posterity

The notion of individual rights is today presumed to be a universal truth. But, in fact, our version of individualism is a European creation only some three centuries old, dating back to John Locke's dissertations in the late 1600s. Countries such as China, with a long tradition of Confucianism, have a more "holistic philosophy." Individuals are seen as a component of the whole society, and their interests are subordinate to interests of the larger group.

Malthus implicitly gave priority to community interests. Intellectuals of his era who had been persuaded to couch moral thinking in terms of the interests of the individual accused him of being a misanthrope. Today, we must reexamine his words. All around us we see politicians who, in the hope of garnering votes, appeal to the selfish individual interests of many. The good of the community, which often lacks a voice and a vote, has been forgotten. But, in time, the abstraction called "community" becomes the reality of posterity, which must suffer for the lack of imagination and courage of its predecessors.

If posterity is to be given a chance, there is a clear need in each nation for the community-oriented ethical thinking that was more common among our ancestors. We must meet the challenge of Charles Frankel's definition of responsibility: "A decision is responsible when the man or group that makes it has to answer for it to those who are directly or indirectly affected by it."

Observers of criminals and the poor have noted that, locked in a seeming inability to give adequate weight to the future, they often succumb to the temptation of present gain. If humankind is not to suffer the same fate, a future orientation must be acquired, or required, by all societies that seek survival.

It must be remembered that birth control is not population control. While techniques of birth control have greatly improved in the last century, the theory and practice of population control seem to have stood still, particularly amongst those with less education. If such groups of people continue to reproduce without discretion, Darwin's natural selection process will in fact be reversed. Like it or not, the issue of coercion must be faced.

Long ago, Aristotle knew that bigger is not better when it comes to the governance of a country. Communication suffers and obedience to the law is more difficult to secure. In addition, as a population grows larger and more diverse, governmental coercion necessarily plays a larger and larger role in human life. Traffic restrictions demonstrate how loss of freedom is an inevitable consequence of unlimited population growth in a limited space.

Coercion is a fact of life in a democracy; unanimity is not required. The United States is governed by restrictive laws that exert mutually agreed upon coercion. However, if the much-praised American inventiveness can be directed into new channels, we should be able to devise reward systems that encourage small families, rather than bring them about through coercion. Errors will no doubt be made, but by sharing in the learning experiences of other nations, we can minimize the cost of our own experiments.

Conclusion

Reform will not come easy. Generally, the pain of political malfunction has to become very bad—almost lethally bad—before we consent to change. The population problem remains a taboo subject for many reasons. Although critical troubles may elicit critical action, chronic troubles are likely to elicit apathy. We search for "technological fixes" for rising levels of pollution, noise, and traffic congestion that should be perceived as signs of overpopulation. Hoping to diminish traffic jams, we build ever more multilane roads and as a result more traffic is attracted to them and traffic congestion gets steadily worse. To confront the population crisis, we must decide that enough is enough.

The preceding pages have been a dissertation on the laws of nature that must be obeyed. Within these limits, there are many ways to control human population—some kinder than others. No definitive answer to "the population problem" will be given here. As Nobelist

Dennis Gabor pointed out, "The future cannot be predicted but futures can be invented." Conceiving a workable system of population control is the work of the future, in which many minds must participate. Making the required political and social changes will involve the human will in a way in which it was not involved when merely technological changes were the focus of attention.

According to M. King Hubbert, a noted geologist who predicted the oil shock of the early '70s, "The foremost problem facing humankind at present is that of how to make the transition from the present exponential-growth phase to the near steady state of the future by as noncatastrophic a progression as possible." Planning for the future demands the best possible assessment of where we are. Instead of focusing on trends, it is important to look at fundamentals. Sentimentality must not compel us to pursue a path of economic insanity. If it is unthinkable to disinvest in practices that bring about a decrease in the resources/population ratio, civilization has truly arrived at a disastrous cul-de-sac.

A future is arriving in which hard choices must be made and temperance must be the guiding ideal. But even if material progress must be throttled down, we need not give up hope of further improvement in the overall conditions of life.

While matter and energy must be conserved, information can grow endlessly. As scarcities of material resources compel the adoption of an economic system that makes better ecological and human sense, music, the arts, literature, science, and philosophy may still flourish and grow vigorously.

The myth of the limitless world is but one of the many myths that have grown up in the protective shadow of the insufficiently examined idea of progress. We are schooled to be naively hopeful of perpetual motion machines but stubbornly resistant to desperately needed social and political changes. But, like it or not, with our world showing increasing signs of ecological and social distress, we must muster the courage to invent, test, and adopt new ways of looking at life.

PART II

RESTRUCTURING FOR
SUSTAINABILITY:
COMMUNITY, ECONOMICS,
AND EDUCATION

Daniel Kemmis

COMMUNITY AND
THE POLITICS OF PLACE

Since the Earth Summit in June 1992, the international community has rallied behind the banner of sustainable development. At this writing, nearly twenty states and several nations have developed strategies for sustainable development, giving us all cause for celebration. But nowhere are efforts to fashion a sustainable society more necessary than in the communities in which we live—our cities, towns, neighborhoods, and even our work places. It is here that many of us can make the largest contribution. Unfortunately, divisiveness and acrimony often characterize public discourse in our communities.

Daniel Kemmis, author and public leader, sees hope. He sees community spirit— our love for the places in which we live—as a potentially powerful unifying force that could help us forge personal and political differences into common vision and common goals essential to rebuild our society from the inside out.

Adapted from Community and the Politics of Place *by Daniel Kemmis. Copyright 1990 by the University of Oklahoma Press.*

The studio lights at the Public Radio station are dim. In their place is an altar of three candles, burning sage, and smoothed river rocks from the nearby Clark Fork and Bitterroot rivers. Surrounding this carefully created center are the four musicians—a drummer, a harpist, a guitarist, and a violinist. Joining them as a fifth member is a poet. As she begins to read her poem about Mount Jumbo—a large, open mountain with folds of coniferous forests that serves as one of the eastern, and very conspicuous, boundaries of Missoula, Montana—the musicians also begin their spontaneous interplay of music and poetic word, notes and spoken voice. The poem ends, lamenting with the violin:

> Luxury homes
> on the back of the sleeping elephant
> who holds the world
> who attaches us
> to heaven.[1]

The "Finding Our Place" improvisational ensemble is a part of a new, unique project in Missoula, Montana. It is a blending of music and storytelling about the place that is and surrounds Missoula, created by the Institute of Culture and Imagination. The institute is striving to revive the lost art of telling our stories, with the hope that they will evoke a response from listeners that helps them identify their sense of commitment to their place of habitation.

The relationship of this project to politics and my book, *Community and the Politics of Place*, is strong. For it is this sense of place, this striving for a sense of community not just within the city of Missoula but extending out and including the country that helps define it, that is central to the book and deserves more attention and detail. "If you know where you are, you know who you are," says Wendell Berry. Terry Tempest Williams takes this a step further with, "If you know who you are, then you can share that in story." The storytelling project of the Institute of Culture and Imagination attempts to help us find who we are through stories of place.

As detailed in *Community and the Politics of Place*, the "where" takes on not only a present geography but a history that helps identify the "who." Let us try to find out "where" we have come from in our political understandings of community. Maybe it too will shed a little light on who we are.

The Loss of Public Life, the Loss of Place

Place is a subject much talked about, especially in the inland of the West, a place that is undergoing another population boom from the far western communities of Seattle, Portland, Sacramento, and Los Angeles. Old-timers—who are now becoming a rare breed—talk about how the hills where they once hunted elk are now being overtaken by subdivisions, one ironically called Elk Hills. They lament the recent time they bush-whacked to their secret trout-fishing hole only to find three other anglers there, casting in the same hole. And a hunting season on mountain lions has been proposed in areas on the very outskirts of Missoula, because sightings of the cats have increased near the city's boundaries, as those boundaries have pushed themselves into prime lion habitat.

But a loss of place doesn't necessarily mean just a loss of physical habitat, physical land, physical space. Loss of place connotes a loss of the *sense* of place, a loss of feeling a connection with the land around you, what it means to you, brings to you, gives to you. This sense of place is being eroded all across the country as we, as a culture, orient instead to the local mall, the McDonald's, and television advertising that tells us what we're missing by not buying the latest VCR.

But there is an underlying current of connection to place that is waiting to be re-exposed and reclaimed. In Montana's preamble to its Constitution, the writers ordain the government of the state to achieve certain specific ends, as most constitutions do. However, the preamble goes on to say, "We the people of Montana, *grateful to God for the quiet beauty of our state, the grandeur of its mountains, the vastness of its rolling plains*, and desiring to secure to ourselves and our posterity the bless-ings of liberty for this and future generations do ordain and establish this constitution" (emphasis added). Public life, this preamble implies, can be reclaimed only by understanding, and then practicing, its con-nection to real, identifiable places.

Concomitant with the loss of sense of place is the loss of a sense for public life and public interaction. Government of any size—local, state, national—is viewed skeptically these days, and participation in the labyrinth of political bureaucracies is waning at best. Political apa-thy, not involvement, covers the general population in a thick passion-less malaise. Incumbent bashing is a growing phenomenon in political elections.

The "public" in the republican government that Thomas Jefferson and others worked so hard to help define in our Constitution is disap-pearing. This loss began with Jefferson's losing of the philosophical battle to Madison and his Federalist cohorts. Our contemporary con-cept of the public life, of public politics—and the resulting sense of dis-connectedness from such—was subtly shaped by these early, and very fundamentally different, philosophies that helped established the political framework of forming colonies into United States.

The Jefferson/Madison Battle

The basic question that Jefferson and Madison attempted to answer through the creation of the United States Constitution was this: Should the burden of solving public problems rest most directly on citizenship or on government? The two arrive at radically different answers.

Jefferson, writing a steady stream of letters from his ambassador's post in Versailles, France, was adamant that the people, the citizenry, had not only the duty but the right to be involved in solving their own problems. To Jefferson, this approach was truly republican. Taking on none of the contemporary political party connotation, the "republican" tradition rested squarely upon a face-to-face, hands-on approach to problem-solving, with an implicit belief that people could rise above their particular interests to pursue a common good.

This republican approach to public policy required a high level of interaction among citizens. In particular, it assumed that citizens were presented with many opportunities and much encouragement to rise above a narrow self-centeredness. John Winthrop, the first colonial governor of Massachusetts, called this approach to government "making other's conditions our own." It was a politics of engagement in which people were *engaged* with one another on an emotional level. They worked out solutions for the common good, putting aside their individual needs for the needs of the whole.

How does this more selfless attitude develop? To Jefferson and the civic republicans, as they came to be known, agriculture was the key. Jefferson thought that the way people made their living had much to do with the development of a sense of responsibility, and that farming developed it most consistently. What bothered Jefferson about the nonfarming activities of commerce and manufacturing was the disconnectedness and the anonymity that seemed necessarily to accompany them. Jefferson saw clearly that those who made their living through these activities were wholly dependent upon the choices of utter strangers, known only as "consumers." Jefferson was appalled by the thought of large numbers of people making their living by depending solely upon the choices of other people with whom they had no social or moral ties of any kind.

Farming, on the other hand, by the mere essence of the work itself, developed "civic virtues": plain honesty, industry, and perseverance. Jefferson saw that the new Constitution, as presented by Madison and others, placed little value upon such civic virtues. This was a retreat from republican principles for which, Jefferson believed, the war with England had been fought.

The thread that Jefferson and the civic republicans hung on to was a phrase in the Constitution, kept there by Madison and others most likely to appease these civic republican desires. Guaranteed to all states in the Constitution was a "republican form of government." Jefferson could foresee that the vast, open lands of the frontier would be at once a source of new states, and that those states would be republican in the most fundamental sense because open lands would draw people into agriculture, at least as fast as they were drawn into cities and factories. Republican principles would thrive "as long as agriculture is our principal object, which will be the case, while there remains vacant lands in any part of America."[2]

The obvious question is: What happens to Jefferson's ideals when all of the vacant land is gone, an inevitable process that surely even Jefferson was aware of? We will deal with that question in a minute.

For there was another view of how these United States were to be governed, of how the Constitution would be written and interpreted. James Madison and Alexander Hamilton were the leaders of the Federalists, a group that was skeptical at best about the ability of individuals to come to a common decision. They believed that the *causes* of conflict could not be removed, that conflict is simply a part of human nature, and believed only in controlling its *effects*. They were fearful that a majority, having come to a decision in a "republican" way (engaged with each other, working out a solution for the common good) would evolve into a tyrannous insurrection. As a result, the Federalists devised political systems whereby citizens would be kept apart—large-scale decision-making bodies instead of small-scale, face-to-face bodies in the republican style—where there was little room for common goals, the common good and, therefore, the dreaded tyranny of the majority.

It was at this point that Madison shrewdly turned the republican ideal of open land for the creation of republican states to his advantage. He argued precisely the same point that Jefferson had urged—that the frontier lands of this country were necessary for the healthy expansion of the country—but for a different end. For Madison and the Federalists, an extensive territory was an excellent hedge against tyranny, especially against the tyranny of the majority. "Extend the sphere, and you take in a greater variety of parties and interests; you make it less probable that a majority of the whole will have a common motive to invade the rights of other citizens; or if such a common motive exists, it will be more difficult for all who feel it to discover their own strengths and to act in unison with each other."[3]

Where those advocating a republican form of government stressed the term "public" as meaning that everything appears in public and can be seen and heard by everyone, Madison abandoned the idea of citizens beholding, let alone acting upon, the public interest. It was their private interests that he wanted them to behold, to understand, and to pursue. To this end, the Federalists advocated a series of checks and balances within government, where government was structured to balance private pursuits of individuals so cleverly that the highest good would emerge without any one individual having willed its existence.

Let us return now to Jefferson and his adamant feeling towards open lands. Remember that the western territories, which at that time meant all lands west of the eastern seaboard colonies, seemed almost limitless. To Jefferson these lands were necessary for the establishment of a strong agrarian population, a series of farming communities that would evolve naturally by virtue of their civic values into states with republican forms of government, as guaranteed by the Constitution.

Yet Jefferson must have realized that even the vast lands of the western territories had, eventually, to be filled up. In fact, just a century after Jefferson penned his letters to Madison, the most remote region of the Louisiana Purchase had been admitted to the union. The admission of these states marked the closing of the old American frontier.

Meanwhile from across the ocean had come a response that, point for point, was exactly the opposite of Jefferson's. Georg Wilhelm Friedrich Hegel argued that a real republic would become possible in America "only after the immeasurable space which that country presents to its inhabitants shall have been occupied, and the members of the political body shall have begun to be pressed back on each other." Hegel even contradicted Jefferson's fundamental argument that civic virtues are more effectively transmitted in rural than in urban settings: "Only when, as in Europe, the direct increase of agriculturists is checked, will the inhabitants, instead of pressing outwards to occupy the fields, press inwards upon each other—pursuing town occupations, and trading with their fellow citizens; and so form a compact system of civil society, and require an organized state."[4]

With the closing of the old frontier, the issue between these two views of civil society would seem to have been firmly joined. If Hagel was right, a civil society could now at last emerge. But if Jefferson was closer to the mark, things would now be likely to become less civil. Let us follow a bit more of our political history to see more clearly where we are in these terms, and who we have become.

The Populist Campaign

All was not lost for Jefferson's civic republican ideals as the frontier lands diminished. Almost ironically, with the "closing" of the frontier in the 1890s—with Montana and the Dakotas (1889), and Wyoming and Idaho (1890) being populated enough to be admitted to the Union—came a strong, land-based political movement that came close to establishing itself as the civic republican philosophy that Jefferson envisioned for the country. But the populists, as they came to be known, suffered a defeat from which they, and with them Jefferson's agrarian ideals, never recovered.

The presidential election of 1896, like any political election, can be analyzed in a variety of ways. For our purposes, it represents a turning point in political history, a classic battle between the Jeffersonian ideals of agrarian, engagement-oriented politics, represented by William Jennings Bryan, and the growing political philosophy of commercial and industrial interests that shapes our contemporary political scene, represented in 1896 by William McKinley.

It might be stretching it to say the election of Bryan could have changed history, but the course of American politics certainly would have shifted, at least temporarily. It is probable that the momentum of capitalist politics would have caught up to the civic republicans. But this is all conjecture. The relevant point that relates to our look at contemporary political thought is that the defeat of Bryan was a decisive setback for the principles of self-government, according to Lawrence Goodwyn in *The Populist Movement*. McKinley and his party ran the first mass advertising campaign that set the course of modern political spending.

Big money and big commerce were the winners in this race. What was lost? The fundamental faith of ordinary people in their ability to govern themselves.

Coupled with the growth of U.S. imperialism, which enabled the United States to look outward, again, to a new "frontier," came a significant increase in regulatory bureaucracy which heightened the mechanistic and diminished the face-to-face dimensions of public life. So at the beginning of the twentieth-century citizens were once again "kept apart" by the government's political framework.

Now, at the end of the twentieth century some citizens are calling for a renewed commitment to small-scale, personal-engagement politics based on a sense of *habitation*, a sense of where one is based, a sense of place. In the end, of course, the point is not what Jefferson or Madison thought, but what we can, should, and will do with the part of the world we call home.

A New Sense of "Being Public"
Our democratic faith has been weakened by a political system (a system that operates with increased regulatory bureaucracy and large-scale government) that frustrates public involvement in the processes of change. The more frustration, the fewer people become involved. For example, Montana has attempted for ten years to pass a wilderness bill for the state, only to be gridlocked time and time again. Public interaction—our way of being public at hearings, public testimony, and public meetings—is unsatisfactory. What do we do?

What "we" do depends upon who "we" are, or who we think we are. It depends, in other words, upon how we choose to relate to each other, to the place we inhabit, and to the issues that inhabiting raise for us.

To Montanans and others in this dry, windy, cold, hot, and remote western region, the place is still largely unpopulated, precisely because of the harsh physical conditions. Even with the increase in "immigrants" to the inland West, studies are showing that a high percentage leave after two to three years due, in part, to unrealistic expectations of climate and more romantic notions of the West not being fulfilled. It seems to come naturally, then, that people tend to define themselves in terms of the land that surrounds them. This is a step in the direction of defining who "we" are.

Wallace Stegner says:

Angry as one may be at what heedless men have done and still do to a noble habitat, one cannot be pessimistic about the West. This is the native home of hope. When it fully learns that cooperation, not rugged individualism, is the quality that most characterizes and preserves it, then it will have achieved itself and outlived its origins. Then it has a chance to create a society to match its scenery.[5]

"Cooperation, not rugged individualism . . ." and "a chance to create a society to match its scenery." Powerful words. But what is missing in our society's ability to change?

In an attempt to understand how to cooperate, how to operate as a republic, let's look at the word itself. The Latin phrase for "republic" was *res publica*, the "public thing," a fairly meaningless phrase at first glance. Hannah Arendt says this about the relationship of the public and *res publica*:

To live together in the world means essentially that a world of things is between those who have it in common, as a table is located between those who sit around it; the world, like every in-between, relates and separates men at the same time.

The public realm, as the common world, gathers us together and yet prevents our falling over each other, so to speak. What makes mass society so difficult to bear is not the number of people involved, or at least not primarily, but the fact that the world between them has lost its power to gather them together, to relate and to separate them. The weirdness of this situation resembles a spiritualistic seance where a number of people gathered around a table might suddenly, through some magic trick, see the table vanish from their midst, so that two persons sitting opposite each other were no longer separated but also would be entirely unrelated by anything tangible.[6]

This vanishing table is the "thing" that would make a "public" possible. It is just this that is suggested by the Montana preamble, where the eminently tangible mountains and plains of the state play precisely the role of gathering people together by simultaneously relating and separating them. Arendt herself does not use the natural world, but rather the human world to define what gathers us together.

The U.S. preamble (and indeed most of what we now call "public" life) attempts to dispense altogether with that gathering and separating "thing." We have severed the public from its republican context. In the process, we have made any real public life all but impossible.

Our question, then, is what happened to the public thing: How did the table vanish? Part of the answer lies in what happened to our understanding of public life at certain key periods in our political history, described in the previous sections. But the demise of public life has to be understood in terms of space (or place) as well as time. Putting it more positively, public life can be reclaimed only by understanding, and then practicing, its connection to real, identifiable places. This is not a particularly easy way for most of us to think about public issues. Thinking of politics in historical terms is second nature, but we tend to be more dubious about the propositions that political culture may be shaped by its place, as well as by its time.

And so we have two parties at the table, the rugged individualist and those who endorse the regulatory bureaucratic approach. What is particularly ironic in the West is that a substantial amount of land has been set aside as federal (public) land; that the land became public precisely for the public good, to protect against the negative impacts of individuals who wanted to do their own thing, be it overharvesting of timber, mining next to pristine rivers, or drilling in the midst of sensitive wildlife habitat. But the two parties at the table have lost the table itself. They have lost the process of how to gather around it, and both feel incredibly frustrated: the individualists feel stymied by what they perceive as overly bureaucratic control, and those inclined to the regulatory approach see their dreams stymied by the process of modern politics, which allows initiatives to be blocked, but doesn't seem to allow genuine progress to be made.

The democratic process, the table, does indeed seem missing. As it stands now, each party has the power to veto each other's initiatives, but none has the ability to create successful initiatives. In 1994, the Wilderness Bill was again introduced to Congress and it was again blocked by both sides. As initiatives are blocked, the willingness to try anything new is diminished.

How our society makes decisions is key. "Public" hearings, which are good in the democratic sense of involving the public, have become simply the place where initiatives are blocked. In fact, any genuine "hearing" is absent, partly because the system of hearings, which rightly fulfills two important components of our due process of law of giving "notice" on decisions and providing "the opportunity to be heard," transfers over the responsibility of *hearing* to the decision maker, a third party, *and the public is therefore not required to hear.* The result? What George Will calls the Cuisinart theory of justice: "A good society is a lumpy stew of individuals and groups, each with its own inherent 'principle of motion.' This stew stirs itself, and in the fullness of time, out comes a creamy puree called the 'public interest.' The endless maelstrom of individuals pursuing private goods produces, magically, the public good."[7]

Will deplores the fact that, in this model, none of the individual participants has responsibility for "willing the social good." They are not expected to do any public willing, and by the same token, they are not expected to do any public hearing. So it is that "public hearings" are curiously devoid of that very quality that their name might seem to imply.

This lack of hearing shouldn't be surprising. It is the result of the Madisonian approach that elevates individual rights over communal, group, or societal rights. This "framework of rights" is the framework of individual rights, and the role of public institutions, then, is to provide this "framework of rights," not to choose or impose the common good, but to uphold individual rights (like the right to privacy, the right to property) against infringement by other individuals, or by the government itself. So this is not a substantive choosing of a common good, but a process of weighing, balancing, and upholding rights. This process, this "due process" (giving notice and giving the opportunity to be heard) replaces direct dealings between parties in conflict. The parties don't have to come to agreement or even to hear each other. They have given this responsibility over to "the process," which prevents face to face problem-solving resulting in the diminished collective ability to get anything done.

An important question here is, Are values purely private? They don't seem to be, for if values are entirely private, then there is no objective way of choosing among them. But herein lies a tension: public decisions are often based on values (and emotions) even though the decisions have to appear to be based on objective facts (rationality). This tension produces all too familiar public scenes—shrillness and indignation of protest or of "public" decision-making and the blocking of initiatives, for protesters realize that they can never win an argument, nor can they lose. This shrillness and lack of forward motion leads to the withdrawal of people from public involvement.

If the privatization of values is at or near the root of this problem, then some conception of shared or communal values must be part of the solution. We must move from "territoriality" (individualism) to "common ground" both literally and metaphorically. Fortunately, there are many ways we can move to common ground, but often we don't realize their existence or realize their potential. Examples abound: 4-H clubs, rural fire departments, and neighborhood watch programs. No one can engage in these social goods in this "practiced way" while maintaining a purely subjective approach to values. Even the homeliest practices instill a sense of the whole, of true "civic virtues" like justice, courage, and honesty.

In the public realm, however, all of these virtues are overshadowed. Robert Bellah and his co-authors in *Habits of the Heart* say that in such instances our language changes from our "second language" of family and tradition to our "first language" of self-reliance. They describe these languages in this way:

> [I]f the language of the self-reliant individual is the first language of American moral life, the languages of tradition and commitment in communities of memory are "second languages" that most Americans know as well, and which they use when the language of the radically separate self does not seem adequate.[8]

Public discourse is couched in the framework of a dichotomy—regulated versus unregulated individuality—and so it is no wonder that people speak publicly in the "first language of individualism." The language of justice and community is pushed to the rear and forced to the forefront is the language of individual survival. The next obvious question then is, What can be done to establish practices that would teach people to act and speak in a truly public way in public?

There are no easy answers, but one aspect is the importance of the specific, the concrete, the tangible which allows values to become objective and, therefore, public. Lawrence Haworth has perhaps best understood the essential connection between the concepts of community and objectivity:

> In any genuine community there are shared values: the members are united through the fact that they fix on some object as preeminently valuable. And there is a joint effort, involving all members of the community, by which they give overt expression to their mutual regard for that object.[9]

Common values, which form the basis for a truly common life, arise out of a context that is concrete in two ways: the actual event or thing which the cooperation produces, such as a 4-H club or a rural fire department, and the actual *places* in which the cooperative efforts took place. To in*habit* a place is to dwell there in a practiced way, in a way that relies upon certain regular, trusted habits of behavior.

Our prevailing, individualistic frame of mind has led us to forget this root sense of the concept of "inhabitation." We take it for granted that the way we live in a place is a matter of individual choice (more or less constrained by bureaucratic regulations). We have largely lost the sense that our capacity to live well in a place might depend upon our ability to relate to neighbors (especially neighbors with a different lifestyle) on the basis of shared habits of behavior. Our loss of this sense of inhabitation is exactly parallel to our loss of the "republican" sense of what it is to be public.

In fact, no real public life is possible except among people who are engaged in the project of inhabiting a place. If there are not habituated patterns of work, play, grieving, and celebration designed to enable people to live well in a place, then those people will have at best a limited capacity for being public with one another. Conversely, where such inhabitory practices are being nurtured, the foundation for public life is also being created or maintained. Wendell Berry's teachings say this about practiced ways of living in places:

> The concept of country, homeland, dwelling place becomes simplified as "the environment"—that is, what surrounds us. Once we see our place, our part of the world, as *surrounding* us, we have already made a profound division between it and ourselves. We have given up the understanding— dropped it out of our language and so out of our thought—that we and our country create one another, depend on one another, are literally part of one another; that our land passes in and out of our bodies just as our bodies pass in and out of our land; that as we and our land are part of one another, so all who are living as neighbors here, human and plant and animal, are part of one another, and so cannot possibly flourish alone; that, therefore, our culture must be our response to our place, our culture and our place are images of each other and inseparable from each other, and so neither can be better than the other.[10]

So we become aware of how places, by developing practices, create culture. The civic republicans, in a sense, take up where this concept leaves off. That is, they recognize the crucial role of practices, not only in the development of culture, but also in the revitalization of public life. Here is how Robert Bellah speaks of what he calls "practices of commitment":

> People growing up in communities of memory not only hear the stories that tell how the community came to be, what its hopes and fears are, and how its ideals are exemplified in outstanding men and women; they also participate in the practices—ritual, aesthetic, ethical—that define the community as a way of life. We call these "practices of commitment" for they define the patterns of loyalty and obligation that keep the community alive.[11]

A New Sense of Place and the Politics of Possibility

What holds people together long enough to discover their power as citizens is their common inhabiting of a single place. In Missoula, part of that place is the basin valley in which the small city lies, and because it is surrounded on all sides by mountains, the area of the valley is finite, limited, and therefore fragile. (The sole-source drinking water aquifer lies a mere thirty feet below the surface.) No matter how diverse and complex the patterns of livelihood which arise within that valley may be, no matter how many the perspectives from which people view the valley, no matter how diversely the people value it, there is, finally, one and the same valley for everyone. There are not many valleys, one for each of us, but only one valley, and if we all want to stay here, in some kind of relation to the valley, then we have to learn, somehow, to live together.

Before they become citizens, then, people become neighbors, and not just as next door acquaintances. The word *neighbor*, in its Old English rendition, meant something like "near dweller." Neighbors are essentially people who find themselves attached to the same (or nearly adjoining) places. Because each of them is attached to the place, they are brought into relationship with each other. Now some people may actually prefer that they had different neighbors, but because neither of them is about to leave and because their dwelling in this place makes them interdependent, they develop patterns for dwelling near each other, for living with each other.

This concept of "living with" is deeply rooted in various inhabitory practices, one of which is the process of consensus building, which has by now developed some fairly standard operating procedures. One of the guidelines often invoked in consensus decision-making is that participants should be looking for solutions that they can all live with. Such an approach can be viewed simply as a matter of compromise and accommodation, and certainly it contains such elements. But the actual practice of finding solutions that people can live with usually reaches beyond compromise to something more like neighborliness—to finding within shared space the possibilities for a shared inhabitation. Such neighborliness is inconceivable without the building of trust, of some sense of justice, reliability, or honesty. This practice of being neighbors draws together, therefore, the concepts of place, of inhabitation, and of the kinds of practices from which civic virtues evolve.

Most people, most of the time, do not think about these features of the art of being neighbors. What they do know is that neighborliness is a highly prized quality of life. Where it is present, it is always near the top of people's lists of why they like a place, and where it is absent, it is deeply lamented. This deep-seated attachment to the virtue of neighborliness is an important but largely ignored civic asset. It is in being good neighbors that people very often engage in those simple, homely practices that are the last, best hope for a revival of genuine public life. In valuing neighborliness, people value that upon which citizenship most essentially depends. It is our good fortune that this value persists.

So it is that places may play a role in the revival of citizenship. Places have a way of claiming people. When they claim very diverse kinds of people, those people must eventually learn to live with each other. That is to say, they must learn to inhabit their place together, which they can only do through the development of certain practices of inhabitation. These practices rely upon and nurture the old-fashioned civic virtues of trust, honesty, justice, toleration, cooperation, hope, and remembrance. It is through the nurturing of such virtues (and in no other way) that we might begin to reclaim that competency upon which democratic citizenship depends.

And so in Missoula, writers and musicians collaborate at the base of Mount Jumbo to tell stories of their place of habitation. It is altogether appropriate in the context of our discussion here that this gathering of people to help spread the art of place is happening at the *public* radio station. The storytelling project is for the citizens of Missoula, the neighbors of Missoula. It is for the people that inhabit this region called the Northern Rockies: the public of this place.

Another Missoula citizen, writing to help save the fragile ecosystem of Mount Jumbo offers this:

> Only a five-minute drive from downtown Missoula and a half-dozen steps past the trailhead, and I already feel the change. Cobalt lupines quietly brush my calves and mind, the streetnoise of just moments ago already fading from memory; the pungent scent of yarrow filters out the diesel fuel and rubber; and my eyes are filled with the smooth, open space of the summer-browned grasses of Mount Jumbo.[12]

[1] Sheryl Noethe, "Untitled," 1.
[2] Thomas Jefferson, *Notes on the State of Virginia*, Query XIX, 157.
[3] James Madison, "Federalist Paper No. 10," 83.
[4] Georg Wilhelm Friedrich Hegel, *The Philosophy of History*, 84-85.
[5] Wallace Stegner, *The Sound of Mountain Water*, 37-38.
[6] Hannah Arendt, *The Human Condition*, 52-53.
[7] George F. Will, *Statecraft as Soulcraft*, 35.
[8] Robert N. Bellah et al., *Habits of the Heart*, 20-21.
[9] Lawrence Haworth, *The Good City*, 86.
[10] Wendell Berry, *The Unsettling of America*, 22.
[11] Bellah et al., *Habits of the Heart*, 154.
[12] Tommy Youngblood-Petersen, *Mount Jumbo: A Preservation Manifesto*, 1.

Thomas Michael Power

THE ECONOMIC PURSUIT OF QUALITY

Conventional economic thinking is widely acknowledged as one of the major driving forces behind many of the world's most pressing environmental problems. One of the chief assumptions about our economy is that it entails only the commercial sector— traditional economic activity—and, more importantly, that environmental and social goals are "noneconomic" and, very likely, detrimental to our economic well-being. Could it be that conventional economic thinking is in error on this issue? Are these conventional ideas based on incorrect assumptions about people and businesses? Would a more comprehensive and realistic view of the economy help steer us onto a sustainable path?

Thomas Michael Power's brilliant analysis of the economy could help to dispel some chief myths about our economy—not just that environmental quality is essential to economic health, but that the more self-reliant a community becomes, the stronger its economy.

An original essay based on The Economic Pursuit of Quality, *published by M.E., Sharpe, Armonk, New York, in 1992.*

The "Official" Economic Model: The Economic Base

One of our most widely shared pieces of economic "knowledge" has been taught and retaught to us since our first encounter with economic geography in elementary school. Most of us remember the maps in our social science books that associated regions with particular types of economic activity. On a map of the United States was an icon of a blast furnace at Pittsburgh; at Detroit, an automobile; in Iowa, corn; in the Pacific Northwest, Paul Bunyan and his blue ox; in Milwaukee, beer; and in the Deep South, cotton.

The economic lesson taught by such maps, which the National Geographic Society still produces, is that one can explain the geographic pattern of settlement by looking at the economic activities that draw people to certain areas and support them there. It is the geographically specialized economic activities that explains why people live where they do. Implicit in this approach is also the assumption that the natural landscape is simply a warehouse of economic resources waiting to be extracted.

The economic theory behind this view has come to be labeled the economic base model. It argues that in order for people to inhabit an area, they need to have the money that allows them to purchase from the larger, external economy things that they cannot easily produce themselves. In order to earn that income, they in turn must successfully market some exportable product. In other words, income from their exports allows people to pay for the imports that make life in that particular location possible and pleasurable.

In that sense, all economic activity is not of equal importance. Spending on locally oriented economic activities (child care, restaurant services, grocery stores) depends upon income that is earned in the export sectors. That export-oriented economic activity is the basic driving force in the local economy. It is primary economic activity while the locally oriented activity is secondary. Export activity drives the rest of the economy in this model.

The importance of primary economic activity is often illustrated by the calculation of an income or employment multiplier that may range from 2.0 to 5.0, depending upon how cautious or exuberant the analyst is. These multipliers show that export activity has an amplified effect on the rest of the economy, triggering cycle after cycle of local spending that puts people to work in locally oriented economic activities.

This familiar view of the local economy also has a not very subtle political message in it—notably, that all economic activities are not equal in importance. Some economic actors are significantly more important than others. A particular minority subset of all economic activities either directly or indirectly butters all of our bread. As a result, primary, usually export-oriented, economic activities need to be nurtured and supported, for without them our communities would cease to be viable and would begin the downward drift towards ghost town status.

Figure 1 depicts this familiar and dominant "extractive" way of looking at the local economy. Extraction from our "natural warehouse" is the primary driving force in the local economy. It provides the exports to external markets that, in turn, inject income into the local economy, triggering multiple cycles of local spending. In this model, the direct employment in extraction and processing and the indirect employment in local economic activities which support the primary industry and its workforce explain why a person is able to live in a particular location.

The View Through the Rear-View Mirror

Export activities usually have a long history in rural areas, often being associated with the original European settlement. Moreover, the common perception of people about their local economy tends to be tied to *past* patterns of economic activity rather than current economic reality. This is not surprising. Individuals, businesses, and the community tend to adjust their behavior and organization to support the dominant economic activities. This is both a matter of survival and the exercise of economic power. In many ways communities form themselves around those dominant "means of livelihood." This creates a shared community vision of what the population "does for a living."

When the pattern of economic activity begins to change, however, there is a considerable lag in the adjustment process. One of the last things that changes is the shared collective understanding of what drives the local economy. In that sense, the shared conventional wisdom about the local economy is a "view through the rear-view mirror," a view tied to a past reality rather than the present pattern of economic activity. This view asserts that what was economically important in the past is of central importance now and into the foreseeable future. From that past perspective, no other set of economic activities appears attractive or viable. Everything else appears unreliable and/or inferior. What could replace mining or ranching or timber in the Old West? What could replace steel and automobiles in Pittsburgh and Detroit?

A rear-view mirror, of course, is a very important safety device on an automobile, especially if one is travelling in congested traffic or changing lanes. A safe driver would not want to be without one. At the same time, it would be dangerous to negotiate through congested traffic travel while *only* staring into the rear-view mirror. To get where one wishes to go safely, one has to primarily be focused upon the traffic and terrain ahead.

It is in that sense that a historically rooted economic base view of the local economy can be dangerous to the economic health of the community. It tends to focus on the past at the expense of the present and the future. If our perspective is limited in this way, the economic well-being of the community may not be protected or enhanced. It could, in fact, be harmed.

Economic Dependence Versus Economic Development

Economic development policy in the United States is a lot like driving a car solely with a rear-view mirror perspective. "More of the same," in the sense of an expansion in an already specialized export industry, rarely can be labeled economic development. Economic development does not consist of increased specialization in a few exports. That is a prescription for dependence and instability because it is through the export industries that fluctuations in the national and international markets are imported into the local economy. Commodity price cycles, general business cycles, and long-term declines tied to technological change all threaten an economy that specializes in the export of a few products. It is the instability that goes with such specialization that explains the lack of prosperity that characterizes most of the United States' mining, mill, or agricultural towns. Most of these specialized export centers have a run-down, decaying look to them. Because of the instability and uncertainly associated with the export markets, both individuals and businesses are hesitant to reinvest in these towns. As a result, these towns look anything but prosperous, even when wages are high.

Truly successful economic development consists of spinning a complex web of locally oriented economic activities that make an area increasingly less dependent upon imports and, as a result, not as dependent upon export earnings. In addition, successful import substitution activities often lead to new exports and the diversification of the economy.

False Assumptions and the Economic Base Model

The economic base model is based on assumptions that are familiar enough to seem quite plausible and unremarkable. The primary assumptions are that people have to move to where jobs are located and

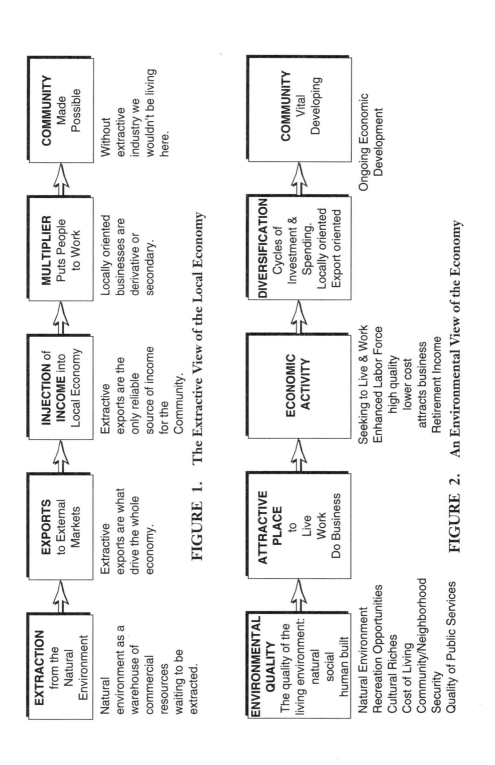

EXTRACTION
from the
Natural
Environment

Natural
environment as a
warehouse of
commercial
resources
waiting to be
extracted.

EXPORTS
to External
Markets

Extractive
exports are what
drive the whole
economy.

INJECTION of
INCOME into
Local Economy

Extractive
exports are the
only reliable
source of income
for the
Community.

MULTIPLIER
Puts People
to Work

Locally oriented
businesses are
derivative or
secondary.

COMMUNITY
Made
Possible

Without
extractive
industry we
wouldn't be living
here.

FIGURE 1. The Extractive View of the Local Economy

**ENVIRONMENTAL
QUALITY**
The quality of the
living environment:
natural
social
human built

Natural Environment
Recreation Opportunities
Cultural Riches
Cost of Living
Community/Neighborhood
Security
Quality of Public Services

**ATTRACTIVE
PLACE**
to
Live
Work
Do Business

Seeking to Live & Work
Enhanced Labor Force
high quality
lower cost
attracts business
Retirement Income

**ECONOMIC
ACTIVITY**

DIVERSIFICATION
Cycles of
Investment &
Spending.
Locally oriented
Export oriented

COMMUNITY
Vital
Developing

Ongoing Economic
Development

FIGURE 2. An Environmental View of the Economy

that job location is dictated by fundamental facts of economic geography, the location of natural resources, transportation costs, and the location of markets. In other words, people must adapt their residential location to a predetermined geographic pattern of economic activity. Unfortunately, those familiar assumptions often are contradicted by economic reality.

The view that people go looking for work, and, as a result, get distributed in a particular way across the landscape matches many of our experiences with the economy. It also matches the focus of those local economic development policies that seek to recruit new businesses or retain existing ones.

But these are not simple, intuitively obvious, assumptions. Stated differently these assumptions are: (1) people do not care where they live; and (2) firms do not care about labor supply.

There is nothing in economic theory or economic fact to support such assumptions. Quite the contrary, we know that both of these assumptions, in general, are wrong.

Consider the first assumption, that people do not care where they live and passively shift their residence to where economic activity is located. It is simply unsupportable. The economic geography of the United States has been transformed during the second half of the twentieth century as a result of the population acting on their preferences for particular types of living environments. How else is one to explain the suburbanization of our metropolitan areas after the Second World War? For the first several decades of this residential relocation, suburbanization represented a move away from both employment and commercial centers. Certainly the negative aspects of living in the central city—congestion, pollution, crime, ethnic conflict, etc.—played a role in these location decisions. So did the positive aspects of suburban and exurban living: lower density settlement, more open, park-like settings, lower levels of social conflict, etc. People had definite preferences for the qualities they desired in their living environments and proceeded to act in the pursuit of those preferences.

Similar things can be said about the settlement of the desert Southwest and the "sun belt" in general. In fact, the term "amenity" was coined by a geographer in Southern California to explain the post-war population boom in that area. The ongoing growth in the economies of many rural counties with particular landscape features during the

1980s despite severe depression in rural areas testifies to the ongoing, broad-ranging impact of the pursuit of preferred living environments on the distribution of economic activity.

Recognizing the elemental economic facts that people care where they live and that businesses care about labor supply can change dramatically how we look at local economic health and local economic development. Attractive qualities associated with the social and natural environments become important determinants of local economic well-being and important source of local economic vitality.

Also consider the second assumption listed above, that firms do not care about the adequacy, cost, or quality of the available labor supply. This view assumes that workers will quickly relocate to wherever there are employment opportunities, and for that reason there will always be an adequate labor supply wherever a firm chooses to locate. Clearly, historical as well as contemporary experience contradicts this view. Industry often relocates in the pursuit of a cheaper labor force. The movement of the textile industry from New England to the rural south earlier in this century, the more recent shift of the meat packing industry from the Chicago area to the rural Midwest, and the current concern with the migration of businesses from the Northeast and North-Central "frost belt" to the "sun belt" and across the border into Mexico are all dramatic examples of industries relocating in pursuit of a relatively inexpensive labor supply. In general, labor supply operates as a powerful force in determining the geographic distribution of economic activity. At the very least, the adequacy, quality, and cost of the local labor supply has a significant impact on an area's economic development.

An Environmental View of the Local Economy

Figure 2 sketches out a view of the economy that emerges if one abandons the false economic assumptions of the economic base model. It is labeled an environmental view because of the importance of people's and businesses' preferences for living environments in determining the location of economic activity. This also provides a dramatic contrast with the extractive view of the economy discussed earlier.

The environmental view recognizes that people have preferences for living environments and satisfy those preferences by moving to preferred social and natural environments. This creates an available supply of relatively low-cost labor because of the relative excess supply of people. That labor supply then attracts economic activity. In addition, new residents are also likely to inject income into the local economy as they expend savings, make investments, and as they seek to "make a living" in those particular areas. Retirement incomes also follow the residential location decisions made by retirees. The net effect on the local economy is expansionary. Entrepreneurs seeking to remain in these areas will explore opportunities to capture dollars that would otherwise flow out of the area by developing a sophisticated array of locally available goods and services. Those businesses that are most successful at displacing imports by serving local needs directly may build on that success and begin exporting to the larger economy.

All of this increases the number of residents that a local economy can support. This increases the "critical mass" of the economy and expands the range of goods and services that can be produced and marketed locally. The more sophisticated local economy reduces the isolation and the cost of inputs that might otherwise be barriers to the relocation of economic activity to the area. This allows ongoing cycles of expansion as long as the area remains a relatively attractive place to live, work, and do business.

This view of the local economy is labeled the environmental view because of the important role being played by environmental quality in both determining local economic well-being and in providing vitality to the local economy. The primary point here is that environmental quality is anything but "non-economic" or "anti-economic" as is often assumed. It is an important driving force in our local economies and it contributes directly to our economic well-being.

Broadening Our Economic Vision:
The Economic Role of the Non-Commercial Sectors

One of the reasons that environmental qualities are often looked upon as non-economic or "anti-economic" (in the sense of undermining economic well-being) is that in common usage, "economic" and the "economy" have come to be synonymous with those commercial business activities that allow us to satisfy our material needs. Figure 3 outlines this "folk economic" view of the economy. According to this view, money flows originating in the world of commerce and finance appear to embody all economic experience. It is here that the jobs and income that allow us to obtain the material means for our individual and collective survival are generated. This economic world is focused on the commercial, the quantitative, and the material. This "economic" world is then contrasted with social, cultural, or moral realms in which non-commercial motivations and activities can play a role. It is also contrasted with the realm of subjective preferences where the pursuit of attractive but discretionary qualities plays a role.

In this context, environmental qualities appear to lie outside the realm of economics both because they are largely non-commercial in character and because they do not appear to be necessary for our biological survival except in extreme circumstances.

The ECONOMY consists of the set of commercial transactions that employ people and generate the income that allows people to take care of their basic needs and, if they are fortunate, also their highest priority wants.

The ECONOMY coincides with the following activities and institutions:

> The World of Commerce
>> Commercial businesses
>> Money flows
>> Finance

> The generation of paying jobs and income

> The production and distribution of the
>> MATERIAL MEANS OF SURVIVAL
>> "bread winner"
>> "bread and butter issues"
>> "bringing home the bacon"
>> "food on the table; roof over heads"

The ECONOMY is focused on the
> COMMERCIAL
> QUANTITATIVE
> MATERIAL
> NECESSITIES

NON-ECONOMIC: Non-commercial realms are "social" or "cultural" or "moral," not economic in character; discretionary qualities are secondary, even trivial, aesthetic considerations.

FIGURE 3.   The "Folk Economic" View of the Economy

But this "folk economic" view seriously conflicts with the basic definition of an economy, namely that the economy is that part of our social organization that develops and uses the available scarce resources to produce and distribute the goods and services that satisfy the needs and desires of the population. The conventional definition of the economy focuses on those institutions that develop and/or protect the scarce resources that are available, transform them into useful goods and services, and then distribute them among the general population in a way that satisfies their diverse needs and desires.

Note that this definition of the economy initially says nothing about commercial business activity, money values, or financial flows. Instead, it focuses upon scarcity and the satisfaction of the needs and desires of the population. Because all scarce resources are not privately owned and bought and sold in commercial markets, one cannot limit the economy to commercial resources. Because it is not only commercial businesses that transform resources into useful goods and services, we also need to look beyond the realm of commercial businesses when we discuss the economy. Finally, because we have preferences for goods and services that commercial businesses do not provide and because the distribution of those goods and services is not always through commercial businesses and markets, we, again, have to broaden our vision of the economy well beyond the world of commercial business, money values, and financial flows if were are going to paint a complete picture of the economy.

Figure 4 provides a more complete view of the total economy by including all sources of scarce resources, all activities that produce valuable goods and services, and all mechanisms used to distribute those goods and services among the population. The social and natural environments figure prominently in this view because, as shown to the left in Figure 4, they are the only available sources of our basic economic "raw materials." Our natural resources flow from the natural environment and our labor productivity flows from the social environment. Non-commercial institutions such as family, schools, not-for-profit organizations, and government also figure prominently because they create the institutional framework that supports our commercial economy and are the sources of considerable economic production themselves, as indicated in the center of Figure 4. Finally, as shown on the right, the social and natural environments are also the source of a broad range of qualities that the population strongly prefers because

Develop and/or Protect SCARCE RESOURCES

The basic "raw materials"

What scarce resources do we rely upon? Who develops or protects them?

Only two sources:

1. **The Natural Environment**

   Privately owned
   marketed (farm land, private timber land, patented mines)
   non-marketed (open spaces, wildlife habitat)

   Publicly owned
   marketed (public timber, mineral, grazing leases)
   non-marketed (wilderness, parks, wildlife watershed)

   Ownership unspecified
   non-marketed (air, waste assimilation capacity, scenic beauty)

2. **Human Skill and Effort**

   Individual and Labor Market (initiative, experience, incentive)
   Family (values, discipline, motivation)
   Culture (attitudes, values, expectations)
   Schools (skills, values, socialization)
   Social Organization (helps determine the productivity of labor effort)

Transform Resources into Useful GOODS AND SERVICES

Choice among a near infinite variety of alternative combinations
What is the full range of goods and services that we value?
Where are these valuable goods and services produced?

Commercial Businesses

Not-for Profit Organizations
educational, medical, research, social, cultural, religious, environmental, recreational, etc.

Families and Households
home-based production
domestic domain

Public, governmental
public enterprise (sewer, water, electricity)
autonomous organizations (schools, Federal Reserve)
government activities (police, courts, welfare system)

Directly from the Social Environment
culture (diversity, richness)
community (neighborly, belonging, security)

Directly from the Natural Environment
climate
landscape
air and water quality
wildlife
outdoor recreation

Distribute Goods and Services among the Population to Satisfy DIVERSE NEEDS AND DESIRES

Conflicting diverse sets of preferences

How do we arrange for these valued goods and services to be distributed among people?

Commercial markets
fee for service

Family & Volunteer Community Orgznizations
largely a non-commercial preserve
internally adopted rules

Not-for-Profit Organizations
user fees (museums, clubs)
special criteria (charitable and service organizations)

Government
user fees (highways, building inspectors, sewers)
need (welfare programs, unemployment compensation)
available to all on demand (courts, police, public schools)

Public Goods
freely available (national security, public health, environmental quality)

FIGURE 4. The Total Economy

they make life more meaningful, satisfying, and diverse. It is only in this larger economic context that fully informed rational decisions can be made about how resource use affects human well-being.

In this larger economic context, conflicts between commercial businesses and environmental protection are not seen as sacrificing "economic value" for "aesthetic value." Instead, such conflicts are more appropriately seen as typical economic tradeoffs involving scarce resources that can be used to produce a variety of alternative "bundles" of valuable goods and services. Some of those goods and services are provided directly by the natural and social environments. Others are produced by commercial businesses. To the extent that they both seek to make use of the same scarce resource base, a straight forward economic choice has to be made. That economic choice is no different than the choice between using a particular piece of farmland to produce wheat rather than hay or the decision to use silver for jewelry rather than photographic film. In the face of scarcity, each decision to use resources in one way involves the sacrifice of what could be produced if those resources were used in any one of the alternative uses. The same is true with the pursuit of environmental qualities. The use of resources to protect or enhance the quality of living environments produces one valued set of goods and services (e.g., scenic beauty or recreation) at the expense of another (e.g., redwood siding or decks). This tradeoff is not evidence of economic irrationality. Quite the contrary, such trade-offs are typical of *all* rational economic choices.

Quantitative Mis-Measures of Local Economic Well-Being

This concept of economic choice has significant implications for how we evaluate local economic well-being. If people strongly prefer a certain type of living environment, one would expect them to make sacrifices in order to obtain it. They may, for instance, pay a higher price for a home in a particular neighborhood or a home with access to a particular amenity such as a park, lake, or scenic vista. These are familiar economic choices that are the "bread and butter" of the real estate profession.

One can access high quality natural or social environments by moving to cities and towns that provide an assortment of amenities. However, in such instances, one often finds that real wages are lower, employment opportunities are more scarce, and/or the cost of living is higher. In fact, attractive areas are likely to have surplus labor supplies that put downward pressure on wages because they serve as magnets for people. Such areas often have higher unemployment rates as well. If land is relatively limited in supply, the larger populations also increase housing costs, a primary determinant of the local cost of living.

High amenity areas, then, are likely to be characterized by some combination of lower wages, higher unemployment rates, and higher cost of living. In fact, it is these and the deterioration of the quality of the living environment caused by ongoing growth that ultimately control the number of people who seek to live in an area. As that "price" rises, fewer potential residents find the area attractive and population flows towards that area slow. To access such high-quality living environments, one has to make an economic sacrifice in terms of the real wages, cost of living, and employment opportunities.

In such a situation, the lower real wages or the higher unemployment rate is not a sign of the lack of economic health or vitality, but of the opposite. The lower real wages are a measure of how attractive the area is to people. It is a measure of the price they are willing to pay to maintain access to the high quality living environment. Rather than being a measure of economic distress, the lower wages are a measure of the value to residents of the services they receive from the natural and social environment.

This suggests that we should not be using per capita income or money wages alone to measure local economic prosperity. If we want to get a full measure of local well-being we have to look not only at monetary income but also the local cost of living and the value of the goods and services residents receive from their natural and social environments. This approach to measuring local economic well-being is indicated in the following formula:

$$\frac{\text{Local Economic}}{\text{Well-Being}} = \frac{\text{Local Money Income}}{\text{Local Cost of Living}} + \frac{\text{Value of Local}}{\text{Non-Commercial}}_{\text{Environmental Qualities}}$$

Economists have labeled wage differences that are due to workers subjective evaluations of alternative working situations as "compensating wage differentials" because they offset the value of site-specific amenities and leave potential residents about as well-off in this particular location as they would be in others.

This type of analysis has two important policy implications. First, low wages are not necessarily a sign of economic distress; there may be no problem that local economic policy needs to solve. Second, such low wages cannot be eliminated by stimulating the local economy; they are not an appropriate target for public economic policy. The latter follows from the fact that the lower wages are associated with a feature of the local area, namely its attractiveness. The wage differential can be eliminated only if one eliminates the attractive features. That would hardly seem to be a rational local economic policy.

Broadening Our Vision of the Economy: Moving Away from Necessities toward Discretionary Qualities

Another reason that qualities associated with the living environment are often treated as non-economic or anti-economic is the heavy emphasis on "necessity" in the prevalent folk economics. The economy is often talked about as primarily providing us with the "material means of life." Economic issues are "bread and butter" issues. People work to "bring home the bacon." They are our "bread winners" who also keep a "roof over our heads." In contrast, environmental concerns are often dismissed as anti-economic with the assertion that "you cannot eat the scenery."

In many different ways the prevailing economic rhetoric tells us that the economy primarily deals with fundamental necessities while environmental and social concerns are secondary. In fact, this is the basis of the claim that economic issues ought to take precedence over "social" or "cultural" or "aesthetic" concerns. As familiar as this association of economics with biological necessity is, there is little evidence to support it. To prove this point, one need only consider what is offered for sale in our premiere commercial institutions: our shopping malls and supermarkets. In the typical shopping mall, despite its hundreds of stores and half-dozen "anchor" department stores, one would be hard pressed to find anything that was necessary for biological survival. Survival clothing or survival food simply are not offered for sale by most businesses. Instead the focus is upon fashionable clothing and tasteful food. The household items offered for sale are also not related to survival: we are offered items to more tastefully decorate our home environments, higher quality video and sound equipment, more sophisticated entertainment, etc., etc.

The eight-mile-long aisles at our supermarkets also are not lined with basic nutrition items necessary for our continued healthy existence. In fact, we pay food producers to strip food value (calories and fats) from our foods so that we can enjoy the consumption of more of them. Many of the food items found in stores actually threaten our health rather than enhance it. The purpose of almost all of it is the pleasure of eating rather than the acquisition of the energy, proteins, vitamins, and minerals that are necessary for survival. If the latter were the focus of our food stores, they would have a dramatically different character.

Our homes are not just shelters. They are living environments, the quality of which is very important to us. We hire residential developers, architects, interior decorators, and landscape architects to help create these attractive environments. And we pay a good part of the cost of our housing for the qualities that are created.

Even our medicine is not aimed primarily at survival. Much of it simply seeks to help us "feel better" even when we have no life threatening illness. It is the quality of our existence that we seek help from medicine in protecting. We try to control the minor "disease" we feel from a variety of inconvenient and harassing maladies. We seek to change our appearance through orthodontics and cosmetic surgery. We seek help in feeling better about ourselves from mental health specialists. And when we are dying, we again raise the issue of whether the quality of the life we would be able to continue to lead justifies heroic measures to keep us alive.

All in all, if one were to sit down and calculate it, not much more than 10 percent of all of our economic activity is focused upon providing us with those things that are necessary for biological survival. The rest of our economic activity is focused upon the production of attractive but distinctly discretionary qualities. It is various bundles of qualities that our commercial businesses produce and offer for sale and that we purchase. Those discretionary qualities are the focus of most of our employment and income and the object of our expenditures.

Not only are qualities the primary output of our economy, they are also the primary inputs. Although the folk economic view of the economy suggests that it is material inputs that are the source of our economic productivity, nothing could be further from the truth. If material inputs were the primary economic inputs, the nations with the most labor intensive economies and largest quantities of raw materials would be the richest and most productive economies. China, India, Zaire, and Mexico should dominate the world economy. They do not. Quite the contrary, much of their populations are mired in poverty.

Empirical analysis of what it is that determines the differential productivities of various economies identify primarily non-material, qualitative inputs: the quality (not the quantity) of the workforce, the state of knowledge, entrepreneurial spirit, legal-political institutions, etc. Skill, work ethic, discipline, knowledge, and responsibility are the inputs, not number of workers or number of worker-hours.

Figure 5 contrasts the material necessity view of the economy with the discretionary quality view. The latter is not a new or novel approach within economics. It is the way that economists analytically look at the world. It is the more popular "materialist/necessity" view embedded in our culture that is out of step with economic analysis and economic reality. This is central to how we think about the economy. If we embrace a material necessity view, we ignore the focus and purpose of most of our economic activity—discretionary qualities such as tasteful food, stylish clothing, attractive homes, comfort, and convenience. We also ignore most of the sources of our productivity. In addition, we mischaracterize many of the choices we face in a way that prejudices the outcome. If we treat the pursuit of discretionary qualities as a relatively trivial interest of the monied leisure class and focus our public economic policies primarily on a quantitative expansion of the volume of material inputs and outputs, we will systematically ignore what it is we most want from our economy and the most productive ways of obtaining what it is that we want.

Discretionary qualities are what we want. They are not the frosting on the economic cake. They are the substance of the cake. They can be treated as secondary economic considerations only at the cost of ignoring the fundamental purpose of our economic activity and the primary resources that propel virtually all that economic activity. This would hardly seem to be a sound basis upon which to base public economic policy. But it is exactly such folk economic attitudes that dominate the discussion of public economic policy.

Confronting the qualitative character of what it is we seek from our economy and what it is that energizes that economy also helps us see a way out of what would otherwise appear to be a nearly hopeless conflict between economic improvement and environmental quality. Within

Folk Economic View	Analytical Economic View
Basic Inputs	**Basic Inputs**
Tons of raw materials processed	Quality of the labor force and leadership
	work ethic
Number of workers	entrepreneurial spirit
	skill, training, experience
Quantity of capital	Quality of organization
	effective cooperation
	motivation
	Quantity of technology
	organization (e.g., assembly line)
	state of applied knowledge
	Quality of the legal structure
	property rights
	contracts
	control predatory behavior
Basic Outputs	**Basic Outputs**
Necessities	Discretionary, subjective qualities
basic food	tasteful food
protect from elements	attractive, stylish clothes
medical care	appealing home environment
	supportive medicine

FIGURE 5. Qualities as the Basic Economic Inputs and Outputs

the context of a material view of the economy the viability of our affluence appears doubtful. After all, the "affluent nations" make up only
about a half billion of the Earth's 5.6 billion aspiring souls. If over the
next two generations that other 90 percent of the Earth's population
succeeds in gaining the material lifestyle of those in the first world, and
the first world modestly improves its material standard of living—say 2
percent per year—the planet will face a twenty-fold increase in the
material demands placed upon it.

That certainly backs us into a corner of doom and gloom. Either the rest of the world's population must not be allowed to improve, or we must surrender our affluence. Economics again seems to implicitly carry a "dismal" message. But fortunately this conceptual corner is unnecessary because it is built around an incorrect definition of the economy, one that sees material production and consumption as its primary *raison d'etre*.

If, as argued above, both the primary inputs to the economy and the primary outputs are qualitative in nature, ongoing economic improvement appears possible over the long run. While the extraction of materials from the Earth and their return to the biosphere as waste may always be disruptive, improving the qualities of our lives may not be. To the extent that those qualities do not have a primary material aspect to them, they can be improved without limit, while adding no burdens to the natural world. Writing a poem, moving gracefully across a dance floor, designing more habitable homes, being better partners and parents, understanding more fully the mysteries embodied in ourselves and the world we inhabit, or engaging more fully both our neighborhoods and nature are not necessarily constrained by material scarcity.

A dynamic and efficient economy could increase access to such valuable qualities while decreasing the material throughput of resources and goods that help enable the pursuit of those qualities. This alternative strategy involves a focus upon the material efficiency with which we pursue the qualities that are valuable to us. Such an economy would simultaneously enhance those qualities that give our lives meaning while alleviating stresses on the Earth. We, at least conceptually, could continue to improve our well-being without having to threaten our communities and the natural world.

Putting the Pieces Together:
Thinking About the Total Economy

If we are going to create a useful local economy, we have to move beyond the popular "folk economics" that most of us have been learning since grade school. It is not that folk economics is flat out wrong; it is incomplete. Figure 6 outlines the ways in which we need to supplement it. To the almost exclusive focus on commercial business activities we have to add the contributions to our well-being flowing from the non-commercial sectors (schools, homes, NGOs, and government) and the natural and social environments. To the unbalanced focus upon the provision of necessities, we need to add the reality that most of what we produce and purchase are discretionary goods and services that primarily make our lives interesting and satisfying rather than simply keeping us alive. Finally, while admitting the material basis and quantitative characteristics of our economy, we need to recognize the qualitative character of what we fundamentally seek (attractive services and activities) and the qualitative nature of our primary economic resources (knowledge, skill, and attitudes). It is only within this more comprehensive view of the economy that effective public economic policy can be crafted. If the more truncated "folk economics" is allowed to set the context, we can be certain the our well-being and that of our communities will be unnecessarily constrained and, very likely, seriously damaged.

Folk View	+	Missing Central Elements = Total Economy
Commercial businesses markets	+	Non-commercial activities and organizations (important sources of well-being)
Necessities	+	Discretionary goods and services (most of our commercial economy)
Material Quantities money, quantities of things	+	Qualities (central economic input and output)

FIGURE 6.   Completing the Economy

Stephan Schmidheiny
with the Business Council for Sustainable Development

CHANGING COURSE
A GLOBAL BUSINESS PERSPECTIVE ON
DEVELOPMENT AND THE ENVIRONMENT

In recent years, business has begun to shift from an adversary in the environmental debate to a proponent of sound environmental practice. Although successes are relatively minor compared to the task that lies ahead, this promising change is vital to achieving a sustainable society.

The change in business practice has resulted in part by a growing recognition of the role that business plays in global environmental deterioration. Business has also come to realize that it too can play a significant role in reversing adverse environmental trends. Perhaps most important, businesses are learning that environmental protection can make extraordinary economic sense. That is, efficiency and other measures that reduce businesses' demand for resources and their output of wastes are not just good for the environment, they are good for the bottom line.

What are some of the steps the business community sees as essential to achieving sustainable development? Can continued economic growth be reconciled with sustainable development?

Stephan Schmidheiny and the Business Council on Sustainable Development offer their perspective on these and other pressing questions in this summary of Changing Course. *Some ideas may seem traditional, even contradictory to the advice given by other authors in this anthology. Others may seem downright radical from the perspective of conventional business practice.*

Changing Course: A Global Business Perspective on Development and the Environment *was published by M.I.T. Press, Cambridge, Massachussets, in 1992.*

Many environmentalists, looking at the damage that they believe has been caused by economic growth, argue that no further growth is desirable. They argue that continued economic growth in the industrial nations could prove devastating to global ecosystems. In fact, most contend that unlimited growth is unsustainable for any organic system, and that for all systems there is a size at which efficiency is optimized.

However, economic growth is absolutely necessary for the foreseeable future for three reasons. First, over one billion people out of a global population of well over five billion live in poverty, according to the World Bank. They are unable to meet daily needs for food, clean water, safety, housing, education, and health care. Alleviating this situation will require economic growth over a vast area of the globe. Second, the global population is expected to double within the next century, most probably within the next forty years. Over 90 percent of this increase is expected in the developing world. Surely economic growth will be crucial to meet the needs of such a rapidly growing population. Third, people do not decide to have fewer children until they are confident that they can keep the children they do have alive and reasonably well. For this, they need adequate food, health care, education, and job opportunities. Again, economic growth is needed to provide these amenities.

Economic growth will also be spurred by the entry of growing numbers of people into free market competitive business systems as capitalism increasingly replaces socialism around the world. All of those entering the market are inspired by the belief that they can make their business grow or prosper. Where this faith is dampened, the ability of capitalism to deliver its benefits, among them widespread opportunity, efficiency, and innovation, are also dampened. So those who theorize that there has been enough growth in the industrial North must devise a whole new market system that can somehow deliver efficiency and innovation while thwarting the legitimate ambitions of efficient and innovative entrepreneurs.

On the other hand, those who believe that the open, competitive market is the best system for all, must prove that this market and its inherent growth are compatible with the goal of *sustainable development*—defined here as development that meets the needs of the present without compromising the ability of future generations to meet their needs. Or they must show how the market system can be refined to be compatible with that sustainable development goal.

Business and Sustainable Development

Many environmentalists argue that business, in its short-term pursuit of profit, is the primary villain on the environmental scene. Certainly all businesses, from peasant farms to multinationals, use natural resources in one form or another. Many use resources wastefully and inefficiently. Many businesses pollute, or they aid and abet pollution by others, for example when banks finance dirty factories.

But there are reasons why business operates as it does. Most businesses function within the laws of the societies in which they are based. In democratic societies, these laws are based on the wishes of the majority of citizens. Most people want to pay as little as possible for all products. Systems of regulations, taxes, and economic instruments tend to favor the low prices at the expense of a cleaner environment. In addition, businesses provide goods and services as cheaply as possible to attract customers and clients. These combined pressures often mean that the environmental costs of operations are not included on balance sheets.

It is as naive to treat business as something separate from society as it is to treat the "environment" as something separate from business. Business operates within a societal setting, the laws and logic of which determine its actions. This is not to claim that business is not responsible for its actions. Within that societal framework, entrepreneurs make decisions, take risks, and adapt strategies by which they are and should be judged. Before business operations can be expected to reflect environmental values though, the operations of society must be altered to reflect environmental values. Because Nature's laws cannot be changed, human laws and human economic systems must be changed to comply with those natural laws, for the violation of those laws eventually puts a stop to all progress, development, and growth.

The necessary changes in laws and economic systems (discussed later) can be most efficiently developed through cooperation among business, governments, and citizens (both in their masses and in their pressure groups, environmental and otherwise). Yet before they can work together for change, each sector must itself change. Individual businesses, traditionally and quite rightly competing with one another, must learn to work together on the long-term issues that affect all of them, such as the pricing of natural resources and international regulations on pollution. Governments must find ways of incorporating the concept of sustainable development in all decisions and all ministries or departments so that the Ministry for Industry is just as concerned with sustainable development as the Ministry of the Environment. And citizens' groups must learn first to work with one another and then to work more efficiently with business and governments, being always careful to focus on issues of high priority.

These prerequisites for change may appear at first glance to be idealistic. But important, positive changes are already occurring due to pressures from business, governments, and citizens' groups:

- Customers are demanding cleaner products, as well as products and services that support the development goals of poorer countries. For example, there are a growing number of investment funds that do not invest in companies making profits in nations ruled by repressive regimes. Although customer demand for such funds waxes and wanes, there is an overall upwards movement.

- Insurance companies are more willing to insure clean companies to avoid paying for possible environmental damage and accidents.

- Banks are more willing to lend to companies that prevent pollution than to those that deal with pollution in traditional ways, which often result in expensive clean-ups or expensive lawsuits, or both.

- Employees, particularly the best and the brightest, often prefer to work for environmentally responsible corporations.

- Environmental regulations are getting tougher and will continue to get tougher.

- New economic instruments—taxes, pollution charges, and tradable permits—are being adopted to reward "clean" companies. Business is calling for the increased use of such instruments that, when well-drafted, appear more cost-effective and less market-distorting than traditional command and control regulations.

None of these trends is compelling by itself, and the strength of each trend varies tremendously from nation to nation but, taken together, they produce a powerful effect. From the business perspective, they are pushing environmental problems up the company hierarchy. Today in the best companies the chief executive officer is also the chief environmental officer. These CEOs are learning that the environment has a part to play in every single business decision—as do the questions of quality and profitability. Many CEOs are beginning to go beyond regulations and are seeking creative ways to improve corporate environmental management. They are encouraging their peers to do the same.

Business has had the advantage of passing through the "quality revolution." Back when companies were focusing only on the end of the assembly line, improving quality meant discarding or fixing rejects; this approach was costly. But once business examined the total system from design on through, it found it could design quality in at the beginning, thus minimizing rejects and saving money. Having done the unthinkable in one area—improving quality while cutting costs—business can now begin to think the unthinkable in another area: decreasing resource use and improving environmental management, while cutting costs.

From a business point of view, the term that best sums up the business approach to sustainable development is "eco-efficiency," coined by the Business Council for Sustainable Development, based in Geneva, Switzerland. The council sought a link between the two ideals of business and environmental excellence. It found that link in the concept of efficiency, which connects business, the environment, and the increasing human needs of this generation and of the larger generations to come. Efficiency keeps companies competitive. It adds the most value with the least use of natural resources, and it is crucial in the fight against mass poverty in the world.

Firms can be said to be eco-efficient when they produce even more useful goods and services while continuously reducing resource consumption and pollution. After studying worldwide business trends, the council agreed that tomorrow's winners will be those who make the most and the fastest progress in improving their eco-efficiency.

Studies suggest that this is as true for countries as it is for companies. Professor Michael Porter of the Harvard Business School researched various aspects of competitive advantage among countries and found that "the nations with the most rigorous [environmental standard] requirements often lead in exports of affected products. . . .The strongest proof that environmental protection does not hamper competitiveness is the economic performance of nations with the strictest laws." Porter noted the successes of Japan and Germany, and that of the United States in sectors actually subject to the greatest environmental costs: chemicals, plastics, and paints.

So there is opportunity in sustainable development, and there is some momentum towards it. The next question concerns the agenda that business, governments, and citizens should follow to maintain and strengthen that momentum.

At the top of the agenda would be establishing a set of "arguing and operating principles" upon which all participants could agree. The first of these might be to adopt the "precautionary principle," which says that a lack of scientific certainty should not be used as an excuse for postponing measures that prevent major, irreversible environmental degradation. For example, there is much scientific debate over climate change, but a radically altered climate would be such a major disaster that it is worthwhile to adopt reasonable measures to insure against it.

A second principle might be a sort of "environmental uncertainty principle." In many cases, we know the direction in which our courses must change, but we do not know the extent of change that will be required over time. So let us start to change direction then fine tune and adapt as time passes. For example, it is obvious that the price of fossil fuels must increase to encourage people to use energy more efficiently and to adopt renewable energy technologies. So rather than wait because we cannot agree on how much gasoline will cost in the year 2020, let us commit ourselves to raising those prices now and adjusting as we go along.

A third principle might be to seek out "no-regret" policies. These include steps such as increased energy efficiency or the development of drought resistant crops, actions that society will not regret even if global warming does not prove to be as threatening as it now seems.

These three principles all involve investments in various types of insurance. Business is good at spotting trends and taking necessary actions. Governments set the frameworks in which businesses operate. The two must work together in implementing these principles.

Pricing the Environment

Business and government must also cooperate to refine the market system so that it more accurately reflects environmental realities. It has often been said that socialism collapsed because it told neither economic nor environmental truth; competitive market economies will collapse unless they can reflect environmental realities.

Environmental degradation is often ignored on a company's balance sheets and is referred to as an economic externality, a phrase that includes everything from damage to human health by the pollution from a power plant to damage to the global climate by greenhouse gases from factories. Both are real, but neither is traditionally included in the costs of doing business.

To adjust markets and business to include such costs, we must incorporate externalities in the costs of doing business. Unfortunately, these costs are often difficult or impossible to establish with mathematical accuracy, but the work must proceed using presently available knowledge and practices. It is far better to have an approximate cost than to value externalities at zero.

Efforts to "internalize" external costs is already underway. The members of the Organization for Economic Co-operation and Development (OECD) agreed to the Polluter Pays Principle (PPP) two decades ago. This says that polluters should bear the full costs of any damage they cause. Unfortunately, governments have been slow to implement this principle.

Environmental costs can be included in the costs of doing business in a number of ways, all of which encourage companies to minimize these external costs. The first, and most traditional, mechanism is command-and-control regulations, such as performance standards for technologies and emission standards. Regulations have served a purpose, and there will continue to be a need for a regulatory framework in all countries, particularly in cases of health risks or risk of serious, long-term damage.

The second mechanism to internalize externalities is self-regulation, whereby corporations or sectors of industry regulate themselves. They can do so through self-imposed standards, monitoring, and pollution-reduction targets. Self-regulation can be cost-effective to society because it saves some of the costs of a large government regulatory mechanism. However, this also calls for trust between government and the business community.

The third general type of mechanism includes a variety of economic instruments such as pollution taxes, tradable pollution permits, and deposit-refund systems (as with glass bottles). Performance bonds, resource-saving credits, differential prices (as with unleaded versus leaded gasoline), and special depreciation provisions also fall within this category. Market mechanisms also include the removal of distorting subsidies and barriers to market activity. Such market mechanisms should be tried more widely because they can decrease the costs, to both business and governments, of the regulatory system. They also can encourage companies to change to even cleaner technologies and to develop those technologies, because it always pays for them to clean up more.

In our view, the best approach entails an optimal mix of command-and-control regulations, self-regulation, and economic instruments. The proportions of ingredients in the mix should be determined by considerations such as efficiency and fairness.

Energy

Energy is crucial for human progress. But the production of energy by fossil fuels causes local, regional, and global pollution; and the price of energy rarely reflects the environmental costs associated with its use. Despite the problems associated with fossil fuel use, it would be impossible to return to the low-energy consumption of the past or change energy systems radically without destroying national economies.

Given the importance of energy as both the basis of economic development and a major source of pollution, it is absurd that so few countries have developed rational energy policies. Energy prices are the first component of markets that must be adjusted to reflect environmental costs. For this to happen, long-term, comprehensive national energy plans must be developed. With business playing a large supporting role throughout, these policies should be built on three pillars: increased energy efficiency, a more sustainable mix of energy sources and consumer patterns, and a long-term energy strategy for developing nations.

Increased efficiency would buy time for the development of new and renewable energy sources. One way to increase efficiency is to increase the price of electricity so that it reflects the replacement cost of new plants. This would encourage companies to build more efficient power plants. Governments and businesses could work together to improve appliance standards and building codes, to provide better information about the energy consumption of appliances, and to encourage consumers to look at the total life-cycle cost rather than just the purchase price when considering a product.

The most immediate priorities in energy policy are to reduce the environmental impacts of fossil fuels in order to encourage energy conservation, while reducing the risks of operating existing nuclear power plants in central and eastern Europe. We believe that the next generation of businesses depends on developing clean coal technologies, a safe nuclear industry, biomass-based energy, solar energy sources, and further hydro-power development.

The Developing World

Developing countries have special needs in terms of sustainable development. But unless these nations are put on a sustainable path, their problems will affect all parts of the globe: through general instability, outpourings of refugees, and outpourings of pollution.

Business sees several main, inter-connected problems of grave importance to developing countries. First, rapid population growth cannot be sustained by many poor nations. Of the about 144 million children born each year on the planet, 126 million are born in the developing world. In our view, all successful programs to reduce population growth have included measures to improve the standard of living of the poor and to decrease infant mortality rates so parents will have the confidence to have fewer children. Given the chance, we think that businesses can reduce population growth by fostering economic growth in a socially and ecologically sound way. Business can also create jobs, provide training, and help absorb as many people as possible into the modern sector of the economy. This will help nations keep up with population growth and could even slow the rate of growth over time.

Other major problems are economic and financial systems where governments attempt to manage and manipulate businesses, banking, and the markets in general. We think that if governments can open markets, they can harness entrepreneurial energy for development. Opening markets means having relatively few rules, but seeing to it that those rules are clear, enforced, and applicable to all.

Trade

The problems plaguing many developing nations lead directly to the issue of the role of trade in sustainable development. Unless nations trade, they cannot develop; and unless nations develop economically, they cannot protect their environments, clean up environmental damage, or make efficient use of resources. Thus, we believe that free trade has a role to play in the establishment of sustainable development.

Industrial nations are introducing increasing numbers of standards, regulations, and economic instruments to internalize environmental costs. If these are not coordinated through international negotiation, they could create barriers to trade. Goals such as environmental protection and sound resource management cannot be forced by one nation upon another nation through means such as unilateral trade measures. They can be achieved through the negotiation of international environmental agreements. Carefully drawn, these need not threaten trade or the trading system. If such treaties are not forthcoming, the pressure for trade barriers will mount.

Capital Markets

Unbeknownst to many, capital markets, such as stock and bond markets, could play an important role in sustainable development. Sustainable development requires long-term investments that respect environmental and development needs in both industrial and developing countries. Most of the investment will come from stocks and bonds.

As nations begin to internalize environmental costs, the ways in which capital markets value corporations will begin to change. Increasingly, companies that further the cause of sustainable development will be perceived as more valuable in the marketplace and will, therefore, attract more investors. The emerging capital markets in the developing world could become powerful tools for development. Making markets and emerging companies more open, efficient, and competitive should be a high priority for business and governments. One way to stimulate some of these changes is by internalizing environmental costs, thus producing more accurate signals for individual and institutional investors, bankers, and insurance companies.

There are clear signs that the financial community is beginning to take environmental issues into account. This is partly because legal changes in the United States and Europe transfer environmental liability to parties not directly responsible for the environmental damage. Banks, for example, may be held legally responsible if their borrowers have caused environmental damage but cannot pay. Concern over the insurance risks inherent in unsustainable development has also made insurance companies more sensitive to the needs of investing in sustainability. The recent growth of "green" funds, and the support of these investment vehicles from some large pension funds, shows that many investors are becoming more aware of the social and environmental issues involved in economic development.

The Corporate Agenda

All governments set the frameworks in which businesses operate. But business must take a leadership role in helping government set the framework, always aware of the opportunities for improved competitiveness through eco-efficiency.

In general, over the past twenty years the business community has tended to be overly cautious and conservative in its approach to the environmental challenge. Society can no longer afford this. Change by business itself is less painful, more efficient, and cheaper for consumers, for governments, and for businesses themselves. By living up to its responsibilities, business will be able to help society shape a reasonable and appropriate path towards sustainability.

Integrating the principles of sustainable development into corporate operations, and making enterprises eco-efficient, is a multi-faceted process. Chief executive officers must recognize that there can be no long-term economic growth unless it is environmentally sustainable. They and their colleagues must ensure that all products, services, and processes contribute to sustainable development.

Commitment to sustainable development will inevitably involve reorganizing, restructuring, and redesigning many processes and detailed systems within a corporation. Thus, companies in the "sunset" industries need not face the same fate as the goods and services they provide, if they can develop environmentally sound substitutes. Old constraints can be turned into new opportunities, such as diversifying from power supply into energy conservation. And new business opportunities can be created by applying corporate assets to new services. Several companies that have developed new pollution-control technologies for their own uses have marketed these technologies to others.

Companies must maintain the trust of society, which is necessary to sustain business operations. More than ever before, business is being challenged by a much broader and more diverse group of people who have a stake in corporate actions. Broadly, these "stakeholders" include not only customers, employees, and shareholders, but also suppliers, government, neighbors, the wider community, and public interest groups. Involving these people with all their differing views and concerns usually leads to better decisions and more universal support for their implementation. Prosperous companies in a sustainable world will be those that are better than their competitors at adding value for all their stakeholders, not just for customers and investors.

Individual business leaders can make a difference, but they cannot transform these goals into realities without a critical mass of other committed individuals. When viewed within the context of sustainable development, environmental concerns become not just a cost of doing business, but a potent source of competitive advantage. Enterprises that embrace the concept can realize the advantages in more efficient processes, improvements in productivity, lower cost of compliance, and new market opportunities. Businesses with vision may expect to reap advantages over competitors who lack it. Ultimately, companies that fail to change will very likely become obsolete.

Business management is changing in ways that make progress towards eco-efficiency easier. First, boards of directors and top management are becoming more concerned with integrating the internal and external dimensions of a business, providing new vehicles for stakeholder participation. Second, organizational structures are evolving toward broad network designs that are being stimulated by advancing communications and computer technology. These enable new policy messages to be communicated throughout large, decentralized multinational organizations. This helps support the creation of a corporate culture of sustainability. Third, an organizational learning culture is being developed. This culture is based on an appreciation of the need to constantly rethink and be open to relearning the fundamentals of every aspect of business.

Corporations need to report their progress towards sustainability. The baseline standard for reporting is stated in the International Chamber of Commerce principle of "compliance and reporting." This principle encourages business first to measure environmental performance, to conduct their own regular environmental audits and assessments of compliance, and to periodically provide appropriate information to the board of directors, shareholders, employees, the authorities, and the public.

More and more companies are recognizing that environmental management requires the minimization of risks and impacts throughout their products' life cycles. This realization is creating an industrial system based on "reconsumption"—the ability to use and reuse goods in whole or in part over several generations. The new philosophy of environmental management also recognizes that environmental considerations must be fully integrated into the production process. Careful choice of raw materials, operating procedures, technologies, and human resources all play a part in improved eco-efficiency. These efforts lead to pollution prevention and mean that environmental concerns, like profitability, become a cross-functional issue that everyone in the corporation promotes.

Pollution prevention involves four types of actions. The first is good housekeeping, that is, operating machinery and production systems in the most efficient manner, a basic task of management. Second is materials substitution—replacing a harmful material with a more benign one. This strategy offers the prospect of completely eliminating hazardous wastes. The third is emissions reductions through manufacturing modifications. An example would be simplifying production technology by lowering the number of process stages. The fourth is resource recovery. In essence, this means that emissions can be reduced by keeping the polluting agents within the production system and reusing them in the same or other processes. Some industries have already established complex "industrial ecosystems" in which the waste from one process becomes the feedstock of another.

As companies become better at preventing pollution and husbanding resources, attention is shifting from problems caused by production to those caused by the product itself. Corporate environmental responsibility no longer ends at the factory gate. It extends from cradle to grave in a management process called product stewardship. Managing a product life cycle for minimal environmental impacts poses tough conceptual and operational challenges for business. Each step in the life of a product—production, packaging, transport, disposal of packaging, use of product, disposal of product—has different implications for the environment.

Business, research institutes, and governments are working to develop life-cycle analyses (LCAs) or "eco-balances" to evaluate the cradle-to-grave implications of different product options. Life-cycle analysis implies life-cycle responsibility. A combination of increasing external pressures and growing internal commitment has made some leading companies ensure that their products are made, used, and disposed of (or recycled) in the most environmentally compatible ways.

But sustainable development means more than reducing pollution and life-cycle responsibility. In the years ahead, business will be challenged to move toward "zero pollution emissions" and to redirect product development to better meet social needs, including those of the poor. The goal is to make the manufacture, use, and disposal of products more compatible with sustainable development.

Steve Van Matre

EARTH EDUCATION
A NEW BEGINNING

Environmental education is one of the newest disciplines in our educational system. It took hold first in colleges and universities in the 1970s and then spread to primary and secondary education. But is environmental education delivering on its promises? Are students becoming better Earth citizens?

Steve Van Matre says no. He contends that, for the most part, environmental education has failed to create generations of citizens who live their lives in environmentally responsible ways. Environmental education has failed to teach students how natural systems operate and that the ecological system is really our life support system. It has also failed to show how individual actions contribute to the destruction of these systems and how responsible individual action can eliminate or greatly reduce our impacts.

In Earth Education *Van Matre does not simply tear apart the environmental education, he offers a constructive alternative that, among other things, could help students understand the importance of the environment to their lives. It also seeks to show students how lifestyle changes can profoundly influence the fate of our environment.*

To the staunch supporter of environmental education, Van Matre's views may seem insulting. To those who can look at them objectively, though, there is much to be learned. Egos should be set aside in favor of creating a system of education that actually does what it sets out to do.

For the past twenty years we have been led to believe that there is a significant educational response underway around the world for dealing with the environmental problems of the Earth. This is not true. Right from the start that effort has been co-opted and diluted and trivialized. Now we are on the verge of losing a whole generation of planetary citizens who could have set the course for a different future. There is not much time left. *Earth Education* is about a new path that the world's largest group of professional educators in the environmental field has already taken. It is called the Earth Education path, and anyone can follow it in developing a genuine educational program made up of magical learning adventures. We hope you will join us.

I am afraid parts of our account are not going to be much fun to read. I have agonized over my approach here for some time, and I have listened to all manner of contrary advice. But I am convinced that environmental education has become little more than mush to so many people that if I don't make our case strongly enough, folks will just stir us in with all the other educational supplements available. Besides, as you will see, we no longer believe we are environmental education; we think we are an alternative to it.

Environmental education may well have been the most important movement of this century in terms of the health of our home, the troubled planet Earth. Listen to what our political leaders were saying in the United States a couple of decades ago at the beginning of that effort:

> The Congress of the United States finds that the deterioration of the quality of the Nation's environment and of its ecological balance poses a serious threat to the strength and vitality of the people of the Nation and is in part due to poor understanding of the Nation's environment and of the need for ecological balance. (Public Law 91-516)

It seems pretty clear in retrospect that what people were talking about in the sixties and early seventies was that the inhabitants of the Earth did not understand how life functions here (the big-picture ecological systems); they did not grasp how their own lives were directly connected to and supported by those systems; and they did not understand how they were going to have to change their lifestyles in order to live more in harmony with those systems—systems that governed all life on this small self-contained vessel they shared. In short, the Earth was in trouble, and we were the problem.

So what happened to our original sense of mission and purpose? The call seemed loud and clear in the beginning, but somewhere along the way it faded into a vague, almost unrecognizable whisper.

One popular idea that surfaced early on was to cause endless problems. This was the position that environmental education was process not content. The advocates of this approach said we should use an environmental perspective to tie all learning together. No one ever demonstrated exactly how to do this, but it sounded good in the telling. I suspect that is why we should have been suspicious from the beginning; it sounded *too* good. In fact, becoming truly integrated in an overall approach to education has been the recurrent dream of educators for centuries. Add to this the supplementalist approach that teachers were going to "infuse" every part of the curriculum with environmental education, and you have a recipe for failure.

The next time you decide to fly somewhere, as you board the plane, poke your head in the cockpit and ask the pilot where he learned how to fly. If he responds, "I guess I got a little piece of it in math class; we worked out the lift on the wing of the plane there. And I remember we talked about the history of flying in history class, too. Oh, I wrote a report on it in English. It was pretty good. I got a B." Would you stay on board? Well, folks, that's exactly what the supplemental and infusion approach is asking all of us to do. Environmental education was the most important learning of the millennium, and we were asked to do it by just sprinkling our messages throughout the curriculum and somehow the learners would put them all together and end up living more lightly on the Earth. How can anyone really believe that?

You see, it is one thing to infuse some environmental messages into your math lessons or language arts exercises, but just exactly what does this mean for environmental education as process in the end? No one has ever done this on any scale, and I doubt that anyone ever will, because we never approach any learning that we are really serious about in our societies in such a fragmented way. In practical terms, infusion appears to have meant diffusion. There's little doubt that that is exactly what has been accomplished.

And please spare everyone the sophistry contained in the line, "We teach students how to think, not what to think." Or even worse, the argument that it is unethical for us to impose our values upon them. We make them go to school don't we? We don't ask them if we are imposing on their values when we teach them how to write, do we? I want them to learn how to read. I want students to be able to describe our form of government. I want them to understand how this planet functions ecologically. And I also want them to cherish all life. I want them to use less energy and consume less material in their own lives. I want them to respect the wisdom of age, but suspect the arguments of adult comfortability. In the end, I want them to live more lightly on the Earth. Influencing their values is exactly what I have in mind.

While I am at it, what is really meant by multidisciplinary anyway? What do people mean when they say environmental education is a part of all subjects? Which parts of environmental education are what parts of which subjects, *please?* And since about one out of every ten families moves each year (in the United States at least), what happens to the thousands of transfer students in this approach? Finally, it is hard enough to pin some people down on the learning outcomes for a specific subject, so what happens to measurement and evaluation when your intended outcomes are a part of everything else? How do we know if we are succeeding?

You know, it is a bit ironic when you think about it. Our environmental education leaders say people need to be multidisciplinary in dealing with environmental problems, but isn't that what the schools claim they were educating us to do all along? Didn't we have to take all those other courses (like history and sociology) because they would supposedly give us insights and skills from lots of different disciplines in order that we could be multidisciplinary later on in solving life's problems? I don't get it. If this approach hasn't worked, why not say so (that would be one way to free up the bloated school curriculum). If it did work, then why not do it in something called environmental education?

Somewhere along the way, when we weren't looking I suspect, someone changed the nature of multidisciplinary, from multidisciplinary in terms of problem solving to multidisciplinary in terms of learning. In other words, instead of being something you could do after you had mastered the disciplines, it became something you supposedly got en route to mastering them. In this new version, environmental education became a sort of subliminal bonus in all your courses. (Actually, I suppose one might argue environmental *action* should be multidisciplinary, but to say environmental *education* should be would mean something entirely different).

Let me digress for a moment to explain my personal observation about what all this philosophical hot air has created. In the past fifteen years I have traveled around the world eight times and conducted almost five hundred sessions on our work. I doubt that there is anyone out there who has been to more sites and centers in this field. And during that time I have learned that it doesn't do much good to ask people if they are doing environmental education. Everyone claims that they are. You have to ask them instead exactly what they do to get that job done. When you really boil down their responses, what most people are calling environmental education is conducting a couple of outside activities, putting up a poster on the bulletin board, and picking up litter in the spring. Really, that's it. All of it. That's what has become of environmental education in the vast majority of cases.

Unfortunately, litter pick-up has practically nothing to do with environmental education. The task is not just to pick up the litter, but to figure out where all that junk comes from. But the major point I want to insert here is that a couple of activities, a poster in the hallway and a litter pick-up campaign in the spring, *do not* a program make.

Before I go any further I guess I should make sure you understand what we mean by a learning program. That is a much overworked term in our field. Sadly, almost any collection of activities—regardless of how insipid, unrelated, ineffectual—can be, and often is, referred to as an environmental education program. It is strange. You wouldn't claim you had a satisfactory reading program if most of your learners couldn't read at the end, or an adequate drivers training program if they ended up unable to drive, but many leaders will say they have a complete environmental education program even though most of their learners don't end up doing anything specifically to live more lightly on the Earth.

We at the institute believe that a genuine learning program is a carefully crafted, focused series of sequential, cumulative learning experiences designed with specific outcomes in mind. I think those are the characteristics of most learning programs, and it doesn't matter whether it is a program for learning how to play tennis, how to speak another language, how to do mathematical division . . . or how to live more lightly on the Earth.

To summarize: We at the Institute for Earth Education are convinced that supplemental and infusion has turned out to equal superficial and ineffective. By their very nature it should be clear that these methods will simply not accomplish what education must urgently accomplish. What we desperately need in our field are genuine learning programs—programs designed specifically to achieve the outcomes that environmental education set its sights on in the beginning. And we need lots of them, for different settings and situations. We simply cannot afford to wait.

We believe people can make real changes most easily in their own lives. If enough individuals are making those changes (like people did when they switched to buying smaller cars), won't the nature of the problems also begin to change? Too simplistic? I'm not so sure. Is it our task to educate everyone about the nature of the current environmental issues and all their ramifications (and in the process be multidisciplinary, I suppose), or do we educate them about how life works, and about how they and why they can, and should, make changes in their own lifestyles (and deal with the environmental issues in that context)?

Perhaps we teachers are focusing too much on the overall environmental problems and not enough on individual lifestyles (particularly with the youngsters). I guess it is easier to talk about land use in general than it is to talk about the problem of individual consumption in specific. Isn't it interesting though how many people quote René Dubos, "Think globally, act locally," then ask the kids to tackle the acid rain problem? For that matter, how many *adults* can absorb and utilize all the multidimensional understandings of any major environmental issue?

Sometimes it seems like the more we examine one of these problems the further away we get from solving it. After all the discussion, all the inputs, and all the sessions at a national environmental education conference on acid rain, what do you say to your learners when you return home? What do you want them to do? Understand that it's a big problem? Congratulations, they probably got the idea.

I am not arguing against educating people about the big issues, but I think it is the easy way out for us. Shouldn't we educators focus our attention in our conferences on developing the education programs and let other groups tackle the ramifications of acid rain? Shouldn't the issue that we focus on and call to public attention be the lack of adequate funding and support for genuine environmental education programs? What I'm trying to say is why do we have conferences on acid rain in *this* field when the average person on the street doesn't even understand the water cycle? I believe we need to help our learners build (and internalize) the big picture of how life works ecologically first, then ask them to work on their own environmental habits.

In brief, why can't we develop the broad-based environmental education programs and let the environmental action groups (which we individually support) spearhead work on the current issues? Isn't it a cop-out for us to ask a ten-year-old if we should ban the SST, or if abortion is the solution to population control (as one current set of materials recommends)?

As an educational consultant in the seventies, I had the task of working with a new world history teacher at a local high school. Reports were that he was spending about one-half of his course reading the Pentagon Papers with the kids. When I challenged him about the use of so much time for this purpose, he replied that most people didn't even know where Vietnam was, let alone why we were fighting there, and besides, his students were interested in the topic. I tried to get him to see that there was nothing wrong with tying into the current interest in Vietnam, but why not use what was happening in that part of the world as an illustration of some fundamental principles that could then be applied elsewhere later on? Because he had brought up the future, I added that the reason people at the moment didn't know anything about Vietnam was probably because twenty years before their world history teacher was spending all his time on the Korean War instead of the underlying principles that govern lots of similar events over time.

However, my explanations seemed to fall on deaf ears. It took me a while to figure out that this particular teacher had not learned any fundamental principles about world history himself and thus could not really understand my point. Sadly, we are so used to dealing with only the more visible manifestations of any current issues that we seldom take the time to examine it more deeply. Much of the issues approach to environmental education is guilty of the same offense. A group of students working on water quality, for example, often end up knowing a lot about that topic and little or nothing about other, equally important facets of their own impact upon the Earth.

At one of my workshops a few years ago, a participant asked me if our approach was more accurately described as training or education. Although I didn't want to get bogged down in that philosophical quagmire at the time, I think our Earth Education work, like much of education in general, represents a bit of both approaches. On one hand, we want to change certain behavioral patterns, breaking some bad environmental habits and forming some good ones. And it is obvious that we are making some judgments ourselves about what particular habits need attention. However, on the other hand, we are trying to equip the students with some broad-based understandings and appreciations that will provide an underlying rationale for such immediate changes, and will motivate them to continue operating in a similar fashion on their own in the future.

I think the major problem we teachers have with many of the environmental action projects is that the students appear to start where they should really end. Because they never developed any broad-based understandings and appreciations, nor examined their own environmental habits to see how they were contributing to the problems, students come away with neither the education nor the training needed for the future. Surely, in some cases they may have used the specific issue they were involved in as a way of working back to larger principles, but for the most part, they probably ended up with some fairly narrow understandings of one particular issue. And chances are good that many of them never did make the connection between what they did at home in the evening with the issue they were addressing at school in the afternoon. Naturally, this doesn't hold true for everyone and, depending upon the teacher, some students may have become more involved in environmental concerns by coming through the back door like this. I just think a front door approach is more effective for more students over the long run.

When we were designing our Sunship Earth program, I said at the outset that I did not want students returning home to write their legislators or picket their factories. Why? Because that's our responsibility as adults. If anything, maybe the kids should be writing their educational authorities and picketing their schools. That is where they are and that is where they can make a real difference. Schools are often very energy intensive and wasteful institutions in our societies; so why not encourage the kids to start there and make some changes in their own behavior?

Another concern I have with much of the issues-oriented environmental education is that it tends to externalize the problems. Environmental problems are viewed as the result of something or someone out there, rather than within us as individuals. It encourages the perspective that if only *they* would do this, or if *they* hadn't done that, then everything would be fine. But that's not true; we are the *they* we complain about later.

For example, one investigation project that has been written up had the kids collect samples of litter from their neighborhood streets. After analyzing it, they concluded that much of it came from the local fast-food place. So they put their data together and presented it to the manager of the restaurant who subsequently agreed to put out more waste containers. End of project. Two cheers for everyone.

Actually, this may have been an adequate social studies activity for how to effect change, but it totally misses the point as an environmental education activity. If we are really serious about the mission of environmental education, then we simply must get from litter pick-up to fast-food put down. That is the real issue, and it is certainly one in which kids can make a significant difference.

Frankly, getting a group of kids fired up to make some changes in their surroundings is a fairly easy task, but when it's all over will they make any changes in their own lives? True, they may have learned a bit more in some of these projects about how to organize and implement their ideas, but what will this mean if they never change their own environmental behavior? I have a feeling that a lot of these issues-oriented activities generate a spurt of short-term attention (often with an accompanying media blurb and the endorsement of some "cornucopian" group), but result in very little long-term individual change. In the end, the kids get charged up briefly about implementing some environmental improvements in their own area, while continuing to spend their money at the local fast-food joint.

Finally, I can just hear someone reading this section and saying, "Now, Steve, haven't there been some successes?" Sure there have. Although we disagree with the placement of the environmental action projects in the overall structure of a comprehensive program, it has probably been in this area where the most notable achievements have occurred. Lots of environmental projects (beyond the beautification variety) have made real dents in the environmental problems we face. And lots of teachers and leaders have labored selflessly to make such good things happen. You can find both cooperative and confrontational examples of successes in schools and centers everywhere.

I don't mean to sound like nothing good has ever happened at any center or in any classroom, but overall it has not been enough, and I think it is the approach we have used that explains why. In a sense, we have squandered the goodwill and energies of a generation of teachers and leaders. If those of us who lay claim to providing some leadership in this field would have gotten our act together sooner and spoken out earlier, we might have been able to refocus the movement into more productive paths for everyone's sake.

In short, there is little doubt that every center, and every environmentally oriented classroom has some good things going on but, because of a flawed, piecemeal approach, the cumulative effect in either case seldom reaches the synergistic level necessary to promote the kind of fundamental changes needed in our societies.

So where are we going with our alternative? After years of frustration with the educational side of the environmental movement, but with good feelings about the soundness of our earlier Acclimatization work, we at the Earth Education Institute have started over. Earth Education aims to help people build an understanding of, appreciation for, and harmony with the Earth and its life. And anyone can set up an Earth Education program. Anytime. Anywhere. It doesn't have to be one of ours either. People can create their own. We just hope they will try to make it a genuine Earth Education *program* that is a carefully crafted, focused series of sequential, cumulative learning experiences designed with specific outcomes in mind.

Earth Education is the process of helping people live more harmoniously and joyously with the natural world. To help explain its components we have developed a structural logo, a three-sided pyramid representing the whys, whats, and ways of Earth Education. The three points on each side of the pyramid represent one of the three components of either the whys, the whats, or the ways.

Let's begin with the reasons for our existence. Each of the three "whys" of Earth Education—preserving, nurturing, training—has two facets: *preserving* the Earth for ourselves and for itself alone; *nurturing* people who have been deprived of a healthy relationship with the Earth and enriching those who have not; and *training* individuals who can make changes in their own lives and preparing them to serve as teachers in helping others.

Environmental Education Versus Earth Education

Environmental Education (*tendencies*)	Earth Education (*aims*)
* supplemental and random	* integral and programmatic
* classroom based	* natural world based
* issues oriented	* lifestyle oriented
* focuses mainly on developing secondary concepts and conducting environmental studies projects	* focuses largely on developing "ecological feeling" based on a combination of mental and physical engagement with the natural world
* activity based	* outcome based
* claims to teach how to think, not what to think	* claims to instill values and change habits
* relies heavily upon conducting group discussions to achieve its instructional objectives	* relies primarily upon participatory educational adventures to achieve its instructional objectives
* integrates the inputs (messages) and consolidates the applications (projects)	* consolidates the inputs (messages) and integrates the applications (projects)
* infused with "cornucopian" management messages and views	* infused with the ideals of deep ecology
* accepts a wide range of definitions and intentions	* rejects becoming everything to everyone

Please note the use of the qualifying terms in the headings above (i.e., environmental education tends to be and Earth education aims to be). We realize that there are exceptions to these characteristics on both sides of the chart. However, in general we think you will find they represent accurate descriptions of the two movements.

Principles of Earth Education

the "whys"

```
          /\
     nurturing
       /    \
preserving  training
     /_____\
```

Preserving
We believe the Earth as we know it is endangered by its human passengers.

Nurturing
We believe people who have broader understandings and deeper feelings for the planet as a vessel of life are wiser and healthier and happier.

Training
We believe Earth advocates are needed to serve as environmental teachers and models, and to champion the existence of Earth's nonhuman passengers.

the "whats"

```
            /\
     understanding
        /     \
   feeling   processing
       /_____\
```

Understanding
We believe in developing in people a basic comprehension of the major ecological systems and communities of the planet.

Feeling
We believe in instilling in people deep and abiding emotional attachments to the Earth and its life.

Processing
We believe in helping people change the way they live on the Earth.

the "ways"

```
          /\
     structuring
       /     \
  immersing  relating
     /_____\
```

Structuring
We believe in building complete programs with adventuresome, magical learning experiences that focus on specific outcomes.

Immersing
We believe in including lots of rich, firsthand contact with the natural world.

Relating
We believe in providing individuals with time to be alone in natural settings where they can reflect upon all life.

Preserving

Earth Education exists to preserve the extraordinary richness and biotic health of the third planet from the sun by changing the perspective and habits of its most dangerous passengers.

Tragically, the health of this marvelous oasis in the universe is now in great danger. The human species has become so pervasive and grown so powerful and arrogant that it presently threatens much of the other life with which it shares its garden-like vessel. Estimates vary, but many environmental scientists believe that the human passengers on board are destroying the other kinds of life on the vessel at the rate of at least one species each day.

Nurturing

Earth Education aims to help people develop a better sense of relationship with the natural world. Improving upon this personal contact and connection lies at the heart of everything we do. We believe many people have become estranged from the places and processes that actually support their lives. Helping them restore a harmonious and joyous relationship with the Earth is therefore our most important task.

A Zen master once said that Zen was the art of making the concrete and the abstract one and the same. In Earth Education, this is what we are trying to do with the understandings and the feelings. We believe wisdom lies in fully grasping our ecological relationship with the Earth—using both our head and our heart—and once achieved, such wisdom brings a happiness uncommon in the modern world.

Training

If you are already an Earth advocate, we want to help you become an Earth Educator. But genuine teaching for the Earth cannot be performed in isolation. As leaders, we have to play out the role in our own lives personally and be willing to take the stage publicly on behalf of our beliefs. As we see it, there are three facets to the role of the Earth Educator: teacher, model, and champion. They are the hidden side of the pyramid in our logo; the three points the whole edifice of Earth Education rests upon.

Now that we have taken a look at the "whys" of Earth Education, we should move on to the "whats." There are three content areas in our work: the understandings, the feelings, and the processings. In other

```
                                    /\
                                   teacher
**We believe:**                   /      \
                              model      champion
   An environmental teacher is . . .   /_____\
   a person who helps others understand and appreciate and
   change.

   An environmental model is . . .
   a person who demonstrates forming good environmental habits
   and breaking bad ones.

   An environmental champion is . . .
   a person willing to publicly defend another life that cannot
   defend itself.

A basic premise of Earth Education is that if we can get individuals to
*re-cognize* the Earth (conceptualize it differently), then they will want to
*re-present* it to others (communicate it freshly). Consequently, we have to
train the leaders first so they can train others.
```

words, an Earth Education program must include building some basic
ecological understandings, developing some good feelings about the
Earth and its life, and processing those understandings and feelings in
specific behavioral changes at home and at school.

Understanding

To understand life on the third planet from the sun, you have to
understand the flow of light energy bathing the planet each day, how it
is captured and utilized, and how it powers the great cycles of the
building materials of all living things—the air, the water, and the soil.
Together, that energy and those materials combine in varying amounts
in different places and times across the surface of the Earth. From the
beginning, variations in the quality and quantity of energy and available materials have given rise to various communities of life whose
inhabitants continually interrelate with one another as they go about
obtaining their own energy and material needs. Within those percolat-
ing pools of life there is the constant ebb and flow of change. Things
change one another, they change their surroundings, and their surroundings, in turn, change them.

In short, all living things draw upon sunlight energy for their existence, and each represents a temporary ordered arrangement of matter interacting with its neighbors. Each builds up, then breaks down as the materials of its own body inexorably crumble over time.

In sum, four key understandings explain the basic functions of life on this planet: the flow of energy, the cycling of matter, the interrelating of life, and the changing of forms. It is these broad brush strokes that we must focus upon in explaining the big picture of life on Earth.

Feeling

It may sound strange, but when it comes to the Earth, we are going to have to use it to save it. That is the paradox we now face. I think it is going to be impossible to convince large numbers of people of the necessity of preserving natural communities if they have had no contact with them. Yet our species has grown so prolific on our diet of old sunlight that our numbers alone threaten to fatally wound any natural area that receives us. We are like Lenny and his puppy in Steinbeck's novel, *Of Mice and Men*. If very many of us start loving it, we may kill it. But in this case, if we don't, it will die anyway, killed by those who never loved it.

The solution to our dilemma appears to be to figure out more and better ways of introducing people to the natural world, then proceed to implement such programs with great caution. However, before we can figure out the ways, we need to determine exactly what we want folks to take home with them. It's one thing to talk about the importance of cultivating good feelings about nature, but quite another to pin down exactly what those feelings are.

After many years of work in this area, we in Earth Education have concluded that there are four primary feelings we want people to hold: a joy at being in touch with the elements of life, a kinship with all living things, a reverence for natural communities, and a love for the Earth.

Processing

When it comes to the real crux of our environmental crisis, I do not think we can blame people for not understanding what's going on. Everywhere they go they are assailed by descriptions of the problems: endangered species signs at the zoo, save the prairie campaigns at the club meetings, raptor rehab programs at the nature centers, environmental degradation documentaries on television, etc., but no one ever tells them that it is their lifestyles that are causing the problems. No one ever says, "Hey, the way you live is the reason for all this. That is the primary cause of our trouble."

The point is that understanding and feeling are not enough if people don't incorporate them into their personal lives. They have to act upon those understandings and feelings in direct ways. So the third "what" of Earth Education is the processing of the other two—absorbing those insights and relating them to our own lives on a daily basis. And just as in the other sections, we have identified four components that we must focus upon: internalizing understandings for how life works on the planet, enhancing feelings for the Earth's richness of life, crafting more harmonious lifestyles, and planning environmental actions.

Unfortunately, the twelve parts of the "whats" end up being a lot to hold on to, but thinking of them as "the head, the heart, and the hands" will help you. There are four understandings—energy flow, cycling, interrelationships, and change (the head); four feelings—joy, kinship, reverence, and love (the heart); and four processings—internalizing, enhancing, crafting, and planning (the hands). And remember, Earth Education sets out to do what environmental education appeared to

© I•E•E

want to do but didn't. So we must not make the same mistakes ourselves. The point of Earth Education is change. If there is no change, there is no point.

Finally, there are three "ways" Earth Education uses to achieve change: structuring, immersing, and relating.

Structuring

Structuring is our way of talking about the skeletal framework of Earth Education programs. Of course when we use that term, we are talking about building complete programs that include all three of our "whats" (the understandings, feelings, and processings). We are talking about how we design our learning experiences for each of those components in a focused, sequential, cumulative fashion. And since we want our programs to serve as powerful springboard experiences for what takes place at school and home, we are also talking about how we make those activities interactive and dynamic. Finally, we are talking about how we put those pieces together in a whole—an overall program that is so carefully crafted and so rich in detail that it becomes synergistic, or more than the sum of its parts.

Immersing

One of the major differences between Earth Education and environmental education is how we get our participants out there and "immerse" them in the natural systems and communities of the Earth.

In *The Earth Speaks* I shared a story about St. Francis of Assisi who suddenly began ringing the church bell late one night in his village. When the awakened townspeople rushed to the tower to see what was wrong, St. Francis called down to them to look up, right then, at the beautiful moon overhead. Shut up inside their homes they had been missing one of the Earth's supreme treasures.

We need bellringers like this in Earth Education. We need to awaken people to the marvels and mysteries of daily life that they are missing. However, there is a bit more to it than that. If we are going to help people build a joyous relationship with the Earth again, we have to accomplish three major objectives. First of all, like St. Francis, *we have to get people out there*, only a bit farther away. You cannot accomplish what we are talking about inside most cities. You have to be "immersed" among the wild and growing things, in direct contact with the elements of life. Next, *we have to help people take in more of what is around them* out there. Lots of folks have gone someplace where they were closer to the natural world, but never really touched, or were touched, in turn, by it. Walking along on an asphalt path chattering away about something else will not get the job done. And finally, *we have to make sure people have a good time* while they are there. We want people to remember their experience as a joyous one. It will not do us much good if they decide it was not fun, and they don't want to go back.

Relating

Another way we could have stated the third of our "ways" would have been to say we want to provide individuals with time to be alone in natural settings where they can reflect upon all life, *including their own*. In other words, we want to help our learners relate both *with* and *to* the other life of the Earth. We want them to relate *with* it personally on an affective level, relate *to* it individually on a cognitive level, then examine their own lives in light of both experiences (it's feeling the processes and processing the feelings).

We use solitude experiences to help us accomplish this interplay between the understanding, the feeling, and the processing. And we often suggest that our participants spend a portion of such time writing in a journal or log or diary to help them sort out some of their thoughts and feelings about their own relationship with the Earth. However, even though solitude experiences are an important "way" of processing things, we also want to make sure our learners don't spend all of their time out there locked in on some head trip either. I know that must sound confusing, especially because of what I just said about writing in a journal, but keep in mind the dual purpose of these experiences. To accomplish our goal of helping people relate *with* the natural world we are going to have to help them get out of their heads (and into their surroundings) during some of their time out there as well.

Please take one more look at those nine crucial components of Earth Education:

WHYS	WHATS	WAYS
preserving	understanding	structuring
nurturing	feeling	immersing
training	processing	relating

If we have sparked your interest and you would like to develop your own Earth Education program based on these components, then the last chapter of *Earth Education* takes you through seven steps for doing so. Or, you might want to preview one of the model Earth Education programs we have already published, and centers around the world have implemented. Our annual *Earth Education Sourcebook* provides more information on these options.

Ten Characteristics of an Earth Education Program

An Earth education program:

1. hooks and pulls the learners in with magical experiences that promise discovery and adventure (the hooker).
2. proceeds in an organized way to a definite outcome that the learners can identify beforehand and rewards them when they reach it (the organizer).
3. focuses on building good feelings for the Earth and its life through lots of rich, firsthand contact (the immerser).
4. emphasizes major ecological understandings (at least four must be included: energy flow, cycling, interrelationships, change).
5. gets the descriptions of natural processes and places into the concrete through tasks that are both "hands-on" and "minds-on."
6. uses good learning techniques in building focused, sequential, cumulative experiences that start where the learners are mentally and end with lots of reinforcement for their new understandings.
7. avoids the labeling and quizzing approach in favor of the full participation that comes with more sharing and doing.
8. provides immediate application of its messages in the natural world and later in the human community.
9. pays attention to the details in every aspect of the learning situation.
10. transfers the learning by completing the action at school and home in specific lifestyle tasks designed for personal behavioral change.

Most of all, I hope we can welcome you home. As should be obvious by now, we believe that many of those people today who call themselves environmental educators are actually doing other things. The term environmental education has been so misused and abused that we have given up on it. Perhaps someday that side of the field will sort itself out and begin rectifying its current image as merely an umbrella for outdoor interests. We wish them well. We even hope our work might be of some assistance in their efforts.

Meanwhile, we want to get on with the urgent task of Earth Education. It is an alternative designed specifically for those who are serious about an educational response to our environmental crisis and are willing to make the personal sacrifices necessary to see genuine, broad-based educational programs implemented for that purpose. The goal of helping people develop a better sense of relationship with the Earth, while learning to live more lightly upon it, is too important to let it get lost out there amidst a plethora of unrelated groups and committees and reports. We are making a home for it. Won't you join us?

David W. Orr

ECOLOGICAL LITERACY
EDUCATION AND THE TRANSITION
TO A POST-MODERN WORLD

Ecological Literacy *is really two books in one. The first half is a treatise on sustainability—one that raises important questions and defines key issues. The second half is a thoughtful and engaging critique of higher education—not just environmental education, but the entire educational system of the United States. This analysis also offers a wealth of constructive criticism aimed at making modern education real—that is, grounding our entire educational experience in the realities of the modern world, most notably the urgent challenge of learning to live sustainably on the Earth. According to David Orr, this task will require a fundamental rethinking of the basic principles of higher education, a revamping of outdated curricula, and even a change in the day-to-day operations of the university so that it models a sustainable activity.*

Ecological Literacy: Education and the Transition to a Post-Modern World *by David W. Orr was published by SUNY Press, Albany, New York, in 1992.*

Higher Education and the Challenge of the Twenty-First Century

In *Earth in the Balance,* Vice President Al Gore proposes making "the rescue of the environment the central organizing principle for civilization." If the environment and humans, which depend on it, are to be rescued, however, those now being educated will have to do what the present generation has been unable or unwilling to do: stabilize world population; stabilize and then reduce the emission of greenhouse gases, which threaten to change the climate (perhaps disastrously); protect biological diversity; reverse the destruction of forests everywhere; and conserve soils. They must learn how to use energy and materials with great efficiency. They must learn how to run civilization on sunlight. They must rebuild economies to eliminate waste and pollution. They must learn how to manage renewable resources for the long-term. They must begin the great work of repairing, as much as possible, the damage done to the Earth in the past seven hundred years of industrialization. And they must do all of this while they reduce worsening social, ethnic, and racial inequities. No generation has ever faced a more daunting agenda.

A constituency able and willing to do these things must be educated into existence. That constituency must be smarter, better informed, more creative, and wiser than earlier generations. It must comprehend systems and patterns. It must be farsighted, yet practical. It must be able to tell the difference between ecological sense and nonsense. And it must be politically effective.

Much of the current debate about educational standards and reforms, however, is driven by the belief that we must prepare the young only to compete effectively in the global economy. That done, all will be well, or so it is assumed. But there are better reasons to reform education that have to do with the rapid decline in the habitability of the Earth. The kind of discipline centric education that enabled us to industrialize the Earth will not necessarily help us heal the damage caused by 150 years of industrialization. In *Preparing for the Twenty-First Century*, Paul Kennedy reaches broadly similar conclusions, calling for "nothing less than the re-education of humankind."

But we still educate the young for the most part as if there were no planetary emergency. It is widely assumed that environmental problems will be solved by technology of one sort or another. Better technology can certainly help, but the crisis is not first and foremost one of technology. Rather, it is one within the minds that develop and use technology. The disordering of ecological systems and of the great biogeochemical cycles of the Earth reflects a prior disorder in the thought, perception, imagination, intellectual priorities, and loyalties inherent in the industrial mind. Ultimately, then, the ecological crisis has to do with how we think and with the institutions that purport to shape and refine the capacity to think. The ecological crisis, in other words, is a crisis of education not one in education; tinkering won't do.

Despite all of the clear evidence of spreading environmental problems, this message has not made much headway in the vast majority of colleges and universities. In the words of Dartmouth professor Noel Perrin, "Most colleges act as though they have all the time in the world . . . neither trustees nor the administration seem to believe that a crisis is coming." Historian Jaroslav Pelikan in *The Idea of the University* goes farther, questioning whether universities will "address the underlying intellectual issues and moral imperatives of having responsibility for the Earth and to do so with an intensity and ingenuity matching that shown by previous generations in obeying the command to have dominion over the planet." Why should institutions of higher education, full of smart and learned people, be so slow to respond to the largest issues on the human agenda for the coming century? There are, I think, three primary reasons, no one of which is new.

First, we have organized both curriculum and research by fragments called disciplines, sub-disciplines, and departments, each of which deals only with small pieces of the total picture. This is fine until we need to understand patterns and whole systems, which is the business of no single discipline, department, or specialized field. As a result, larger trends and patterns tend to be ignored within a discipline-centric context. For example, from newspapers, journals, and books the following "random" facts recently crossed my desk:

- Male sperm counts worldwide have fallen by 50 percent since 1938 and no one knows exactly why.
- Human breast milk often contains more toxic substances than permissible in milk sold by dairies.
- At death human bodies often contain enough toxic chemicals and heavy metals to be classified as a hazardous waste. The same is true of the bodies of whales and dolphins that recently washed up on the banks of the St. Lawrence River and the Atlantic shore.
- Fungi have declined throughout the world and no one knows why. The same is true of populations of amphibians worldwide even where the pH of rainfall is normal.
- Roughly 80 percent of European forests have been damaged by acid rain.

- From mining and manufacturing, U.S. industry, according to Paul Hawken in *The Ecology of Commerce*, creates some 11.4 billion tons of hazardous wastes each year.
- Ultraviolet radiation reaching the ground in Toronto is now increasing at 5 percent per year.

From the perspective of any single discipline, these facts appear to be random. In truth they are not random at all, but are part of a larger pattern that includes shopping malls and deforestation, glitzy suburbs and ozone holes, crowded freeways and climate change, overstocked supermarkets and soil erosion, a gross national product of $5.6 trillion and superfund sites, technological wonders and insensate violence. In reality there is no such thing as a "side effect" or an "externality." These things are threads of a whole cloth. The fact that we see them as disconnected events or fail to see them at all is evidence of a failure to educate people to think broadly, perceive systems and patterns, and live as whole persons.

There is a second and related reason having to do with the rise of discipline-based professionalization. Whatever the gains in standards and quantity of knowledge, the net effect of professionalism has been to narrow scholars intellectual focus and encourage conformity with standards set by the elite in a particular field. Publication and research have come to be valued more highly than good teaching and service to the institution or the community. The full costs of professionalization, according to Alan Mermann of the Yale School of Medicine, include the failure to engage problems in the local community and a crippling "alienation from each other and from what is healthy for ourselves."

Modern scholars described by Mermann tend to think of themselves as professionals, part of the established order, not critics of it. For the consummate professional scholar, under professional and administrative pressures to secure large grants, the rule of thumb is that if it has no obvious and quick professional payoff leading to tenure, promotion, higher salary, or higher standing in the profession, don't do it.

The ideal of the broadly informed, renaissance mind has given way to the far smaller idea of the academic specialist. The resulting narrowness, "methodolatry," and careerism have rendered many unwilling and unfit to ask large and searching questions. In addition, whereas intellectuals once addressed the public, today professional scholars now talk mostly to each other about matters of little or no consequence for the larger society. Moreover, the professionally induced fear of making a mistake or being thought to lack rigor has rendered much of the professorate toothless and confined to quibbles of great insignificance. One sure way for a young professor to risk being denied tenure is to practice what philosopher Mary Midgley calls "the virtue of controversial courage," the very reason for which tenure was created.

Third, colleges and universities have not yet responded with "intensity and ingenuity" to the environmental crisis because their leaders have not been bold and visionary enough. This explains in part why institutions of higher education, in Stan Rowe's words (in *Home Place*), have shaped themselves "to an industrial ideal—the knowledge factory." Few professors bothered to question the foundational assumptions of higher education that dated back to Descartes and Bacon, the disciplinary structure of knowledge, the growing dependence of higher education on corporate and government funding, or the implicit belief in the human domination of nature. Few, if any, asked how the knowledge that their institutions propagated and dispensed fit with our responsibility for the earth and the ecological agenda looming ahead.

Reinventing Higher Education

What would it mean for colleges and universities to respond with "intensity and ingenuity" to the ecological challenges looming ahead? The answer, I believe, has three parts. It means, first, rethinking the foundational principles of higher education. In doing so we must recognize that all education is environmental education, by which I mean that students are taught in various and often unintended ways that they are part of or apart from natural systems. Furthermore, the goal of education is not the mastery of knowledge, but the mastery of self through knowledge—a different thing altogether. In the conduct of teaching, we must also acknowledge that the process of learning is often as important as the content, and that institutions teach by what they do as well as by what they say.

Second, an intense and ingenious response to environmental challenges requires rethinking the conventional curriculum. The ecological crisis is, in large part, a crisis of design. We've made things—farms, houses, cities, technologies, and whole economies—that do not fit harmoniously within their ecological context. One of the principle tasks of education in the coming century is to foster ecological design intelligence, which requires a careful meshing of human purposes with the larger patterns of the natural world. It also requires a careful study of those larger patterns to inform human purposes. The ecological design arts are the set of perceptual and analytic abilities, ecological wisdom, and practical wherewithal that will enable the young to make things that fit in a world of microbes, plants, animals, and entropy.

According to David Wann, author of *Biologic*, designing with nature means incorporating intelligence about how nature works into the way we build and live. Design applies to the making of nearly everything that directly or indirectly requires energy and materials, including farms, houses, communities, neighborhoods, cities, transportation systems, technologies, economies, and energy policies. When human artifacts and systems are well designed, they are in harmony with the ecological patterns in which they are embedded. When poorly designed, they undermine those larger patterns, creating pollution, higher costs, and social stress. Bad design is not simply an engineering problem, although better engineering would often help. Its roots go deeper.

Good design everywhere has certain common characteristics, including:

1. right scale
2. simplicity
3. efficient use of resources
4. a close fit between means and ends
5. durability
6. redundancy
7. resilience
8. solving more than one problem

Moreover, good ecological design promotes human competence instead of consumer dependence. Where good design becomes part of the social fabric at all levels, unanticipated positive side effects (synergies) multiply. Good urban design, for example, minimizes the use of automobiles by putting jobs, recreation, schools, and shopping in close proximity. Fewer automobiles mean:

1. more people walk and bike, leading to a more physically fit population;
2. less urban congestion, hence more civility;
3. cleaner air, hence better health;
4. lower emission of CO_2, hence less risk of climate change; and
5. fewer accidents, hence lower insurance costs.

And by using less gasoline we will have fewer oil spills, which helps to preserve biological diversity, balance trade deficits, and improve the economy. But when people fail to design with ecological competence, unwanted side effects and disasters multiply.

Ecological design requires the ability to comprehend patterns that connect, which means getting beyond the boxes we call disciplines to see things in their larger context. It requires, in other words, a liberal education, but nearly everywhere the liberal arts have become more specialized. Design competence requires the integration of firsthand experience and practical competence with theoretical knowledge, but the liberal arts have become more abstract, fragmented, and remote from lived reality. Design competence requires us to be students of the natural world, but the study of nature is being displaced by the effort to engineer nature to fit the economy instead of the other way around. Finally, design competence requires the ability to inquire deeply into the purposes and consequences of things to know what's worth doing and what should not be done at all. But the ethical foundations of education have been diluted by the belief that values are merely personal opinions.

All of this is to say that liberal arts institutions have not been vigorous enough in their response to the rapid decline in the habitability of the Earth. A more adequate response would aim to equip students to do the work of rebuilding households, farms, institutions, communities, corporations, and economies that (1) do not emit carbon dioxide or other heat trapping gasses; (2) operate on renewable energy; (3) do not reduce biological diversity; (4) use materials and water with high efficiency; (5) recycle materials and organic wastes; (6) restore damaged ecosystems, and (7) promote sustainable local and regional economies. These objectives will require significant changes in the skills, aptitudes, and abilities fostered in the conventional curriculum.

Third, an intense and ingenious response to the ecological challenges ahead means rethinking how institutions operate, buy, invest, and build.

Operations

The same institutions that purport to induct the young into responsible adulthood ought not to undermine the health and sustainability of the world their students will inherit through their daily operations. Colleges and universities take in vast amounts of energy, food, water, materials, and they dispose of large amounts of waste in a variety of forms. Every institution ought to conduct an audit of these resource flows to determine its total environmental impact. For example, how much CO_2 is emitted per student per year? How much paper is used? How much water is consumed? An audit will also indicate ways in which environmental impacts as well as costs can be reduced through greater efficiency in the use of resources and operational changes that close waste loops, eliminate hazardous chemicals, and adopt management practices with lower environmental impacts.

Purchasing

In the academic year 1987–88 colleges and universities bought $114 billion worth of goods and services, according to the *Chronicle of Higher Education*. For the most part these expenditures were made without much thought for their environmental impacts. If environment is to become the "central organizing principle" for higher education, however, buying power should be used to leverage the development of sustainable local and regional economies. Food served on college campuses, for example, seldom comes from land farmed sustainably. Whatever the price paid by the institution, its real cost to society, measured in both ecological and human terms, is much higher. Buying food locally, on the other hand, encourages the development of sustainable agriculture in the surrounding region, improves the quality of food served in campus dining halls, promotes local economic development, and eliminates the economic and ecological costs of providing transportation, refrigeration, and processing. The same benefits result from other institutional purchases whenever it is possible to substitute local resources, materials, and products for those imported from distant sources.

Investment

College and university endowment funds in 1993 totaled $73.9 billion. As with purchases, the vast majority of this money is invested without much regard for environmental impacts. An "intense and ingenious" response to looming ecological problems would require trustees and administration officials to screen institutional investments to determine whether or not they promote the transition to a sustainable economy. Aside from the more obvious investment criteria having to do with the environmental practices of particular companies, there are good reasons to use a percentage of investments to leverage sustainable development throughout the region in which the institution is located. Investments in regional energy efficiency, in particular, may offer attractive opportunities for high returns with short payback times.

Campus Architecture

It is widely assumed that learning takes place in buildings but that none occurs as a result of how they are designed or by whom, how they are constructed and from what materials, how they fit their location, and how and how well they operate. Academic architecture is in fact a kind of crystallized pedagogy, and buildings have their own hidden curriculum that teaches as effectively as any course taught in them. Students should be involved in the design, construction, and operation of academic buildings. That effort can be a liberal education in a microcosm that includes virtually every discipline in the catalog. The act of building is an opportunity to stretch the educational experience across disciplinary boundaries and across those dividing the realm of thought from that of application. It is an opportunity to work collectively on projects with practical import and to teach the art of "good work." It is also an opportunity to lower life-cycle costs of buildings and to reduce a large amount of unnecessary damage to the natural world caused by careless design.

Conclusion

As we approach the year 2000 the vital signs of the Earth are virtually everywhere in decline. The big numbers are working against us: population growth, the extinction of species, deforestation, desertification, soil loss, acid rain, toxic substances, and the possibility of rapid climate change. But these trends need not prove fatal to the human prospect if we are able to summon the courage and the moral energy necessary to respond with foresight and wisdom. For their part, however, colleges and universities have done little to prepare their graduates to deal with the challenges ahead. The question, still unanswered, is whether they are capable of responding with "intensity and ingenuity" at all.

To some, such a response to the challenges of the twenty-first century appears to be utterly unimaginable. To others, however, it looks a great deal like what Winston Churchill once called an "insurmountable opportunity." It is an opportunity to revitalize and enliven curriculum and pedagogy. It is an opportunity to create a genuinely interdisciplinary curriculum. It is an opportunity to redesign the campus to reduce costs, lower environmental impacts, and help catalyze sustainable economies.

In fact, a revolution in education is gathering momentum. It is apparent in the conferences sponsored by the Student Environmental Action Coalition that have drawn thousands of students from campuses all over the United States. It was evident in the February 1994 conference sponsored by Yale University students who organized the "Campus Earth Summit." It is evident in the rapid growth of environmental studies programs on campuses virtually everywhere. It is evident in growing student enrollments in environmental studies courses and participation in campus environmental projects. Increasingly, students realize that their inheritance is being spent carelessly and sometimes fraudulently. But a sizable number know in their bones the truth of Goethe's words that "whatever you can do or dream you can, begin it. Boldness has genius, power, and magic in it."

Sources

Editors of the Chronicle of Higher Education, 1992. *The Almanac of Higher Education*. Chicago: University of Chicago Press.

Gore, Albert, 1992. *Earth in the Balance*. Boston: Houghton Mifflin.

Kennedy, Paul, 1993. *Preparing for the Twenty-First Century*. New York: Random House.

Mermann, A., 1992. *The Pharos*, summer.

Midgley, M., 1989. *Wisdom Information and Wonder*. New York: Routledge.

New York Times, October 20, 1993.

Perrin, N., October 28, 1992. "Colleges Are Doing Pitifully Little to Protect the Environment." *Chronicle of Higher Education*.

Pelikan, Y., 1992. *The Idea of The University*. New Haven: Yale University Press.

Rowe, S., 1990. *Home Place: Essays on Ecology*. Edmonton: Newest Publishers.

Smith, A., 1992. *Campus Ecology*. Los Angeles: Living Planet Press.

Wann, D., 1994. *Biologic: Revised Edition*. Boulder: Johnson Books.

PART III

BLUEPRINT FOR SUSTAINABILITY:
LEARNING TO LIVE AND
PROSPER WITHIN LIMITS

Helena Norberg-Hodge

ANCIENT FUTURES
LEARNING FROM LADAKH

In our frantic rush to satisfy a seemingly insatiable desire for progress, many people view science and technology as powerful saviors. However, some critics believe that these forces, combined with an undying belief in the primacy of continued economic growth, are fueling an environmentally unsustainable form of development in the industrial world. Making matters worse, many industrial nations are exporting unabashedly western development strategies to the developing nations. While GNPs of the developing nations may show gains from such activities, the lives of the people, the culture, and the environment often crumble under the weight of the wholesale exportation of western ways.

In Ancient Futures, *Helena Norberg-Hodge tells of a people of Ladakh in northern India that once thrived in a high-altitude desert, living off the land, satisfying their needs with locally raised livestock and food produced during a brief four-month growing season. Her story tells of the profound changes that have occurred as western ideas and western ways have invaded this once sustainable community, changing not just the way people live but also the way they think.*

Ancient Futures *clearly describes the Ladakhi plunge from contentment to anxiety as the people of Ladakh moved from a sustainable, cooperative, agricultural system to an increasingly westernized, money-based culture. However, the main theme of this story is not about the pathology of westernization. It is about steps people can take, lessons we can learn, to create a humane, sustainable future. The lessons come not so much from science, technology, and economics, but from the practices and beliefs of ancient cultures themselves.*

Like others who have studied ancient cultures, Helena Norberg-Hodge argues that we might have just as much to learn from them as they do from us, perhaps more. Our future might be tied more to adopting ancient ways—community and close ties to the land, for instance—than continued material wealth and technological advancement that is blind to ecological limits.

Ancient Futures: Learning from Ladakh *by Helena Norberg-Hodge was published by Sierra Club Books, San Francisco, in 1991.*

Why is the world teetering on the edge of social and environmental breakdown? What are the roots of our crises? Were things better in the past? Or worse?

Experiences over nearly two decades in Ladakh, an ancient Buddhist culture on the Tibetan Plateau, have dramatically changed my perspective on these questions. In Ladakh I have had the privilege to experience another, saner way of life and to see my own culture from the outside. I have lived in a society based on fundamentally different principles and witnessed firsthand the impact of the modern world on that culture.

Before Ladakh, I assumed that human beings were essentially selfish, struggling to compete and survive, and that more cooperative societies were nothing more than utopian dreams. Now I know otherwise. Furthermore, I view my own industrial culture in a very different light.

When I first came to Ladakh in 1975, I was one of the first outsiders in several decades to visit the region. The rugged mountain geography and government policy had largely sheltered Ladakh from western influences, and it was like coming to the Hopi culture in America before the Spaniards had arrived. Life in the villages was still based on the same foundations that had supported it for centuries.

I learned the language in my first year and was thus able to see the culture "from the inside." The more I learned, the more impressed I became. Using little more than "stone-age" technologies and the scant resources at hand, the Ladakhis managed to *prosper* in a high-altitude desert that at first seemed incapable of sustaining human life. Barley, wheat, and vegetables—grown on terraced fields carved from the desert and irrigated with glacial meltwater—had kept the population well fed from generation to generation. Goats, sheep, yaks, cows, and donkeys supplied the Ladakhis with meat, milk, wool, hides, and animal power. Village houses—made of stones and mud brick—were large and graceful. Elegant carvings adorned the windows and doors.

This was a healthy, sustainable culture: there was virtually no waste or pollution; cultural practices rooted in an awareness of resource limits had kept population within the bounds that the land could support. Crime, unemployment, and homelessness were essentially unknown. The status of women was high, and old people were productive members of society until the day they died. The sense of community, in large measure a consequence of the strong local economy, was all-embracing. Perhaps most remarkable of all was the amount of leisure that people enjoyed. Despite the difficult environment, the Ladakhis' intimate knowledge of their ecosystem enabled them to provide all their material needs in just the four-month agricultural season, leaving them eight months of the year for visiting family and friends, for music and storytelling, for festivals and parties.

After several years in Ladakh, I came to understand a fundamental difference between Ladakhi society and my own industrial culture. Unlike us, the Ladakhis truly *belonged* to their place on the earth. They were bonded to that place through intimate daily contact, through a knowledge of their immediate environment with its needs and limitations, and the knowledge that they were dependent on it for their livelihood. Just as importantly, everyone, including aunts and uncles, monks and nuns, belonged to a highly interdependent community. A mother was never left on her own, separated from all her children; a grandmother or grandfather was never cut off from the flow of everyday life; a farmer was never left to work his fields alone without the help of others. Ladakhis knew they were inextricably connected to others and to their surroundings, a knowledge that was reinforced by the teachings of Buddhism. As a result, the Ladakhis were more emotionally healthy, more secure, than any people I had ever known. They were confident in themselves and proud of their culture, and they expressed a joy in life that could be seen in everyone from the youngest child to great-grandmothers.

In recent years, however, sudden and dramatic change has come to Ladakh. Efforts are underway to "develop" the region, and the local economy is being dismantled. Local agriculture now seems "uneconomic" because of a glut of heavily subsidized grains and packaged foods, trucked into Ladakh over the Himalayas. As a consequence, many Ladakhis are abandoning farming.

The introduction of western-style schooling is beginning to erase the local knowledge that had been handed down from generation to generation. Children no longer receive the location-specific education that taught them how to use local resources, how to notice the subtle microclimates within the village, how to recognize the way soil varies from field to field. In the new schools, children are trained for specialized jobs in an urban economy. Those jobs are scarce, and many of the children I met in my first years, though "educated," are now unemployed and alienated.

A new tourist trade is bringing thousands of westerners to the region every year—people who appear to the Ladakhis to be fabulously wealthy without ever having to work. Films, television, and advertising similarly portray images of an idealized, urban way of life that makes traditional life seem primitive and shabby by contrast. As a result, people who once considered themselves wealthy now feel poor and deprived. Individual self-esteem and cultural pride have been eroded. The young in particular are growing ashamed of being Ladakhi and are becoming increasingly insecure.

Ladakh's environment is also straining under the weight of modernization. The thin air in Leh, the capital, is choked with diesel fumes from trucks carrying the goods that Ladakh now "needs"—not only staple foods, fossil fuels, and cement, but also packaged candies, fizzy drinks, and plastic toys. In the traditional village everything comes from the Earth and returns to the Earth, but in urban Leh the detritus of a consumer culture piles up in the streets and on the open dumps outside of town. In much of urbanized Ladakh, the once-pristine water is no longer fit to drink.

The messengers of development—tourists, advertisements, and film images—are implicitly telling the Ladakhis that their traditional practices are backward and that modern science will help them stretch natural resources to produce ever more. Development is stimulating dissatisfaction and greed, and in so doing, it is destroying an economy that had served people's needs for more than a thousand years.

Since development first came to Ladakh, I have watched the gap between rich and poor widen; I have watched women lose their self-confidence and power; I have watched the appearance of unemployment and inflation and a dramatic increase in crime; I have watched population levels rise, fueled by a variety of economic and psychological pressures; I have watched the disintegration of families and communities; I have watched people become separated from the land, as self-sufficiency is gradually replaced by economic dependence on the outside world; and I have watched violent conflict arise between Ladakhi Muslims and Buddhists, after five hundred years of harmony and cooperation.

As one of the last subsistence economies to survive virtually intact to the present day, Ladakh has been a unique vantage point from which to observe the whole process of development. Its collision with the modern world has been particularly sudden and dramatic. Yet the transformation it is now experiencing is anything but unique: essentially the same process is affecting every corner of the world.

"Development" is the name given to a process of planned change by which the standard of living is supposed to be raised through technological advance and economic growth. The development of Ladakh, as everywhere else in the world, involves a massive and systematic restructuring of society that presupposes enormous and continual investments in infrastructure: paved roads, a western-style hospital, schools, a radio station, an airport, power installations. At no stage is it questioned whether or not the result of these tremendous efforts will constitute an improvement on what had existed before. It is like starting from zero, as if there were no infrastructure in Ladakh before development. It is as if there were no medical care, no education, no communication, no transport or trade. The intricate web of roads, paths, and trade routes, and the vast and sophisticated network of irrigation canals maintained over centuries are all signs of a living, functioning culture and economic system, signs that are treated as though they simply do not exist. Ladakh is being rebuilt according to western guidelines—in tarmac, concrete, steel . . . and dollars.

Development works on the assumption that the introduction of cash is invariably an improvement. The more money, the better. This may be true for those dependent on the mainstream economy (and even this is a debatable assumption), but it is certainly not true for the millions of people living within, or benefiting from, a subsistence economy— that is, a non-monetized economy based on a direct relationship with natural resources. For these people, who are able to produce their own food, clothing, and shelter, there is a significant reduction in the quality of life once they relinquish their own culture and independence for an unstable monetary income.

The situation in the traditional parts of Ladakh and in the neighboring Himalayan kingdom of Bhutan vividly illustrates the shortcomings of defining human welfare in monetary terms. In each case, the standard of living is quite high when compared with most of the Third World. People provide their own basic needs and still have beautiful art and music, and significantly more time for family, friends, and leisure activities than people in the West. Yet the World Bank describes Bhutan as one of the poorest countries in the world. Because its gross domestic product (GDP) is virtually zero, the country is ranked at the bottom of the international economic order. In effect, this means that no distinction is made between the homeless on the streets of New York and Bhutanese or Ladakhi farmers. In both cases there may be no income, but the reality behind the statistics is as different as night and day.

This one-dimensional view of progress, widely favored by economists and development experts, has helped to mask the negative impact of economic growth, while blinding us to the value of locally based economies in both the North and the South. Moreover, it has disguised the fact that development programs, far from benefiting people in the Third World, have in many cases served only to lower their standard of living.

Farmers in Ladakh and elsewhere in the Third World who previously grew a variety of crops and kept a few animals to provide for themselves—either directly or through the local economy—are now encouraged instead to grow cash crops for distant markets. In this way, they become dependent on forces beyond their control—huge transportation networks, oil and agro-chemical markets, and the fluctuations of international finance. Over the course of time, inflation obliges them to produce more and more to secure the income that they now need in order to buy what they used to grow themselves.

Throughout the world, the process of development has displaced and marginalized self-reliant local economies in general, and small farmers in particular. In the industrialized world, more than 90 percent of the population has been pulled away from agriculture. Now the same process is occurring in the Third World, only much more rapidly, as rural subsistence is steadily eroded.

The promise of conventional development is that by following in the footsteps of the "developed" countries of the world, the "underdeveloped" countries can become rich and comfortable too. Poverty will be eliminated, and the problems of overpopulation and environmental degradation will be solved. This argument, as reasonable as it may seem at first glance, in fact contains an inherent flaw, even deception. The fact is that the developed nations are consuming essential resources in such a way and at such a rate that it is impossible for "underdeveloped" areas of the world to follow in their footsteps. When one-quarter of the world's population consumes three-quarters of the world's resources, and then in effect turns around and tells the others to do as they do, it is little short of a hoax. Development is all too often a euphemism for exploitation, a new colonialism. The forces of development and modernization have pulled most people away from a sure subsistence and got them to chase after an illusion, only to fall flat on their faces, materially impoverished and psychologically disoriented. A majority are turned into slum dwellers—having left the land and their local economy to end up in the shadow of an urban dream that can never be realized.

Development is in the process of reducing all the diverse cultures of the world to a single monoculture. It is based on the assumption that needs are everywhere the same, that everyone needs to eat the same food, to live in the same type of house, to wear the same clothes. The same cement buildings, the same toys, the same films and television programs find their way to the most remote corners of the world. Across the world, "Dallas" beams into people's homes and pinstripe suits are *de rigeur*. Recently, I've seen almost identical toy shops appear in Ladakh and in a remote mountain village in Spain. They both sell the same blonde, blue-eyed Barbie dolls and Rambos with machine guns. Even language is being homogenized, because it is necessary to learn English to be part of the modern "global community."

One way in which this process is promoted is that rural peoples all over the South are given a grossly distorted impression of modern life—one of ease and glamour, where everyone is beautiful, everyone is rich. They see the fast cars, the microwaves, and the video machines. Advertising and the media are telling people what to do—in fact telling them what to *be*: modern, civilized, and rich. What they don't talk about are the "side-effects" of this way of life: the environmental deterioration, the psychological stress, the drug addiction, the homelessness. People who have been presented with only one side of the development coin are left vulnerable and eager for modernization.

In the last few decades, diverse cultures from Alaska to Australia have been overrun by the industrial monoculture. This is a tragedy of many dimensions. With the destruction of each culture, we are erasing centuries of accumulated knowledge, and as diverse ethnic groups feel their identity threatened, conflict and social breakdown almost inevitably follow.

Returning each year to the West, I have become increasingly aware that the pressures of economic and technological change are bearing down even on our culture in a similar way; we, too, are being "developed." Today, even though only 2 or 3 percent of the population is left on the land, small farmers are still being squeezed out of existence; and even though industrialization has pared the extended family down to a small nuclear unit, our economy is still chipping away at it. Technological advance is continuing to speed life up, while robbing people of time. Increased trade and ever greater mobility are furthering anonymity and a breakdown of community. In the West, these trends are labeled "progress" rather than development, but they emanate from the same process of industrialization that inevitably leads to centralization, social degradation, and the wasteful use of resources.

The over-reliance on the gross domestic product (GDP) as a prime indicator of social welfare has not only rationalized destructive development in places like Ladakh, it has also led to misguided public policy in the industrialized world. Every time money changes hands—whether from the sale of tomatoes or a car accident—it is added to GDP and we count ourselves richer. Policies that cause GDP to rise are thus often pursued despite their negative impact on the environment or society. A nation's balance sheet looks better, for instance, if all its forests have just been cut to the ground, because felling trees makes money. And if crime is on the increase and people buy more burglar alarms or governments build more jails, if we put the sick and elderly into costly care institutions, if we seek help for emotional and stress-related problems, if we buy bottled water because tap water has become so polluted—all of these contribute to GDP and are measured as economic "progress."

The situation has become quite absurd: rather than eating a potato grown in your own garden, it is better for the economy if you buy a potato grown on the other side of the country, which has been pulverized, freeze-dried, and reconstituted into brightly colored potato balls. Consuming in this way, of course, means more transportation, more use of fossil fuels, more pollution, more chemical additives and preservatives, and more separation between producer and consumer. But it also means an incremental increase in GDP and is therefore encouraged.

"Progress" based on economic and technological development has reached an advanced stage in the West. Wherever we look, we can see its inexorable logic at work—replacing people with machines, local interdependence with global markets, country lanes with freeways, and the corner shop with a supermarket. Governments everywhere—regardless of their political hue—are encouraging an *acceleration* in these changes through support for a globalized economy. Long-distance trade receives heavy subsidies—in particular, to maintain and expand networks of communication and transportation. Swedish biscuits and New Zealand apples compete with local produce in the United States and France only because of an energy-intensive system laden with hidden subsidies and ignored pollution costs. Meanwhile, trade agreements like NAFTA, GATT, and Maastricht—justified by the rhetoric of "free trade"—are leading to ever greater centralization of economic and political power. National governments are handing over more and more control to supranational institutions such as the European Community and the World Bank. Such organizations are so far removed from the people they are supposed to represent that they are incapable of responding to their diverse interests.

In Ladakh, the effect of this pattern of centralization is readily apparent. In the decentralized village-scale economy, individuals had a real influence on the important decisions affecting them. They depended on people they knew, and on local resources they controlled themselves. Nowadays, as they are drawn ever more tightly into the socio-economic structure of India, each individual becomes just one of 800 million; as part of the global economy, one of over 5 billion. Their influence over the political and economic forces that affect them is being so reduced that they are essentially powerless.

Globally, this sort of political change is a reflection of an economic centralization that threatens to allow multinational corporations to outstrip even governments in their influence and power. Such trends are extremely disturbing because these corporations lie outside the realm of democratic control. Organized labor and environmental pressure groups are no match for giant, highly mobile corporations. Legislation that protects workers' rights or bans toxic chemicals can be rendered useless when companies relocate their operations to a part of the world with less stringent controls.

Though the problems facing society today are potentially catastrophic, we still have an opportunity to steer toward social and ecological balance. But if we are to do more than simply treat symptoms, it is important that we understand the systemic nature of the crises facing us. Under the surface seemingly unconnected problems such as ethnic violence, pollution of the air and water, broken families, and cultural disintegration are closely interlinked. Understanding that the problems are interrelated can make them seem overwhelming, but finding the points at which they converge can, in fact, make our attempts to tackle them a great deal more effective. It is then just a question of pulling the right threads to affect the entire fabric, rather than having to deal with each problem individually.

The fabric of industrial society is to a great extent determined by the interaction of science, technology, and a narrow economic paradigm—an interaction that is leading to ever-greater centralization and specialization. Since the Industrial Revolution, the perspective of the individual has become more limited while political and economic units have grown larger. I have become convinced that we need to decentralize our political and economic structures and broaden our approach to knowledge if we are to find our way to a more balanced and sane society. In Ladakh I have seen how human-scale structures nurture intimate bonds with the earth and an active and participatory democracy, while supporting strong and vital communities, healthy families, and a greater balance between male and female. These structures, in turn, provide the security needed for individual well-being and self-esteem.

The changes we need to make can greatly enrich our lives. Yet they are often treated, even within the environmental movement, as sacrifices. The emphasis is on giving things up and making do with less, rather than recognizing how much we have to gain. We forget that the price for never-ending economic growth and material prosperity has been environmental breakdown, spiritual and social impoverishment, psychological insecurity, and a loss of leisure and of cultural vitality. We think of ourselves as "having everything" and are surprised when young people turn to drugs or strange cults to fill the void in their lives.

Currently, the emerging global economy and the growing domination of science and technology are not only severing our connection to nature and to one another but are also breaking down natural and cultural diversity. In so doing, we are threatening our very existence, because in the natural world, diversity is an inescapable fact of life. Indeed, biologists are now corroborating the life-sustaining importance of species diversity, and many are speaking out about the danger of erasing it for the sake of short-term gain.

In a modern setting, it is easy to believe that economic development has actually *increased* diversity. Large-scale transportation and communication make trade far easier, bringing together a vast array of foods and products from different cultures. However, the very system that facilitates this multinational, multicultural exchange of goods is actually helping to *erase* diversity. Lingonberry and pineapple juice are giving way to Coca-Cola, woolen robes and cotton saris to blue jeans, yaks and highland cattle to Jersey cows. Diversity does not mean having the choice among ten different kinds of blue jeans all made by the same company.

Cultural diversity is as important as diversity in the natural world and, in fact, follows directly from it. Traditional cultures mirrored their particular environments, deriving their food, clothing, and shelter primarily from local resources. Even in the West today, there are still remnants of local adaptation to diversity. In the American Southwest, you find flat-roofed adobe houses, which are ideally suited to the extremes of the desert climate, while in New England the houses are made of wood and have peaked roofs designed to shed the rain and snow. The cuisines of different cultures still reflect local food sources, from the olive oil prevalent in Mediterranean cooking to the oatmeal and kippered herring on the Scotsman's breakfast table.

Without retreating into cultural or economic isolationism, we can nourish the traditions of our own region. A true appreciation of cultural diversity means neither imposing our own culture on others, nor packaging, exploiting, and commercializing exotic cultures for our own consumption.

One of the most effective ways of reviving cultural differences would be to lobby for a reduction in unnecessary trade. At the moment, our tax money is spent to expand transport infrastructures and to increase trade for the sake of trade. We are transporting across whole continents a vast range of products, from milk to apples to furniture, that could just as easily be produced in their place of destination. What we should be doing instead is reinforcing and diversifying local economies. By reducing and eliminating subsidies for long-distance transport, we would cut waste and pollution, improve the position of the small farmer, and strengthen communities in one fell swoop.

What exactly is "local" and what is "necessary" as opposed to "unnecessary" trade are issues that cannot be defined in absolute terms. But the crucial point is that the *principle* of heavily subsidized trade is one that needs critical reassessment. It is in robust, local-scale economies that we find genuinely "free" markets; free of the corporate manipulation, hidden subsidies, waste, and immense promotional costs that characterize today's global market.

The trend toward a globalization of the market not only concentrates power and resources in ever-fewer hands, but contributes directly to ever-greater dependence on urban centers. Even though the numbers of people living in many western cities may actually be falling, the pull to the center is increasing. This manifests itself in the growth of suburbia— regions devoid of any connection to the land or real sense of community and entirely dependent on the economy of the urban areas to which they are linked. Living and working outside the reach of these urban centers is becoming increasingly difficult, and commuters are traveling farther and farther to reach their place of employment. Outside the urban orbit, whole regions suffer severe decline, and as a result small towns and rural villages all over the industrialized world are dying.

To reverse these trends we need to encourage demographic as well as economic decentralization. This would involve a succession of changes in the whole socio-economic system. It is important to remember, however, that we are not talking about dismantling a static entity but rather about steering in the direction of change. The scale of our society is growing year by year, and the logic of centralization is progressively being carried to new extremes. The pace is such that we would need to actually implement plans for decentralization simply to stay where we are now. That alone would be a significant achievement.

While decentralization is the most important *structural* change we need to make, it would need to be accompanied by a corresponding change in world view. Increasing ecological distress has clearly demonstrated wide-reaching interconnections in natural systems, but most academic institutions continue to perpetuate ever more narrowly focused specialization. This reductionist perspective is, in fact, one of the root causes of the malaise of industrial culture. Paradoxically, a trend toward smaller-scale political and economic units might help us to develop a broader world view—one based on interconnectedness. Instead of narrowing our vision, an intimate connection to community and place would encourage an understanding of interdependence. When you are dependent on the Earth under your feet and the community around you for your survival, you experience interdependence as a fact of daily life. Such a deep experiential understanding of interconnectedness—feeling yourself a part of the continuum of life—contrasts starkly with the analytic, fragmented, and theoretical thinking of modern society.

We need to return to a more empathetic relationship with the living world and learn to see broader patterns, process, and change. Nowadays, one biologist does not speak the same language as another, unless they are both studying the same kind of fruit fly. How can we understand life by breaking it into fragments and freezing it in time? Our static and mechanistic world view has reached its limits, and some scientists—particularly quantum physicists—now speak of a paradigm shift away from the old "building block" view of reality to a more organic one. In direct opposition to the trend in mainstream culture toward greater specialization, we need to actively promote the generalist—the one who sees connections and makes links across different disciplines.

In this regard, one of the most hopeful trends is the increasing respect for more feminine values and ways of thinking. Research into women's thought patterns is substantiating the assertion that the feminine point of view places greater emphasis on relationships and connections, both in terms of empathy and abstract thinking. Such a perspective is obviously not the exclusive property of women, and in recent years men have begun to value more consciously this more feminine perspective. However, for hundreds of years this more contextual way of thinking has not only been neglected, but severely undermined by industrial culture. The dominant perspective of our society is now out of balance, and a shift toward the feminine is overdue.

This shift would bring with it an emphasis on experiential knowledge. To a much greater extent than men, women can be said to form their abstractions from personal experience. Interestingly enough, the same can be said of the Ladakhis and many traditional and nonwestern cultures. To understand the complexities of the natural world, theory must be grounded in experience. Experiential learning is based in messy reality, with its untidiness, its ever-changing pattern, its refusal to conform to our expectations. As such, it inevitably leads to humility. If our studies were conducted less in the laboratory and more in the field—in the fields, in fact—scientific and technological advance would proceed more cautiously. If we learned to examine the potential effects of new technologies in context, over time, we would be less likely to set off destructive chains of unintended effects.

Today mainstream culture—led by government and industry—moves relentlessly toward continued economic growth and technological development, straining the limits of nature and all but ignoring fundamental human needs. The goal, it seems, is to free ourselves from our past and from the laws of nature. Yet a significant counter-current, comprising a wide range of groups and ideas, is keeping alive the ancient understanding that all life is inextricably connected.

At present, this counter-current is still a minority, but it is growing in strength as more and more people begin to question the whole notion of progress. The formation of Green parties and the rise in membership in environmental organizations indicate widespread commitment to environmental protection. Around the world, thousands of grassroots groups are working to revitalize communities and locally based economies, while millions of people have shown their opposition to "free trade" and the further globalization of the economy. Eco-villages, based on a strong sense of community and a close connection to the Earth, are springing up across the industrialized world. From Gaia Theory to the philosophy of Deep Ecology, challenges are arising to the mainstream scientific/reductionist world view. In fields as diverse as economics and psychology, the view of humans as isolated, atomized individuals is being abandoned in favor of the ancient notion that we are in fact embedded in community and in nature.

These trends are often labeled "new," but, as Ladakh has shown, in an important sense they are very old. They are, in fact, a rediscovery of values that have existed for thousands of years—values that recognize our place in the natural order, our indissoluble connection to one another and the Earth. Yet the modern-day mantra, "we cannot go back, we cannot go back," is deeply ingrained in our thinking. Of course we could not go back, even if we wanted to, but our search for a future that works is inevitably bringing us back to certain fundamental patterns that are in greater harmony with nature—including human nature.

Perhaps the most important lesson of Ladakh has to do with happiness. It was a lesson I was slow to learn. Only after many years of peeling away layers of preconceptions did I begin to see the smiles and laughter of the Ladakhis for what it really was: a genuine and unhindered appreciation of life itself. In Ladakh I have known a people who regard peace of mind and *joie de vivre* as their unquestioned birthright. I have seen that community and a close relationship to the land can enrich human life beyond all comparison with material wealth or technological sophistication. I have learned that another way is possible.

James Swan

NATURE AS TEACHER AND HEALER
HOW TO REAWAKEN YOUR
CONNECTION WITH NATURE

Creating a sustainable society requires many changes in the way we conduct our daily lives as well as profound changes in the way we conduct commerce. It also requires profound changes in attitudes—how we view one another and how we view the Earth. More than anything, we need to kindle a sense of reverence for the Earth and a sense of belonging.

To James Swan reverence and a sense of belonging comes from love, but how do people develop a love for nature? Does our future really depend on developing a love or kinship with nature?

Swan explores traditional cultures and the transcendent experiences among their members, which inspire kinship and respect for nature that are the norm in their societies. In this riveting account, which is as much biography as it is an exploration of the fascinating world of human psychology, Swan also explores the barriers that stand in the way of developing a love or kinship with the natural world amongst us moderns. He outlines a course of action designed to promote a reconnection to the living planet and its subtle, life-affirming rhythms.

An original essay based on Nature as Teacher and Healer: How to Reawaken Your Connection with Nature *by James A. Swan, published by Villard-Random House, New York, in 1992.*

Pulitzer Prize-winning biologist René Dubos likened our ecological state of affairs to that of a frog, who when hopping gaily along chanced to jump into a bucket of warm water. This body of water seemed rather pleasant to a cold-blooded creature, and so the frog went swimming about merrily. In time, the water grew warmer, and the frog responded by becoming more active and happy as his metabolism increased. However, the frog was unaware that he had jumped into a kettle of water being heated on the stove, and over time the temperature increased and increased, then suddenly the water came to a boil and the frog was cooked.

Dubos presents this story in his book *Man Adapting*, a penetrating analysis of the human tendency to acclimate to environmental conditions that may not be acutely toxic but in the long run are detrimental to health.

Adaptation is part of human nature. We must adjust to the ever-changing cycles of nature to survive. People become complacent about negative environmental conditions when the detrimental consequences are not readily apparent, and there is no basis for comparison.

Growing up on Grosse Ile, Michigan, a cigar-shaped island that lies where the Detroit River flows out into Lake Erie, I came to know the validity of the Dubos's thesis only too well. Grosse Ile is downwind and downstream from the massive Detroit automobile manufacturing complex. In the 1950s and 1960s, dustfalls at the north end of the island often averaged 120 tons per square mile per month. When you awoke on a winter morning and saw orange snow, you knew that the previous night a steel mill had vented its stacks. Black snow was caused by soot from either a coal-burning electrical power plant or a coke oven. The siding on white homes on the north end of the island would turn salmon in a year or two. Paint on your car would pit. Like many people in that area, as a child I suffered from chronic bronchitis until my family moved to the south end of the island when I was twelve. Fifteen years later, when I directed a public opinion survey of people living in the Downriver Detroit area, we found that the incidence of chronic respiratory illnesses was eight times the national average. Until after the first Earth Day in 1970, no one in the Downriver Detroit area said much about the obvious air pollution. Smoke billowing out from industrial smoke stacks meant prosperity.

Our new home on the south end of Grosse Ile was on a canal that led directly into Lake Erie. Living on the water, I saw a new ecological demon. Several times a year boat owners would wake up to find the sides of their boats coated with a black oily substance, a telltale sign of a night-shift engineer flushing an oil tank some place upstream, hoping the dark of night and the silent dilution of the mighty river would save the company the expense, time, and trouble of waste reclamation. This was only the easily perceptible tip of the iceberg. In the 1950s, quietly, communities all along the Detroit River stopped drawing their drinking water from the river due to growing waste discharges. As a replacement, the towns teamed up with Detroit to build a water supply pipeline all the way to Lake Huron to get potable water from an upstream source that was still pristine. A 1964 International Joint Commission report declared that the lower twenty-six miles of the Detroit River were "polluted bacteriologically, chemically, physically, and biologically, so as to interfere with municipal water supplies, recreation, fish and wildlife propagation, and navigation."

Wildlife biologist George Hunt, from the University of Michigan, estimated that as many as ten thousand waterfowl would die every winter when migrating flocks of ducks, geese, and swans landed in oil slicks in the middle of the night. As a high school science project, I experimented with different ways to try to remove oil from the feathers of waterfowl that were so coated with crude oil that they could not fly. Once when there was an especially bad slick in the early winter before the river froze up, the Michigan Department of Natural Resources recruited volunteers to scatter corn in the shallow waters on the east side of Grosse Ile, hoping to attract migrating whistling swans away from the black stream of death that lurked along the west shore of the island. In those days we always bought Canadian fishing licenses to fish on the Canadian side of the river, because the river was cleaner there. Fish caught from the American side of the river up through the late 1960s often had chemical tastes due to phenol and other waste chemicals poured into the river in the millions of gallons.

Despite sizable damage to the natural environment, personal health, and property, there was almost no opposition to air and water pollution in southeastern Michigan in the 1950s and 1960s. Like the frog, people had adapted and accepted pollution as a price of prosperity. There were no organized groups campaigning against air and water pollution in that area until the UAW created the Downriver Anti-Pollution League in the late 1960s. People made good money working in the factories of southeastern Michigan and with it they bought property in northern Michigan for vacation homes. The Detroit River was still pretty to look at, and the price of waterfront property was quite high and rose faster than overall market values. Poorer people who lived in the inner city of Detroit simply came to accept gray-blue as a normal sky color, I learned when in the late 1960s I conducted surveys on the perception of air quality in the Detroit area.

When I went to college at the University of Michigan I was 35 miles upwind and upstream in Ann Arbor. Detroit was a distant haze in the eastern sky, but nonetheless I was determined to do something about the polluted conditions that I had grown up with. I began as a wildlife biology major and then switched to conservation education, figuring that people needed help to wake up to what was going on. For my master's thesis in resource planning and conservation I studied the socio-economic costs of water pollution in the lower Detroit River area. I found millions of dollars worth of damage, but virtually no one who wanted to take issue with what was going on. What struck me from my studies was how pollution originates from human decisions and the attitudes and values that shape them. I attended a conference where René Dubos spoke, heard him tell the frog story, and decided that if I was really going to be an effective environmental educator, maybe I should study psychology to see what factors would move people to value, even love, nature more so that we would not adapt and boil in our own effluents.

The University of Michigan allowed me to create a joint Ph.D. program in natural resources and psychology, so I began taking graduate courses and reviewing the literature. What I soon discovered was that there was no psychological literature about the love of nature, and next to nothing about the effects of environmental conditions on people or how environmental attitudes and values are formed. I put together a program of classes on perception and survey research and created a dissertation on awareness of air pollution among Detroit inner city high school students. In this project, I asked the question if there was any relationship between how much knowledge a person had about air pollution and how concerned they were about air quality. What I found was that there was no statistical relationship between knowledge and concern. It was then clear that education alone would not be sufficient to rally support for the environment. What was needed to build an ecological conscience was something else, which I set out to study.

In the early 1970s, after I had graduated and begun teaching college, I went to a convention where I chanced to meet the pioneering psychologist Abraham Maslow. Maslow had had the important insight that most psychological theory was based on the study of animals and people with mental illness and learning disabilities; there was no psychology of human healthiness. So, to expand our concept of human nature, for a number of years he studied the potentiality of people to be extremely healthy and productive. As a result, he coined the term "self-actualization" to describe people who seemed to be exceptionally psychologically healthy, and in the process helped give birth to the fields of humanistic and transpersonal psychology to describe the more positive dimensions of consciousness and health.

I told Maslow of my interest in what made people feel deep personal love and concern for nature. He listened and told me two things. The first was that all the self-actualized people he had studied seemed to have a deep reverence for nature and took delight in natural beauty. Then he advised that I should seek out people who seem to have a deep love for nature and from that population perhaps I would learn what made people in general care deeply about the natural world. His advice has inspired some twenty years of research that has included surveys of hundreds of people, numerous interviews, studies of biohistories of committed environmentalists, nearly a decade spent as a psychotherapist, and cross-cultural studies with Native American Indians, the Innuit, Polynesians, Asians, and Africans. This diverse research has led to some conclusions about the love of nature and how it is formed, which I will briefly summarize.

Pathways to Nature Kinship

The love of nature is something that people write about, talk about, and act upon, but we know precious little about its origins. For some people, protection of nature is a deep and central issue in life, a touchstone of consciousness and commitment that moves them with a passion to make great personal sacrifices and undertake lifelong commitments to action. They may take on careers in support of environmental issues, often at lower wages than in other fields. They spend time, money, and resources to aid what they believe is the wise use and protection of the ecology of the planet, when they could be doing other things. Some of the names we know well—Barry Commoner, René Dubos, Jacques Cousteau, James Lovelock, Rachel Carson, Robert Rodale, John Muir, Theodore Roosevelt, Henry David Thoreau, and Gifford Pinchot—are just a few of the modern defenders of nature whose dedication is renowned. Many others—like the officers of state and local environmental groups, the people who run local recycling centers and nature centers, organic farmers, and people who spend countless hours with petitions, picking up roadside litter, and leading nature hikes—are less well known but equally important. My research has sought to identify what common developmental forces seem to have contributed to these people expressing passionate feelings on behalf of the Earth.

One conclusion is that our earliest experiences often have a profound influence on later life, and early childhood exposure to environments that evoke feelings of pleasure, awe, and beauty, frequently in the company of a parent or a loved one, appear to be one of the most important roots of the love of nature. David Brower speaks of his childhood when he took his mother on nature walks and became her "eyes" when she was going blind, as a critically important influence on his life's course. Singer Pete Seeger, who has developed the sloop Clearwater to draw attention to water pollution in the Hudson River, as a child loved to play cowboys and Indians in the local woods, choosing to be the Indians because they seemed so close to nature. Scientist Rachel Carson was tutored by her mother at her family farm, devoting much of her early education to nature study. Actor Robert Redford, an ardent conservationist, speaks of an early vacation trip to Yellowstone National Park as being a strong influence on his lifelong work on environmental issues. Psychiatrist Carl Jung, who helped us better understand the symbols of our unconscious, reports a number of his earliest memories involve scenes of natural beauty, thus helping him in later life appreciate the importance of nature to mental health. Many people, such as Theodore Roosevelt, and more recent presidents Jimmy Carter and Bill Clinton, as well as Henry David Thoreau, report early memories of hunting and fishing as being among the most vivid and pleasant experiences of their childhood. It seems critical to underscore the primary importance of getting kids outdoors and helping them learn to enjoy nature with respect and wisdom, not fear, as being crucial to kindling love and respect for nature.

Early experiences are an important influence for later life. They establish a perceptual foundation from which to evaluate life situations and give inspiration and guidance which shape choices, regardless what path one takes. One can develop emotional feelings for nature and environmental quality in later life without strong, positive early life experiences in natural settings, but their absence is certainly a handicap to achieving nature kinship, and perhaps emotional health in general.

As people grow and develop they embark on various paths of personal expression, moved by situations and conditions that uniquely suit them. Among the people I have studied, there appear to be five major paths to achieving nature kinship and becoming committed environmentalists as adults.

The first path is intellectual knowledge. The nature writings of John Muir, Henry Thoreau, Ralph Waldo Emerson, John Burroughs, and Aldo Leopold inspire many people, as do the modern eco-activist writings of Paul Ehrlich, Thomas Berry, Edward Abbey, Barry Commoner, and Rachel Carson, as well as magazine stories and television documentaries by Jacques Cousteau and others. In my research, many people say they enjoy nature writing and programming, but few people say that educational materials are the primary moving forces that *launched* their commitment to environmental action. Books, radio, and television more often help support and inform environmental attitudes, but they do not seem to be original motivational forces for adopting the attitudes. Perhaps this finding is changing as more and more people live in cities and do not have daily exposure to nature, but without some kind of underlying emotional root in nature, ecological concerns tend to be lumped into social issues in general, with whichever is in vogue, or currently heavily reported in the mass media, getting the highest degree of attention.

The second is social justice. Many people whose lives are moved by concerns about social justice see environmental problems as one more example of the kinds of flaws that arise from our social system, including racial inequality, women's rights, and poverty. Often people who are especially concerned about social justice issues may not be ardent nature lovers or well-schooled naturalists, although they may see themselves as environmentalists. Some, like Ralph Nader, take on ecological issues as they relate to consumer rights and public safety. A number of current leaders of the animal rights crusade openly admit they really are not that fond of animals, but they believe that the treatment of animals is symptomatic of the overall violent nature of modern society, which is not morally or ethically justifiable to them. Some of the popular entertainers who perform benefits on behalf of environmental causes seem to come more from a social justice background than one of having great familiarity with nature and ecology.

The third path is threats to health. Some people become concerned about environmental issues when they find their lives and property threatened by pollution and they are forced to fight back in self-defense. Cesar Chavez's campaign against pesticides was moved more by his feelings about harm being done to farm workers than concerns about fish and wildlife. Barry Commoner's interest in global ecological issues was initially stimulated by concerns about the health effects of atmospheric testing of nuclear devices. Author Debra Dadd, who has become a world-recognized authority on toxic-free living, was forced to give up her career as a professional musician because of chemical sensitivity. Researching a lifestyle that is free of allergenic substances, such as food grown without pesticides and fertilizers, organic cleaning agents, and fabrics and home furnishings made from natural materials, led her to a greater appreciation for nature as a healing force; a pattern shared by others whose initial interests in ecology begin with pollution problems.

The fourth path to achieving a kinship with nature and becoming an environmentalist is the path of health and fitness. In recent times there has been a tremendous growth in interest in health and fitness in the United States. People are making changes to improve their health, including exercising and eating organic foods. Awareness of how environmental factors such as toxic chemicals and air pollution may influence one's health has led many to become concerned about ecology in general. Through his many publications, including the popular magazines *Organic Gardening* and *Prevention*, the late Robert Rodale was a leader in creating awareness of organic living. An important aspect of this path is that it is person-centered more than externally oriented, and as such it is more likely to endure because the emotional motivation for ecological concern is not based on ever-changing social and environmental conditions but ongoing personal health, which is not likely to be a passing fad.

The fifth and last path is that of transcendental experiences. Modern western psychology has had considerable difficulty accepting spiritual experience as part of normal psychology, and yet the psychology of transcendence concerns itself with some of the most important human experiences, such as death, birth, and love. Many aspects of spiritual transcendence, such as seeing visions, hearing voices, communicating with other species, inspired writing and art, and feelings of oneness with the Divine, until recently, have been considered to be symptoms of psychopathology, especially schizophrenia, by modern psychology and psychiatry. Yet when one studies the lives of many environmental leaders as well as healers, artists, religious leaders, and political figures, one finds that special moments of wonder and awe, usually associated with natural beauty, are frequently seen as being pivotal moments in their lives. Aldo Leopold's concern for ecological ethics was inspired by an emotional moment when he had to kill a wounded wolf. Albert Schweitzer's concept of "reverence for life" came to him spontaneously while paddling a canoe through a dangerous herd of hippos. Gifford Pinchot, chief forester in Theodore Roosevelt's administration, conceived of the concept of "conservation" in an ecstatic moment while riding a horse through Rock Creek Park in Washington, D.C.

For some people, such transcendent moments, which Abraham Maslow called "peak experiences," resulted in personal healing. Theodore Roosevelt was troubled by asthma until he was sent for a nature cure at a European health spa followed by an African safari. Rachel Carson was a rather frail person who regenerated her health by periods of solitude at a Cape Cod retreat, moving her to develop a sense of wonder about nature. Chief Justice William O. Douglas, as a youth, "adopted a mountain" as a "second father" to replace the void in his life when his father died. Religious historian Mircea Eliade acknowledged how bathing in mud baths at natural hot springs in Europe seemed to improve the health of himself and his family.

Abraham Maslow concluded that as self-actualization increased, people also tended to have more peak experiences. Research on such experiences finds that they tend to be commonly triggered by encounters with beautiful natural scenes. Nature, then, seems to foster people having peak experiences, and these experiences are integral to mental health and self-actualization, rather than being symptoms of psychopathology.

Nature can be a powerful source of wisdom and health, inspiring us and affirming our self-identity. As Maslow concluded, self-actualization and the love of nature tend to go together, and this conclusion is cause for concern when one considers the overall urbanization of modern society. Recent research shows that the average American spends 84 percent of his or her life indoors, often in air-conditioned environments. The average visitor to a national park does not go more than fifty feet from the road and spends six hours or less in the park, often the most time being spent at the visitor center, restaurant, and bathrooms. People today may know more about ecology than ever before, thanks to the work of environmental organizations and the media, but as my research has shown the simple accumulation of knowledge about ecology and pollution does not necessarily lead to a fondness for nature or an intuitive wisdom about how to live in harmony with nature. An analogy would be that it is one thing to watch love blossom in a feature film, or read about it in a romance novel, but quite another to fall in love and work to preserve the relationship.

The study of ecologically committed people in modern society helps shed light on the formation of an ecological conscience, but such research is inherently biased due to cultural conditioning. The fact that contemporary psychology textbooks do not have lengthy sections about the psychology of love for nature and its importance to human health speaks to a serious blind spot in our understanding of human nature. We must expand the modern psychological paradigm to enable us to appreciate how kinship with nature really works and its importance to the human soul. We need to look cross-culturally to broaden our perspective.

Nature Kinship in Traditional Cultures

Psychiatrist Carl Jung believed that we have two souls, an ancestral soul, which is wise and rooted in nature through sympathies and direct sensory perception, and a contemporary soul that is attuned to the culture in which that person lives. The primary mental diseases of modern humans are associated with loss of contact with the ancestral soul, which is so closely linked with the unconscious. In therapy, the modern person seeks to unravel cognitive blocks and misunderstandings so that the underlying wisdom of the self can make itself known and the splits between mind and body and conscious and unconscious can be healed. Modern education does little with mental functions other than the intellect, leaving us undereducated in other aspects like emotions, intuitions, and sensory awareness.

In a traditional culture sensory awareness is highly prized and developed through educational techniques little understood by contemporary society. Mental disease among traditional peoples is more concerned with the loss of self—falling victim to external forces that pull one away from one's self, or one's intuitive guidance system for life, or becoming swallowed up by the unconscious, which arises from unmediated raw energies of nature. The practice of traditional healers focuses more on driving away negative forces that are pulling people away from right livelihood, which in turn causes distress and restores sympathetic links to positive forces for people who have violated cultural norms, taboos, etc., and need to be reunited with the community norms as established through myths and symbols more than by laws.

The love of nature is at the core of the working psychologies of most native cultures, rather than being a peripheral issue as it is in contemporary psychology. The reason is quite practical; if you are not at the right place at the right time and do not have good food supplies, you will starve. Faced with a reality where weather, tides, seasons of the year, and movements of fish and animals take precedence over the kinds of concerns that preoccupy people living in modern society, consciousness is more predominated by sensory experiences and intuition rather than directing attention to printed words on a page of paper or watching an animated screen.

Genetically and physically we are not significantly different from our ancestors or other cultures. It is not easy to appreciate the different worlds of awareness that may lie so close to us because of the restrictions that modern civilized society places on perception. Modern science, for example, asserts that there are five primary senses and debates the existence of a sixth. According to Oriental wisdom, we have one hundred senses by which to perceive the environment. What can these ninety-five other senses be? They include faculties such as dreaming, awareness of electromagnetic fields, sensing impending weather changes with various parts of the body, interpreting animal behavior as omens, and the ability to readily enter trance states and make symbolic interpretations of external objects, as if in dreams. Modern culture is so tied into visual details and abstract, intellectual thinking that senses such as intuition, touching, tasting, and smelling are largely undeveloped in most modern people, yet there are good examples of how modern people can develop acuity in little-used senses—wine tasting, massage therapists, perfume makers, etc. Cultivating love for nature in modern times will require us to expand the definition of normality to allow for a much wider range of perceptual experience.

Peak or transcendent experiences—moments of awe, wonder and insight, visions and voices, which are prized in traditional cultures and sought through ceremony and ritual—are "abnormal" and suspect as symptoms of mental instability to modern psychology, yet among Eskimos, Lapps, Bushmen, Indians, or Aborigines, if one does not have visions, hear voices, and converse with animals, one is diagnosed as being mentally ill and taken to the shaman, who conducts rituals to induce altered states of consciousness so healing can occur. A careful review of the biohistories of many modern environmentalists shows that they, too, also have frequently had moments of transcendence in nature, which they generally consider to be a cornerstone of deepening their love for nature. Typically, however, modern ecologists are reluctant to openly share their numinous moments for fear of being labeled crazy. Frequently these special experiences occur at places of special beauty and power.

One of the most fundamental elements of environmental perception in traditional cultures is that there are special geographic locations that have an unusual spiritual quality or presence. The act of visiting a place of power is one of the oldest expressions of ecological respect. Even today people are drawn each year by the millions to places, such as Macchu Picchu, Mount Fuji, the Ganges River, the Pyramids, Stonehenge, Lourdes, Mecca, Jerusalem, and Mount McKinley, for reasons they cannot explain, except that these places have a special magnetic attraction for them. My interviews with people who have undertaken such pilgrimages find that at such places people frequently do have experiences that could be called paranormal. Many people report having unusual dreams, hearing voices, and having unusual encounters with animals at places of power. In general, though, one of the most important benefits from visiting special places is inspiration, which aids creativity and even health. One could argue that undertaking pilgrimages to special places is one of the most important acts of nature kinship; perhaps among the earliest ways to seek out how to best live in harmony with nature.

We need to find ways for modern men and women to preserve and enhance their sense of wonder about nature to recover our basic kinship with nature. We need to encourage people of all ages to get out into the natural world and allow themselves to experience the beauty, wonder, and magic that is there. The ancestral soul in each of us needs to be conserved. We must also find ways to have scientific theories expand and integrate perceptions of the non-rational states of consciousness. One example of how modern science and ancient wisdom can work together is to believe that the earth itself is alive. Ancient wisdom all around the world asserts that the Earth is a living being, but modern science has not held this view until a relatively recent challenge by British scientist James Lovelock, developer of the Gaia Hypothesis.

Open a high school biology text and you will find that "life" exists when something can grow, metabolize nourishment, and reproduce. Lovelock concluded that these qualities really need to be integrated into a perspective that looks more at systems than isolated qualities of objects. The defining characteristic of life, Lovelock feels, is the ability to be self-regulating. The Earth has a number of well-known homeostatic systems—oxygen cycle, carbon cycle, water cycle, etc.—and so the Gaia Hypothesis asserts that the entire Earth is a living being that carries us tiny humans through the heavens.

If self-regulation is a defining characteristic of living organisms, one might propose that sacred places are organs of the living Earth which help humans learn to live in greater harmony with nature and themselves, and at the same time inspire us to be more fully human. The mental state of communicating with the Earth may be difficult to comprehend for members of modern society. Contrast our educational system and its training with that of the Pueblo Indians of the American Southwest who, according to tradition, send teenagers to live for up to nine months in an underground room so they can be "born to the second mother, the Earth." During their time in the womb of the second mother the children cannot speak, but must instead focus their attention on sensory experiences. A primary goal of this time in isolation is to learn to listen to the voice of the Earth Mother.

Scientists will debate whether the Earth is alive or not for years to come. Scientific theories are like shoes, we need to find the best fit for our purposes. There is an additional value of viewing the Earth to be alive, however. Carl Jung concluded that all symbols that live in the human unconscious are alive, for in our dreams and visions they can become animated and converse with us. Within each of us, then, there is a living Earth as part of our identity. Science does agree that whenever two or more things come into harmony, energy is exchanged. Believing that the Earth we live on is alive helps to bring the planet into harmony with our inner Earth, this sets up an intuitional sympathy with the Earth, which is an essential element in learning to live in harmony with nature.

Among the Salish Indians of the Pacific Northwest Coast of the United States there is a word "skalalitude," which seems to sum up the mental set of traditional people in regard to nature. Skalalitude means that when you are in proper harmonic relationship with the place where you live, the special places of power that are magnetic to you, and the many creatures of nature, then magic and beauty are everywhere. In a skalalitude state of mind, nature is a force for teaching and healing. To develop the skalalitude consciousness, Indian children are taught to learn to "listen with the third ear, the heart," by spending time alone in wild places, aided by supportive adult teachers.

There is a sense of peace that one feels when you are with people who have a positive harmonic relationship with the Earth where they live. They do not suffer from the stress diseases of modern civilization. In fact, native people who avoid serious injuries from accidents and infections can live to be very old, deriving considerable joy from appreciating the beauty of nature. In the consciousness of native people, when skalalitude exists, nature becomes a source of nourishment and health—a teacher and healer. We cannot go back to the past, but we can and must find ways to bring the consciousness of nature kinship of the past into the present and integrate it with modern society.

Obstacles to Nature Kinship

Developing an ecological literacy is one of the most important fundamental requirements of responsible citizenship that must be mastered by everyone today, but knowledge alone does not automatically lead to ecological respect and stewardship. Intuitions, emotions, and feelings play a powerful role in shaping our thoughts and actions, and we must find ways to allow the rich diversity of human experience to be cultivated and refined into a sophisticated environmental perception if we are to achieve a holistic harmony between nature and humankind.

Both fear and guilt are inhibiting emotional issues that are capable of distorting perceptions of self and reality enough to cause psychosomatic illness on a personal level. Emotional blind spots can restrict our abilities for critical thinking, problem-solving, planning, and development. They can lead to imbalances and diseases on personal and planetary levels. There are special kinds of ecological fears and ecological guilt issues, which if not mastered can lead to projecting our personal problems into creating buildings, towns, highways, waterways, and waste disposal systems that create more pollution and resource misuse. Here I can only briefly touch upon the nature of environmental fears and ecological guilt, but the core issues can be at least recognized in hopes that the serious reader will pursue these in more detail.

The fear of nature is a learned response to a perceived threat, real or imaginary, and nature is not always nice. It can be painful, even a killer. Spiders, snakes, scorpions, and rabid raccoons can kill. Ice storms and tornadoes can destroy homes and crops. Floods, volcanoes, tidal waves, and earthquakes may wipe out entire towns. Bears can attack people. There are some aspects of nature that are frightening, but there are many others that are not threatening but which still may be feared by people if they are not familiar with natural phenomena.

Fear is manifest by the fight or flight response. After early childhood, we learn what to fear and how to effectively express our feelings. Such concepts can be carried into later life, influencing they way we work, act, play, and build our towns and cities. If we learn as children that nature is something to be feared, then as adults we will protect ourselves through architecture and design. It is generally agreed that alienation from self and nature is very widespread today, and alienation, or separation, is caused by fear. Frank Lloyd Wright called modern architecture "cash and carry," implying that it was mechanical, paid little attention to local landforms, and was based more upon expediency and economics than human needs. One wonders how much of our lack of design sensitivity is an expression of the fear of nature translated into sealed, air-conditioned buildings that protect us from climatic change, and cities that offer few or no parks or scenes of natural beauty.

Pest control strategies represent another way that fear can be transferred into action. Insects of all kinds can eat our crops, carry disease, and consume the foundations of our homes, but sometimes we spray with toxic chemicals more out of fear than a real need to protect ourselves. To a farmer who views the world according to a Newtonian-Cartesian mechanical model, which has been the prevailing model of science for many years, coping with an insect pest is a matter of finding the right chemical poison to kill the insect or animal as quickly and cheaply as possible. However, as practitioners of organic gardening have clearly shown, pests can also be controlled by strengthening potential victim plants with added soil nutrients, planting companion plants that naturally repel pests, and introducing natural predators, like lady bugs and praying mantises, to eat the pests. The methods of the organic farmer are all based on an understanding of the dynamics of systems, and the methods of control are rooted in changing natural relationships, letting nature do the work rather than applying poisons that often harm life systems far beyond a single pest.

Learning to think ecologically—in terms of systems rather than simple cause and effect—transforms scientists into tinkerers who experiment with systemic balances. Tinkering requires patience, as well as an attitude that one cannot or should not try to control nature, but rather must work with natural forces and organisms to achieve goals. Tinkering requires patience, tolerance, and ultimately love.

Another fear of nature that keeps many people apart from the wonders of nature, especially wild places, is the fear of being alone and what may happen then. When we are alone and without distractions, such as television, radio, and newspapers, our unconscious becomes more active, sometimes revealing aspects of ourselves that are normally suppressed. Some people are afraid to spend time alone in nature because they fear becoming aware of things they are doing that they really do not like, but do for money or security, such as stay in a bad relationship or job.

Alone in nature, unusual sensory experiences that many people find frightening may also occur. In the movie *Field of Dreams*, Kevin Costner plays a farmer who hears voices from people who are not there and builds a baseball field in a corn field as a result. When he reports his experience to a group of seasoned farmers, no one questions that such things can happen.

A number of research studies have concluded that beautiful natural settings are an important element, for many people, in evoking paranormal experiences. When one has such an experience, one loses control of ego consciousness. This may be very frightening, especially if we are used to living in a world that places high emphasis on controlling our consciousness.

Some fears of nature can be prevented or erased by good educational programs, such as hands-on programs for young children that allow them to touch snakes, lizards, turtles, and frogs; take walks in the woods at night; and learn to tell poison ivy from English ivy. Knowing what to do helps if you meet a bear in the woods.

Modern psychology has devised a number of good strategies for helping people deal with fears. These methods need to be used outside the counseling office to help people feel at ease in natural settings. When unnecessary fears are curtailed, then people can develop feelings of respect and appreciation for nature that lead to what Rachel Carson called "a sense of wonder," which is similar to skalalitude. Studies have shown that spending as little as an hour a week alone in a natural area can have a positive effect on mental health. Learning to conquer our fears of nature is crucial to being able to accept nature as a teacher and healer.

Ecological guilt is the other core issue which, if not controlled or understood, can manifest itself in environmentally destructive behavior. The advice by the late mythologist Joseph Campbell to "follow your bliss" has become very popular. It is great guidance, especially in an age in which social trends seem to change as quickly as the wind shifts direction. Campbell also emphatically said on numerous occasions that "flesh eats flesh." I have yet to see that saying on a bumper sticker, but that wisdom is just as important to ecological harmony.

One of the fundamental psychological issues that all humans must resolve is that life is dependent upon death. Walking, breathing, and even healing yourself, all require killing microorganisms. Building materials and cloth come from once living plants and animals, and if the Earth is alive, then the stone blocks in your fireplace must be alive, or at least were alive before you took them inside.

The wisdom of traditional cultures asserts that everything is alive and has consciousness. Modern science now agrees that plants as well as animals have consciousness. Therefore, even if you are a vegetarian, you must kill to live. We cannot escape being killers, and so the way to make peace with this dark side of human nature is to learn to accept the killer in each of us.

Humans need to cultivate a "reverence for life," as Albert Schweitzer put it, a phrase that came to him one day in a moment of unitive consciousness when surrounded by a herd of menacing hippos. Schweitzer did not like to hunt, but he did eat meat, carried a gun for protection, and shot poisonous snakes and birds of prey that threatened his domesticated animals and pets. He came to formulate the concept of reverence for life as a way to describe an attitude that expresses deep respect for life, but also acknowledges the necessity of killing as a part of the balance of life. Cultivating a sense of reverence for life involves people acknowledging that they must kill to live. As a result of this realization they develop deep appreciation for life in general, and more easily see themselves as part of the food chain, and not separate from it.

Food does not come from the supermarket. Today, the food you eat often travels thousands of miles before it reaches your plate. Learning respect for the food you eat is an essential element in forming an ecological consciousness. If you eat meat, and some people do need to eat meat for their health, then you need to find some way to show respect for the animals you eat. Finding peace with nature begins with loving yourself, and if you deny your personal needs, even for moral or ethical reasons, at some level in your being you will be angry at what you are doing to yourself, and this anger will spill out into your relationships in some way.

There is a sense of peace that comes from eating food that originates from the land where you live. The plants and animals that naturally reside in a bioregion arise from that place as a result of millions of years of evolution. They arise from the minerals of the Earth and carry the subtle signatures of the rhythms and cycles of nature in that place. Eating them results in a sense of rootedness that aids emotional grounding. If each person could grow, gather, or harvest at least some of the food they eat, we would be a much more peaceful and ecologically conscious society.

Creating an Ecological Conscience

In the late 1940s wildlife biologist Aldo Leopold penned *A Sand County Almanac*, a poetic book that chronicles his sensitive observations of the annual cycles of nature and what those observations led him to conclude man must do to live in harmony with nature. He concludes that to conserve natural resources we need nothing less than a new "land ethic" arising from an "ecological conscience" to make conservation become the norm and not the exception.

When Aldo Leopold first wrote *A Sand County Almanac*, the manuscript was passed among a number of publishers who rejected it. When it finally came out, the book did not sell well at all. Reissued twenty years later in the wake of Rachel Carson's chilling warning about the potential dangers of toxic chemicals polluting the environment, *Silent Spring*, and on the eve of the 1970 Earth Day groundswell of popular support for ecology, Leopold's book became a bestseller. Twenty years later, the book still remains one of the classics of environmental literature. Yet the land ethic and ecological conscience that Leopold urged us to create remain as elusive as the ruffed grouse on Leopold's farm.

Today, because the media give us more news of eco-disasters and dangers, people are more aware of the problems of the Earth than ever before. Indifference has been replaced by a sense of urgency that we must act to save the planet. Memberships of large environmental groups has doubled from four to eight million in the last decade, and as many as 25 million other people may be involved at the local level.

Although people are more aware than ever before of ecological problems, this awareness is largely based on secondhand information, taken from media reports based on the sometimes conflicting views of scientists. In addition, large environmental organizations often base their funding appeals on reporting a seemingly never-ending series of new crises that are followed by appeals for financial support to address them. This approach may ultimately mean that environmental organizations may need crises to survive. In the long run, such an organizational personality promotes well-informed futility and cynicism. Political action is an essential part of ecological conservation, but it is essential that environmental organizations go beyond the need to have crises and enemies to survive. They must find new ways to generate and maintain their membership and revenues, or they will become dinosaurs and people will believe that nothing can be done to stop a seemingly endless stream of ecological crises.

Our growing intellectual familiarity with ecology alone is not sufficient motivation to establish an ecological conscience. A land ethic grows from firsthand contact with the soil and the creatures of nature that is gradually integrated with ecological literacy to result in an organic wisdom of nature kinship. Without the primary emotional roots in nature, ecology tends to be just one more topic that a socially responsible person should be familiar with, rather than a guiding force in one's entire life. Ecological responsibility is ultimately a way of life based on preventing environmental problems.

Knowledge of the terms and concepts of ecology is far more important than a great deal of what is taught in schools today, but to seriously follow Aldo Leopold's advice to create a land ethic from an ecological conscience, we need to provide ways for everyone to form an emotional/intuitive bond with the Earth. I want to conclude with suggestions of four ways in which we can help generate an ecological conscience through emotional ties to nature.

The first way is through holistic education. Our schools tend to focus on educating only a small fraction of the human potential—primarily linear, rational-analytical thinking and memorization. This perspective rewards a few, asks many others to conform, ignores many creative and artistic talents, and alienates far too many. Environmental education, ideally, is not a special class or a special unit in a class, but a theme that pervades all of education, ensuring that an integrative social norm, a land ethic, is reinforced everywhere. Educational programs that seek to help build an ecological conscience should address a broad spectrum of human potentiality and should include:

1. Consideration of the many different ways that people learn, offering programs that involve many different skills and abilities that lead to a lifelong commitment to ecological stewardship. Programs and themes should begin in the earliest grades, be geared to the unique mental set of each age group, and be integrated into science, social studies, drama, humanities, art, physical education, and manual skills training.
2. Fostering a positive emotional bonding with nature, which begins with a pleasingly landscaped school site and guided field trips to natural areas at all grade levels. It also includes overnight camping and even wilderness solos in higher grades.
3. Being practical, as well as theoretical—for example teaching students to grow and harvest some of their own food. In the area where I live, one private school operates a five-acre organic garden, run largely by student labor, which supports itself and some school programs through vegetable sales to the public. Units from the science classes are tied into the running of the farm, as are the economics of operating the project. Two other high schools have undertaken stream restoration programs and established salmon runs in those restored streams. A number of schools all around the world have students

conducting air and water environmental quality monitoring, thanks to the Global Rivers Environmental Education Network directed by the University of Michigan School of Natural Resources and Environment.** The more immediately relevant environmental education can be, the more that students will grasp its purpose and value.

4. Respect for cross-cultural differences, including how different cultures all around the world view nature, as expressed in literature and art, as well as cultural customs and religions. This is especially important in a culturally diverse society such as the United States, where each cultural group has its own unique values and customs about nature and all have value in developing nature kinship.

5. Promoting service to the community at large, such as undertaking beautification, recycling, reforestation, and wildlife habitat restoration projects as a regular part of the normal class work.

Another way to help foster a land ethic is through design that seeks to harmonize human activities with nature and to celebrate the uniqueness of each place. Simple interior design decisions, such as placement of windows, colors and textures of walls, and use of art, call to mind sentiments that are refreshing and tied to the natural world, diminishing a feeling of separation between people and nature that is found in many modern buildings.

Frank Lloyd Wright used to claim that he could design a home that would guarantee a divorce in six months. Modern psychological research is finding that Wright was probably right about how the construction of homes can influence people who live there. Simply having windows in hospital rooms seems to decrease the amount time patients need for recovery. Windows in office buildings reduces burn-out in employees. Research is showing that certain structural materials used in buildings can generate environmental fields that are detrimental to health—especially electrical power transmission lines and certain kinds of plastics. These subtle environmental factors become especially important to health when people spend so much time indoors.

The shape and form of the landscape and the placement of human structures should show respect for the uniqueness of nature in that place. In American Samoa, the gymnasium at Samoana High School is built in the shape of a giant turtle and the modern building where the islands' legislature, the Fono, meets, replicates a dome-shaped traditional thatched roof structure, which is called a "fale." This shape also imitates the shape of the volcanic mountains of the islands.

Organic forms and shapes mirror and blend with natural features, creating feelings of peace, harmony, and even inspiration. Walking into a home or building that has been designed as an organic expression of nature in that place creates a feeling of rightness about the design statement that influences emotions and mental activity. It moves you to feel a sense of oneness with that place rather than a vague feeling of disconnectedness that contributes to anxiety and alienation in many people.

In Seattle, Washington, landscape architect Lawrence Halprin has built a park over the top of an interstate freeway that bisects the town. Covering a freeway in itself cuts down on ambient noise and confusing energies, but Halprin has made the park in the spirit of the nearby water-rich North Cascades Mountain Range, weaving evergreen trees and numerous rushing watercourses with boulders into an organic concrete freeform structure that resembles a high mountain valley. The pathways in the park draw people from all walks of life outdoors to eat their lunch, relax, or stroll, uplifting spirits while thousands of cars are speeding by underneath. The great parks of New York and Chicago similarly draw people outdoors, reminding those who live and work in concrete, steel, and glass mountains where life comes from and how important natural beauty is to us all.

Each place on the face of the Earth has a unique character, a blend of subtle forces of earth, wind, water, and climate, as well as the indigenous plants and animals of that bioregion. Public art that captures and expresses the "spirit" of a place establishes the identity of that place and helps unite a sense of community in support of nature in that area. In downtown Eugene, Oregon, not far from the Willamette River, a sculpture of a school of salmon sits above a flowing fountain ringed by a grove of Douglas fir trees. Sited in the middle of several public buildings for Lane County, this art makes a statement about what makes this particular place special, reminding all passersby of the annual migration of thousands of salmon in the nearby rivers, as well as the forested ecosystem that supports successful salmon spawning and is the mainstay of the local economy. In Mill Valley, California, just north of San Francisco, a grove of redwood trees remains in the physical center of town, reminding all of the importance of the giant trees to the identity of the area, which once was a center of logging for northern California.

Festivals to celebrate nature also help generate an ecological conscience. Annual cycles and rhythms predominate the moods of nature, balancing the linear aspect of time, which is much more emphasized in modern society. Festivals are a vehicle by which communities can come together and call attention to certain features of nature, including the seasons and their unique qualities and influences on human life. Festivals are good for business, and they also represent an important opportunity to establish values and set or change social norms, as well as strengthen a sense of community. Festivals that help foster a land ethic should:

1. Harmonize with natural cycles and phenomena. For example, spring flower blooms, fall harvests, migration of birds and fish, and seasonal sports all can be unitive themes for festivals. They remind us of what makes a place special and call us together to celebrate the uniqueness of that place.
2. Set an example of ecological behaviors. Festivals are ephemeral, but they allow us to establish behavioral norms that can be carried on. A cleanup day at the beach can influence recycling, litter prevention, and trash collection the rest of the year. Tree planting and flower planting parties encourage people to landscape their homes. Showcasing organic fruits and vegetables at a farmers' market inspires people to grow more of their own food at home. Readily visible containers for trash to facilitate recycling illustrate how easy it is to recycle when people plan for it.
3. Encourage ecological restoration. Festivals call attention to special features, including history and native plants and animals of an area, and can organize people to action. We need to prevent pollution and protect precious natural resources, but in some places we can actually take steps to restore plants and animals that once were common, creating natural ecosystems that have evolved from the unique climate and soils of that place. Festivals can help us recall just how important the original plants and animals of a region are to the identity of that place.

One example of the power of restoration is the movement to bring back the American bison, which is catching on across America. The plentiful bison, once the most common ungulates on Earth, were replaced by the introduced cow, which is more easily handled but less hardy, and its flesh has a much higher fat and cholesterol content than the native bison. Bison meat is a health food endorsed by the American Heart Association, and buffalo restoration also aids the recovery of the Native American Indian religion, which is so tightly linked with the native creatures of the land, and the mythic images of the American wilderness. It seems no mere coincidence that the symbol of the U.S. Department of Interior is the bison. If there would be a national animal, it should be the bison, for this land once gave birth to a herd that numbered at least 60 million. All across the land there are unique animals, plants, and natural features that can be honored through festivals.

Using arts and entertainment as education is the fourth way to help foster an ecological conscience. The average American spends ten times more time in a movie theater than in museums during his or her lifetime. Television sets are on eight hours a day in many American homes. Music is the universal language. Documentaries are important to educate people about nature and the environment, but since ancient times, it has been the mythic sentiments, expressed through the creative and performing arts, that have most powerfully moved people.

The first environmental education lessons were the songs, stories, dances, and ceremonies that native people used to communicate environmental values and the mythic tales, instructing people in proper livelihood. Whereas boredom is all too often the norm in schools, the place where magic is alive most often is in theater, film, concerts, and even on television. In Mexico and India, soap operas have proven one of the most effective means of public health education. I am waiting for soaps in the United States to focus on issues like population control and pollution as major issues, driving home the point that environmental concern touches everyone. We have musical events that raise money for various ecological causes, but not nearly enough songs, operas, plays, and ballet performances about nature. Nature kinship forms out of enchantment, as much as knowledge.

For many people today, nature is a distant land of wild animals, which is perhaps lightly touched while on vacation or viewed on a television documentary, unless some dire ecological catastrophe blackens the skies or beaches and leaves wildlife and humans devastated. We cannot wait for eco-castrophies to be the sole rallying reason for supporting environmental conservation. People need to individually feel the value of nature in their personal lives. This will lead them to know why the Indians of the Pacific Northwest believe that modern society's greatest sin may be the way it inhibits people from knowing what skalalitude is, and why that state of mind, where nature is a teacher and healer, is so important to the survival of the human species and perhaps the Earth itself.

Nature As Teacher and Healer: How to Reawaken Your Connection with Nature by James A. Swan, published by Villard-Random House, 1992; and in Japan, Nihon Kyobunsha, 1995.

**Global Rivers Environmental Education Project, 721 East Huron Street, Ann Arbor, Michigan, 48104.

Daniel D. Chiras

LESSONS FROM NATURE
LEARNING TO LIVE
SUSTAINABLY ON THE EARTH

Time and again, "experts" boldly proclaim that there are no formulas or recipes to ensure a sustainable future for cities, states, and nations. Such experts typically assert that citizens, business leaders, and elected officials will have to work out the details on a case-by-case basis. Although this logic may be appealing to many individuals, it is not necessarily true. In fact, it could make the task of creating a sustainable way of life more time-consuming and more difficult than it need be.

Sustainability is a fairly well-established pattern among living things. It has evolved over millions of years of biological and cultural evolution. Indigenous cultures, for instance, have lived for thousands of years in harmony with natural surroundings, reaping food and extracting resources in ways that did not foreclose on future genera-tions. Countless living organisms have achieved even greater success, sustaining them-selves for millions of years without wrecking the planet.

Can we learn the secrets of sustainability from our studies of indigenous cultures, natural systems, and life itself? Can we pattern our society after these sustainable communities and yet retain the valuable contributions of science and technology? Would this ecologically based approach make economic sense?

Lessons from Nature: Learning to Live Sustainably on the Earth *by Daniel D. Chiras was published by Island Press, Washington, D.C., in 1992.*

H. G. Wells once wrote that "human History becomes more and more a race between education and catastrophe." Today, the race has reached a fevered pitch, for each passing day thousands of acres of rain forests surrender to bulldozer and chain saw, dozens of species vanish from nature's slate, and millions of tons of greenhouse gases pour into the atmosphere cradling the Earth.

Faced with these and a host of other disheartening social, economic, and environmental trends, many environmental and political leaders have pinned their hopes on educating the world's people—and saving the life support system of the planet—on a notion called sustainable development.

Although sustainable development is not a new idea by any stretch of the imagination, it has gained popularity as more and more people recognize the folly of our present, largely unsustainable, course.

The concept is now widely endorsed by key representatives from business, government, and the environmental movement. Virtually every nation of the world has embraced the notion of sustainable development, as have the World Bank, the United Nations Development Programme, and the U.S. Agency for International Development, all of whose programs profoundly influence the future of the less developed nations of the world.

Although some skeptics view the sustainable development as a passing fad, or, even worse, an attempt at a kind of semantic whitewash that will permit business as usual under a more appealing appellation, others disagree. They see enormous potential in this novel approach to development. I personally believe that the sustainable development movement could spawn a cultural revolution as far-reaching as the Agricultural and Industrial Revolutions. The Sustainable Revolution has the potential to undo much of the environmentally destructive policies and practices that evolved during the previous epochal shifts in human culture, especially the Industrial Revolution with its rampant technological and economic progress that was unwittingly blind to environmental repercussions.

Sustainable development is truly an idea whose time has come. But beyond the hoopla and official chatter, is there any consensus on what it means, and more importantly, what it requires of us?

The popular belief is that there is no standard formula for sustainable development. According to this point of view, each community, each state, and indeed each nation must find its own way. Proponents of this view argue that a sustainable course will emerge from site-specific programs tailored to the specific conditions of each community, state, or nation. To me, this erroneous view at once "complexifies" the task and makes it seem painfully unattainable.

I believe that the challenge of living sustainably on the Earth is fundamentally similar, no matter what the individual cultural, economic, or ecologic conditions. Ultimately, living sustainably on the Earth is a biological challenge. It is the same challenge that faces every organism on Earth from the tiniest bacterium to the magnificent blue whale. That challenge is to live within the carrying capacity of the environment. Quite simply, that means that organisms cannot take more than their surroundings can reliably produce, nor can they produce waste products in excess of the environment's ability to detoxify or dilute wastes to safe levels.

For most species, living sustainably requires no policies and deliberate actions that respect ecological limits. Checks and balances hold populations in balance. But for humans, achieving a sustainable state will require deliberate strategies that allow us to meet our needs while safeguarding the Earth's ecological life support systems.

The best definition of sustainable development comes from the World Commission on Environment and Development whose book *Our Common Future* touched off the recent flurry of interest in the subject. In this seminal work, the authors defined it as "development that meets the needs of the present without compromising the ability of future generations to meet their needs."

According to Webster's *New World Dictionary*, sustainable means "able to be sustained." To sustain, in turn, means "to keep in existence, to maintain, and [to] endure." In other words, the term sustainable implies nurturance, care, and longevity.

Development refers to "advancement" or "improvement." Contrary to what many think, it does not necessarily mean growth. In fact, growth can actually prove to be a detriment to strategies that seek to improve our lot in life.

In sum, then, the term *sustainable development* refers to improvements in human well-being that can endure. Robert Costanza, president and founder of the International Society for Ecological Economics, defines sustainability as a "relationship between dynamic human economic systems and larger dynamic . . . ecological systems in which: (1) human life can continue indefinitely; (2) human individuals can flourish; (3) human cultures can develop; but in which (4) the effects of human activities remain within bounds, so as not to destroy the diversity, complexity, and function of the ecological support system.

According to this definition, sustainable development is a strategy that permits human life to continue indefinitely. It allows individuals and cultures to flourish. Yet for this to occur, it calls on us to find ways to protect the ecological support systems of the planet.

Sustainable development is not simply an environmental strategy, and it is more than an economic strategy. Rather it is an attempt to meet social, economic, and environmental goals simultaneously. To be sustainable, a policy or action must make sense from all three perspectives.

In the past, though, environmental policies have tended to ignore social and economic values—for instance, the need for jobs and economic vitality. Economic policies have also been lacked an environmental ethic.

Sustainable development, in contrast, represents a new way of approaching human development that gives all three concerns equal weight. What are some of the social, economic, and environmental criteria essential to sustainable development? Let's begin with social requirements.

Social criteria are perhaps the least understood and most often ignored considerations in contemporary debate surrounding sustainable development. The most widely discussed social concept is intergenerational equity—or fairness to future generations. Intergenerational equity maintains that the present generation holds the Earth's cultural and biological endowment in common with all generations—past and future. Thus, each generation is a beneficiary of previous ones and a custodian of the planet for future generations. In essence, the Earth is viewed as a priceless heirloom. The recipient of an heirloom has certain rights and obligations. For example, she has a right to benefit from it. But she also has an obligation to convey her inheritance to a successor in as good, if not better, condition than it was received.

When it comes to the Earth, present generations seem to fully exercise their rights, benefiting from the Earth in millions of ways. But they almost universally live in nearly total disregard for their obligations. Economist Herman Daly summarized the situation best when he wrote that most nations are treating the Earth as if it were a corporation in liquidation.

Although not all proponents of sustainable development would agree, the term itself also implies a fairness to present generations—a kind of *intra*generational equity. Some take this to mean that resources should be more equitably distributed—that the rich should use less so the poor can enjoy more. In the very least, intragenerational equity means that wealthy nations should end their exploitation of the world's poor: siting toxic waste dumps in minority communities and exploiting resources of the developing countries, padding the pockets of international corporations while leaving local people impoverished. Intragenerational equity also compels the developed nations to greatly decrease the pollution of the global commons—especially the air and water—the impacts of which are felt around the world or in minority populations within a nation's borders.

In practice, the concept of equity must translate into a long-term, cross-cultural perspective for planning and action. Defining equity solely in terms of human needs is natural, yet inadequate. Lest we forget, millions of species share this planet with us and they, too, depend upon the Earth for sustenance. Do we not have an obligation to protect them as well? Do we not have an obligation to ensure their survival and success?

Fairness to other species—or ecological justice—raises the ante considerably. It is not a widely held principle, but one that is growing in strength with each passing day.

Sustainable development, while highly sensitive to economic needs, turns the principles and practices of conventional economics on their heads. For example, according to a small but growing number of economists, for a policy or action to be sustainable it must make sense in the long term. That is to say, it must be profitable yet environmentally compatible. If an activity seeks short-term profit at the expense of a resource, it is viewed skeptically by proponents of sustainable development.

To make sense economically, products and services must be priced accurately. Today, the cost of most products and services bear little resemblance to their true costs—that is, to the social and environmental costs. Pollution from factories, for example, causes damage where costs are not reflected in the price of the product. Sustainable economics, requires a much better accounting system—including ways to determine the social, economic, and environmental costs of all human activities as well as better mechanisms to incorporate these costs into the price of products.

A better accounting system could permit businesses to incorporate the true costs of production into the price of the products they manufacture, achieving full-cost pricing. If full-cost pricing were put into effect, manufacturers would no doubt find it advantageous to select alternative manufacturing processes or products that meet our needs without wrecking the planet.

Another criterion for judging the sustainability of economic activities is by its disbursement of benefits. To be sustainable, economic activities must meet the needs of a wide number of people, not merely add to the economic output in ways that concentrate wealth in the bank accounts of a few, furthering economic exploitation and an inequitable allocation of benefits.

A growing number of economists are recognizing yet another important criterion by which to judge the sustainability of an economic activity, notably its contribution to the long-term health and stability of economic systems. According to proponents of this view, sustainable development at the local level should entail those strategies that tend to smooth out the boom and bust economic cycles that disrupt our social fabric and raise havoc with our environment. Increasing levels of local and/or regional economic self-reliance, for instance, may foster economic and social stability. Regional self-reliance may mean measures to increase the efficiency of businesses and homes within a region, thus reducing the demand for imported energy and reducing the outflow of dollars. Regional self-reliance, say proponents, may also include measures to put waste products such as newspaper to use, creating a locally usable material and a steady stream of revenue from a product that was once hauled away at great expense.

Sustainability must also be judged by numerous environmental criteria. For example, does a policy or action detract from or enhance biodiversity? Does it disrupt natural systems? Does it pollute the air and water? Clearly, a thousand questions could be asked.

Herman Daly, a leading proponent of sustainable economics, proposed three bottom-line environmental criteria for evaluating the sustainability of human activities. First, human activities must not produce pollution in levels that exceed the planet's ability to absorb or detoxify them. Second, they must use renewable resources at a rate commensurate with their regeneration. Third, they must use nonrenewable resources at a rate equivalent to their replacement by renewable substitutes.

Sustainable development calls for new, integrated approaches to human development that achieve all three objectives—social, economic, and environmental—concurrently. Underpinning sustainable development is a growing recognition that the Earth and its many and diverse ecosystems are more than a backdrop for human activities. And, nature is more than a force to conquer and control.

The Earth is the source of all of our resources and a sink for all our wastes. That is to say, the Earth and its diverse array of ecosystems provide human civilization with a vast number of goods and services that are essential not only to our personal well-being but also to our economic welfare. In addition, natural systems absorb wastes, the unavoidable product of any species. Some economists refer to nature as the biological infrastructure, or *infra*infrastructure, of modern society. Our Earth makes all else possible.

The sustainability movement is an attempt to recast the people vs. environment debate in a framework that acknowledges the interdependence of human and natural systems. On a theoretical continuum from pure economics to pure environmentalism, sustainability is a midpoint that makes sense from both perspectives.

The writings on sustainability, both theoretical and practical, illustrate two basic challenges facing the world community. The first is revamping existing systems and existing infrastructure to make them more sustainable. The second is directing all new growth and development in accordance with sustainable principles.

But how do we go about overhauling thousands of years of "progress" and changing the course of history? Where can we find direction for this monumental task?

William Ruckelshaus, former administrator of the EPA, once wrote, "Sustainability was the original economy of our species." Many ancient cultures lived in a sustainable relationship with the Earth. They had to, he says. If they did not they perished.

Only in recent times (in an evolutionary time scale) has humanity drifted off its sustainable course. Fortunately, the secrets of living sustainably on the planet can still be found in many indigenous cultures that persist in isolated rain forests, deserts, and grasslands. Sustainable principles and practices can also be gleaned from an older source—the workings of nature. After all, as one of my students once noted, nature is the "master of sustainability."

Scientific analysis of why natural systems endure reveals at least six biological principles of sustainability: conservation, recycling, renewable resource use, restoration, population control, and adaptability.

That is to say, natural systems sustain themselves in large part because organisms use only what they need and use resources with efficiency. I call this the conservation principle, but recognize that it has two components—frugality (using what one needs) and efficiency (using resources efficiently).

Natural systems also sustain themselves because they recycle all materials necessary for life. There is no waste in nature. One organism's output is another's food source. Microorganisms ensure that all materials are returned to nutrient cycles to be used again and again.

Natural systems also depend chiefly on renewable resources that can provide a steady supply of materials *ad infinitum*. Sunlight, water, soil, and plant matter are the essential renewable resources of natural systems.

Natural systems and living organisms within them endure because they possess dozens of restorative mechanisms from mechanisms to repair the damage of DNA to mechanisms to revegetate hillsides denuded by mudslides.

Sustainability is also fostered by growth-control measures—that is, through mechanisms that hold populations in check so they live within the carrying capacity of their environment.

Finally, natural systems endure because organisms in them can adapt evolutionarily to change so long as the change is gradual.

These very same principles at work in nature are present in indigenous cultures and are the reason for the long success of hunting and gathering societies.

The biological principles of sustainability constitute a blueprint for a sustainable future. Applied to human civilization—to the very systems that support our lives—they represent our greatest hope for refashioning our society.

Although the notion of tapping into the wisdom of nature may appear bizarre to many, its appeal has not escaped scholars for centuries. Roman poet Juvenal, for instance, wrote, "Never does nature say one thing and wisdom another."

Shakespeare waxed poetic about nature's lessons when he wrote, "And this our life, exempt from public haunt, finds tongues in trees, books in the running brooks, sermons in stones and good in everything."

This very same theme has appeared in more recent writings of American authors. Thomas Paine, for instance, aptly argued that "man must go back to nature for information."

In even more recent times, Wes Jackson and Wendell Berry have spoken eloquently of the need to pattern farming (and other activities) after natural systems.

In *Saving the Earth: How to Shape an Environmentally Sustainable Global Economy*, Lester Brown, Christopher Flavin, and Sandra Postel affirm the wisdom of patterning human systems after nature. They write, "Just as any technology of flight, no matter how primitive or advanced, must abide by the basic principles of aerodynamics so must a lasting society satisfy basic ecological principles." The late Edward Abbey once quipped that "we must learn to think not only logically but biologically."

To create an enduring human presence by mimicking the ways of nature, we must learn to be more frugal—to use only the resources we need and use all resources much more efficiently. To follow in nature's footsteps, we must also recycle virtually all of our waste, returning nutrients to the land from whence they came and turning solid wastes back into useful products. In addition, we must shift from nonrenewable fuels such as coal and oil to clean, renewable resources such as solar and wind energy. We must also restore the damage we have created in the forests, farms, and fields that have historically supplied us with a host of valuable resources. We must then forsake the exploitive frontierist strategies and adopt management techniques that ensure the health and long-term well-being of resources. Last, but not least, we must find ways to curb the burgeoning growth of the human population and check the spread of cities and towns onto ecologically valuable lands. We need land-use efficiency policies to protect wildlife habitat and lands that provide valuable commercial products and ecological services such as flood control.

Natural systems also persist because organisms can adapt to change. For humans, biological adaption is probably not an option. Time is too short. Cultural adaption may be our only hope of creating an enduring human presence. Cultural adaptation requires new policies and practices, new technologies, and new ways of thinking.

Although the idea of applying ecological principles to human society may seem ludicrous, a survey of much of the writings on sustainable development shows that most recommendations comply with nature's laws. Publications from such distinguished organizations as the Worldwatch Institute, the Rocky Mountain Institute, and countless nonprofit organizations contain solutions that fit within nature's strategies. In addition, most of the policies and actions outlined in the *Agenda 21*, the massive set of recommendations generated by the Earth Summit in Rio de Janeiro in 1992, also promote nature's "plan."

The principal goal of sustainable development, eloquently outlined by Vice President Al Gore in his book *Earth in the Balance*, is to realign our relationship with the planet, to create an enduring human presence by bringing human society into line with ecological limits. To do so, we must embrace a systems view. We must look at whole systems and our impact on them.

One of the benefits of this broader picture is that it encourages us to examine root causes in complex networks of cause and effect. Such an exercise could force us to redirect limited financial resources to confront issues where actions will have the most significant impacts.

A systems approach also suggests a restructuring of basic human systems from waste management to transportation to housing. By applying the principles of sustainability to these systems, we can revamp the latter in ways the promote our long-term survival.

Sustainable strategies are not a repackaging of traditional environmental protection efforts; they're a fundamentally new approach that seeks to prevent problems in the first place by addressing systems and striking at the root causes. This, more than any other feature, distinguishes this new approach from earlier attempts at environmental protection.

Interestingly, the biological principles of sustainability—conservation, recycling, renewable resource use, restoration, and population control—confront the key root causes. If you could reduce the environmental crisis to its basics you would find that it is here because, for the most part, we do not use resources efficiently. Nor do we recycle much or restore damage to vital ecosystems. Our use of renewable energy is, for the most part, pitifully inadequate, as are our measures to control population growth and urban sprawl.

The biological principles of sustainability could form the basis of a long-term proactive strategy that fosters lasting solutions, avoiding costly cleanups or end-of-pipe solutions or expensive species recovery plans. Their economic potential is enormous. In most cases, sustainable solutions provide the same service as conventional approaches, but at a far lower cost. They also tend to employ many more people than traditional approaches. And, making them even more appealing, sustainable strategies provide far better environmental gains than traditional approaches.

Economist Robert Costanza argues that "Sustainable development must become our primary long-term policy goal," but to make it so we will need a new kind of leadership. We will need men and women with long-range vision who can help bridge the differences among the people they represent and forge their shared concerns for the environment into strong working relationships. However, we need leaders who not only understand our problems but are also willing to develop root-level solutions, rather than simply continuing the useless patchwork approach that merely passes our problems on to future generations.

To live sustainably, though, it is not enough to change the way we treat the Earth. It is not enough to become better stewards of the planet's resources and ecosystems. We must also greatly improve the way we treat one another, reshaping social structures to foster human dignity and welfare. According to the Worldwatch Institute, those countries where people are the most oppressed, where freedoms and justice are oppressed by military regimes, corrupt governments, or powerful economic forces, have some of the worst environmental conditions.

Although individuals differ in the goals they set for economic and social development, several common goals are virtually universal, according to the authors of *Caring for the Earth*. These include a long and healthy life, education, and access to resources needed for a decent standard of living. They also include political freedom, a guarantee of human rights, and freedom from violence. Many observers therefore assert that sustainability requires an ethic calling for universal justice, freedom, and compassion for one another.

As a final note, it is important to point out that sustainability is not just another environmental issue, it is *the* issue of our times. Creating sustainable communities, economies, and lifestyles—in other words, creating a sustainable relationship with the planet—is *the* challenge of our times.

Sustainable development must become the central thesis of the present decade and the century beyond. To make it so, we must vigorously implement the principles, policies, and practices that will allow us to draw on the most promising technologies and best scientific knowledge we've gained in the Agricultural and Industrial revolutions to create a new cultural synthesis that works as well for people as it does for other species and the planet.

Lester R. Brown, Christopher Flavin, and Sandra Postel

STATE OF THE WORLD

In 1984, Lester Brown, an agricultural economist, launched State of the World, *which has been published annually since that time.* State of the World *today stands as the most important and most enduring inquiry into the condition of the planet.*

*Translated into all of the world's major languages—in fact, more languages than Reader's Digest—*State of the World *is much more than a recitation of the planet's ills, as one might surmise from its title. Rather, it is a collection of recommendations—actual policies and actions that address the world's most pressing social, economic, and environmental issues, such as population growth, global warming, species extinction, poverty, and deforestation.*

In this selection, "Picturing a Sustainable Society," Lester Brown, Christopher Flavin, and Sandra Postel offer a thumbnail sketch of a future that protects and restores the planet, yet permits human culture to meet its needs and to thrive within limits.

"Picturing a Sustainable Society" was reprinted with permission from Brown et al., State of the World 1990, *W. W. Norton, New York, 1990.*

Societies everywhere are slowly coming to recognize that they are not only destroying their environments but undermining their futures. In response, governments, development agencies, and people the world over have begun to try to reverse obviously threatening trends. So far, this has resulted in a flurry of fragmented activity—a new pollution law here, a larger environment staff there—that lacks any coherent sense of what, ultimately, we wish to achieve.

Building a more environmentally stable future clearly requires some vision of it. If not fossil fuels to power society, then what? If forests are no longer to be cleared to grow food, then how is a larger population to be fed? If a throwaway culture leads inevitably to pollution and resource depletion, how can we satisfy our material needs? In sum, if the present path is so obviously unsound, what picture of the future can we use to guide our actions toward a global community that can endure?

That, in essence, is the challenge taken up in this chapter—to draw the outlines of a sustainable society, to describe what it would look like, how it would function. It can, of course, only be a thumbnail sketch. Ideas and technologies yet unknown will fill in many of the gaps. But just as any technology of flight, however primitive or advanced, must abide by the basic principles of aerodynamics, so must a lasting society satisfy some immutable criteria. With that understanding and from accumulated experience to date, it is possible to create a vision of a society quiet different, indeed preferable to today's.

A sustainable society is one that satisfies its needs without jeopardizing the prospects of future generations. Inherent in this definition is the responsibility of each generation to ensure that the next one inherits an undiminished natural and economic endowment. This concept of intergenerational equity, profoundly moral in character, is violated in numerous ways by our current society.[1]

Indeed, there are no existing models of sustainability. For the past several decades, most developing nations have aspired to the automobile-centered, fossil-fuel-driven economies of the industrial West. But from the localized problems of intractable air pollution to the global threat of climate change, it is now clear that these societies are far from durable; indeed they are rapidly bringing about their own demise.

Efforts to understand sustainability often focus on what it is not. Obviously, an economy that is rapidly changing the climate on which its food-producing capability depends is not sustainable. Neither is one that overcuts the forests that provide its fuel and timber. But this negative definition leads to a strictly reactive posture, one that has us constantly trying to repair the consequences of our destructive behavior.

The World Bank, for example, now tries piecemeal to assess the environmental side effects of projects it is considering funding. Not one of its member countries, however, has a coherent plan of action aimed at achieving sustainability, which logically should provide the basis for deciding what investments are needed in the first place. The United States has followed a similar track for the last twenty years. Its National

Environmental Policy Act requires that the environmental impacts of major proposed government actions be assessed. But this, too, is a defensive approach, one that attempts only to avert unwanted effects rather than working positively and consistently toward a sustainable economy.

In taking on the task of sketching an environmentally stable society, we have made several important assumptions. The first is that if the world is to achieve sustainability, it will need to do so within the next forty years. If we have not succeeded by then, environmental deterioration and economic decline are likely to be feeding on each other, pulling us into a downward spiral of social disintegration. Our vision of the future therefore looks to the year 2030.

Second, new technologies will of course be developed. Forty years ago, for example, some renewable energy technologies now on the market did not even exist. Under the pressure of finding a means to slow global warming, researchers are likely to develop a range of new energy technologies, some of which may be difficult to imagine at the moment. In the interest of being conservative, however, the future we sketch here is based only on existing technologies and foreseeable improvements in them.

Our third assumption is that the world economy of 2030 will not be powered by coal, oil, and natural gas. It is now well accepted that continuing heavy reliance on fossil fuels will cause catastrophic changes in climate. The most recent scientific evidence suggests that stabilizing the climate depends on eventually cutting annual global carbon emissions to some 2 billion tons per year, about one-third the current level. Taking population growth into account, the world in 2030 will therefore have per capita carbon emissions that are one-eighth the level in western Europe today.[2]

The choice then becomes whether to make solar or nuclear power the centerpiece of energy systems. We believe societies will reject nuclear power because of its long list of economic, social, and environmental liabilities. Though favored by many political leaders during the sixties and seventies, the nuclear industry has been in decline for over a decade. Only ninety-four plants remain under construction, and most will be completed in the next few years. Meanwhile, worldwide orders for new plants have slowed to a trickle. The accidents at Three Mile Island and Chernobyl and the failure to develop a safe way to store nuclear waste permanently have turned governments and citizens alike away from nuclear power.[3]

It is of course possible that scientists could develop new nuclear technologies that are more economical and less accident-prone. Yet this would not solve the waste problem. Nor would it alleviate growing concern about the use of nuclear energy as a stepping stone to developing nuclear weapons. Trying to prevent this in a plutonium-based economy with thousands of operating plants would require a degree of control that is probably incompatible with democratic political systems. Societies are likely to opt instead for diverse, solar-based systems.[4]

The fourth major assumption is about population size. Current U.N. projections have the world headed for nearly 9 billion people by 2030. This figure implies a doubling or tripling of the populations of Ethiopia, India, Nigeria, and scores of other countries where human numbers are already overtaxing natural support systems. Either these societies will move quickly to encourage smaller families and bring birth rates down, or rising death rates from hunger and malnutrition will check the population growth.[5]

The humane path to sustainability by the year 2030 therefore requires a dramatic drop in birth rates. More countries will do as China has done, and as Thailand is doing: cut their population growth rates in half in a matter of years. As of 1990, thirteen European countries have stable or declining populations; by 2030 most countries are likely to be in that category. For the world as a whole, human numbers will total well below 9 billion. We assume a population of at most 8 billion that will either be essentially stable or declining slowly—toward a number the earth can support comfortably and indefinitely.[6]

The last assumption we make is that the world in 2030 will have achieved a more equitable and secure economy. Unless Third World debt can be reduced to the point where the net flow of capital from industrial to developing countries is restored, the resources and incentives to invest in sustainability will simply be inadequate. In the final section, we briefly discuss issues related to jobs, economic growth, and social priorities, recognizing that major changes in other areas will be needed as well.

In the end, individual values are what drive social change. Progress toward sustainability thus hinges on a collective deepening of our sense of responsibility to the earth and to future generations. Without a re-evaluation of our personal aspirations and motivations, we will never achieve an environmentally sound global community.

Powered by the Sun

During the seventies and eighties, policymakers assumed that changes in the world energy system would be driven by depletion of the world's fossil fuel resources: as we gradually ran out of oil, coal, and natural gas, we would be forced to develop alternatives. Such a transition would have been comfortably gradual, extending over more than a century. But now the world faces a new set of limits. Long before fossil fuels are exhausted, rising global temperatures from their use could spell an end to civilization as we know it.

The world energy system in the year 2030 is likely to bear little resemblance to today's. No longer dominated by fossil fuels, it will be run by solar resources daily replenished by incoming sunlight and by geothermal energy. And it will be far more energy-efficient.

In many ways, the solar age today is where the coal age was when the steam engine was invented in the eighteenth century. At that time, coal was used to heat homes and smelt iron ore, but the notion of using coal-fired steam engines to power factories or transportation systems was just emerging. Yet only a short time later the first railroad started running, and fossil fuels began to transform the world economy.

In the late twentieth century, then, is the dawn of the solar age. Many technologies have been developed that allow us to harness the energy of the sun effectively, but these devices are not yet in widespread use, and their potential impact is barely imagined. When it comes to solar technologies, today's political leaders, still captivated by coal and nuclear power, are akin to the steam engine's eighteenth-century skeptics.

Countering such skepticism are glimmerings of the new age. Some nations—Norway and Brazil, for example—already obtain over half their energy from renewables. And these resources are available in immense quantity. The U.S. Department of Energy estimates that the annual influx of currently accessible renewable resources in the United States is 250 times the country's annual use of energy.[7]

Solar power is by nature diverse; the mix of energy sources will reflect the climate and natural resources of each particular region. Northern Europe, for example, is likely to rely heavily on wind and hydropower. The economies of northern Africa and the Middle East may instead use direct sunlight. Japan and the Philippines will tap their abundant geothermal energy. And Southeast Asian economies will be powered largely by wood and agricultural wastes, along with sunshine.

Although some countries are likely to import renewable energy, the enormous oil-related bills that characterize modern trade relationships will dwindle. And renewable energy sources are to a large extent inflation-proof: solar, wind, and geothermal power plants require no fuel and so are not vulnerable to fuel price increases.

Due to the abundance of sunlight, direct conversion of solar energy will be the cornerstone of a sustainable world energy system. Not only is sunshine available in great quantity, but it is more widely distributed than any other energy source, renewable or fossil fuel. By 2030, solar panels will heat most residential water around the world, following the model of Japan and Israel, which already use them extensively. A typical urban landscape will have thousands of collectors sprouting from rooftops, much as television antennas do today. And passive soar architecture may by then cut artificial heating and cooling needs to virtually zero in millions of buildings.[8]

Solar thermal power is one means of harnessing sunlight. It uses mirrored troughs to focus sunlight onto oil-filled tubes that convey heat to turbine and generator that then produce electricity. An eighty-megawatt solar thermal plant built in the desert east of Los Angeles in 1989 converts an extraordinary 22 percent of the incoming sunlight into electricity. It does so at a cost of eight cents per kilowatt-hour—a third less than the twelve cents per kilowatt-hour cost of power from new nuclear plants.[9]

Forty years from now, solar thermal plants may stretch across the deserts of the United States, North Africa, and central Asia. As the technology becomes widespread, these regions may become large exporters of electricity. They may also become suppliers of hydrogen fuel, which can be manufactured in desert solar plants and shipped by pipeline to run automobiles in distant cities.

Photovoltaic solar cells are a semiconductor technology that converts sunlight directly into electricity without using the mechanical processes involved in solar thermal conversion. Currently, photovoltaic systems are less efficient and four times as expensive as solar thermal power is. But they are already used in many remote locations, and the cost is likely to decline rapidly. Systems with efficiencies approaching 20 percent may soon be available, and scientists hope to bring costs down to less than ten cents per kilowatt-hour by the end of this decade.[10]

The key advantage of photovoltaics is their versatility. They can be used not only in large electricity plants but to power small water pumps and rural communications systems. As they become economical, the completion of the solar revolution will be possible: all Third World villages can be electrified with this technology. Unlike communities today, these villages will not have to depend on extended power lines connected to centralized plants. Rather, they will contain their own power sources—photovoltaic electric systems with battery storage for lighting and other uses in the dark evening hours.[11]

Using this technology, homeowners throughout the world may become producers as well as consumers of electricity. Indeed, photovoltaic shingles have already been developed that allow roofing material itself to become a power source. As costs continue to decline, many homes are apt to get much of their electricity from photovoltaics, and in sunny regions residents will sell any surplus to the utility company for use by others.[12]

Wind power is an indirect form of solar energy, generated by the sun's differential heating of the earth's atmosphere. The cost of wind energy has already fallen by 70 percent during the eighties, to six to eight cents per kilowatt-hour, making it close to competitive with new coal-fired power plants.[13]

Engineers are confident that they will soon have improved wind turbines that are economical not just in California's blustery mountain passes, where some wind farmers are already generating thirty thousand dollars worth of electricity per hectare annually, but in vast stretches of the U.S. northern plains, the U.K. North Sea Coast, and central Europe. Among the regions where major wind farms are now on the drawing boards are West Germany and the state of Gujarat in India.[14]

The United States could be deriving 10 to 20 percent of its electricity from the wind by 2030. Wind power is likely then to rival hydro as a low-cost form of energy, and so attract new industries into windswept regions. These businesses will be set up to take advantage of the wind whenever it is available, such as in the middle of the night, when electricity demand is normally quite low.[15]

The wind resources of the U.S. Great Plains—which have long pumped water for millions of cattle—may one day be used to generate vast amounts of electricity for sale to Denver, Kansas City, and other major cities. On the better sites, income from electricity sales could dwarf the thirty dollars or so per hectare from cattle grazing, tempting many cattle ranchers to become wind farmers as well.[16]

For hydropower, which now supplies nearly one-fifth of the world's electricity, prospects for future growth are most promising in the Third World, where the undeveloped potential is still large. Small-scale projects are likely to be more appealing than the massive projects favored by governments and international lending agencies in past decades. In deciding which hydropower resources to develop, environmental issues such as land flooding and siltation will play an important role. These considerations will likely keep most nations from developing their total potential, though hydro will still be an important energy source.[17]

Living green plants provide another means of capturing solar energy. Through photosynthesis, they convert sunlight into biomass that can be burned. Until the industrial revolution, wood supplied most of the world's energy. Today, it still provides 12 percent of the total, chiefly in the form of firewood and charcoal in developing countries.[18]

The use of bioenergy will surely expand during the next forty years, but its growth will be constrained. With many forests and croplands already over-stressed, and with food needs pressing against agricultural resources, it is unrealistic to think that ethanol derived from corn or sugarcane, for instance, can supply more than a tiny fraction of the world's liquid fuels.

One promising approach is to grow energy crops on marginal lands not currently used for food. Land that is too steeply sloping or not sufficiently fertile or well watered for crops might support trees that are periodically harvested. The wood could then be burned directly in a wood-fired power plant or converted to ethanol; the Solar Energy Research Institute has already developed a process that brings the cost of wood-derived ethanol down to $1.35 per gallon.[19]

In the United States, for example, the 13 million hectares of marginal cropland retired under the Conservation Reserve Program could be planted in trees that would yield as much as 265 million barrels of ethanol each year. Equivalent to 10 percent of current U.S. gasoline consumption, this amount will be a far larger share of supplies in the energy-efficient world of 2030. Since in any given year most of the land would be covered by trees, there would be a carbon storage benefit as well.[20]

Biomass energy thus has a major role to play, although resource constraints must be kept in mind. The conversion efficiency of the photosynthetic process is only a fraction of that of direct solar technologies. And there are substantial pressures on biological systems already, as well as new stresses likely to be exerted by global warming. Projects will have to be carefully chosen and properly managed.

Geothermal energy employs the huge reservoir of heat that lies beneath the earth's surface, making it the only renewable source that does not rely on sunlight. For this reason, geothermal resources must be tapped slowly enough so as not to deplete the accessible reservoir of heat, and thus be truly renewable. Continuing advances will allow engineers to use previously unexploitable, lower-temperature reservoirs that are hundreds of times as abundant as those in use today. In the future, many countries may find themselves where Kenya, Nicaragua, and the Philippines are today—getting much of their electricity from geothermal resources.[21]

Virtually all Pacific Rim countries, as well as those along East Africa's Great Rift and the Mediterranean Sea, are well endowed with geothermal energy. Iceland, Indonesia, and Japan are among the nations with the greatest potential. Geothermal energy can provide not only electricity that is transmitted long distances, but also direct heat for industries that locate near accessible heat reservoirs.[22]

Land use will inevitably be shaped by the development of economic systems based on renewable energy. Solar technologies are land-intensive, but no more so than those based on fossil fuels. In fact, if all the land devoted to mining coal is included, many solar technologies actually require less area than coal power does.[23]

A one-thousand-megawatt solar thermal facility, for example, would require twenty-four square kilometers of land. Meeting all U.S. electricity needs with this technology would thus require about twenty-nine thousand square kilometers, an area one-tenth the size of Arizona. Although wind farms that produce an equivalent amount of power would cover a wider area, they would not really occupy the land in the same way; indeed, cattle-grazing and other activities could go on as before. Moreover, solar, wind, and geothermal systems will use land that may not be much in demand today—windy mountain passes or stretches of dry desert. Land values, traditionally determined largely by agriculture, ranching, and forestry prospects, will be influenced by energy production potential as well.[24]

Nations now constituting what is called the Third World face the immense challenge of continuing to develop their economies without massive use of fossil fuels. Yet they have an advantage in being less hooked on oil, coal, and gas, and so their transition to the solar age will be easier. One option is to rely on biomass energy in current quantities but to step up replanting efforts and to burn the biomass much more efficiently, using gasifiers and other devices. Another is to turn directly to the sun, which most of the Third World has in abundance—solar ovens for cooking, solar collectors for hot water, and photovoltaics for electricity.

In both industrial and developing nations, energy production inevitably will be much more decentralized, breaking up the huge industries that have been a dominant part of the economic scene in the late twentieth century. Indeed, a world energy system based on the highly efficient use of renewable resources is liable to be not only more decentralized but also less vulnerable to disruption and more conducive to market principles and democratic political systems. In ecological terms, it is the only kind of world likely to endure for more than a few decades.

Efficient in All Senses

Getting total global carbon emissions down to 2 billion tons a year requires vast improvements in energy efficiency. Fortunately, many of the technologies to accomplish such reductions are already at hand and cost-effective. No technical breakthroughs are needed, for example, to double automobile fuel economy, triple the efficiency of lighting systems, or cut typical heating requirements by 75 percent. Technologies developed in the decades ahead will undoubtedly allow even greater gains.[25]

Automobiles in 2030 are apt to get at least one hundred miles per gallon of fuel, four times the current average for new cars. A hint of what such vehicles may be like is given in a recently developed prototype, the Volvo LCP 2000. It is an aerodynamic four-passenger car that weights just half as much as today's models due to the use of lightweight synthetic materials. Moreover, it has a highly efficient and clean-burning diesel engine. With the addition of a continuously variable transmission and a flywheel energy storage device, this vehicle could get ninety miles to the gallon.[26]

Forty years from now, Thomas Edison's revolutionary incandescent light bulbs may be found only in museums—replaced by a variety of new lighting systems, including halogen and sodium lights. The most important new light source may be compact fluorescent bulbs that, for example, use eighteen watts rather than seventy-five to produce the same amount of light. The new bulbs, already available today, not only reduce consumers' electricity bills, they last over seven times as long.[27]

In 2030, homes are likely to be weather-tight and highly insulated, greatly reducing the need for both heating and cooling. Superinsulated homes in the Canadian province of Saskatchewan are already so tightly built that it does not pay to install a furnace; a small electric baseboard heater is more than adequate. Such homes use one-third as much energy as modern Swedish homes do, or one-tenth the U.S. average. They have double the normal insulation and airtight liners in the walls. Mechanical ventilation systems keep the air fresh. The most welcome change for residents may be the almost complete elimination of utility bills.[28]

Inside these homes, people will have appliances that are on average three to four times as efficient as those in use today. Probably the greatest savings will come in refrigeration. Commercial models now on the market can reduce electricity use from 1,500 kilowatt-hours per year to 750: other models under development would bring that figure down to 240 kilowatt-hours. Gains nearly as great are possible in air-conditioners, water heaters, and clothes dryers.[29]

Industry will also be shaped by the need to improve energy efficiency. Steel-making is likely to rely heavily on efficient electric arc furnaces that require half the energy of the open hearth ones of today. Some energy-intensive materials, such as aluminum, may be used only in select applications, replaced in large measure by less energy-intensive synthetics. Vast improvements in the design and maintenance of electric motors could by themselves eliminate the need for hundreds of large power plants around the world.[30]

Cogeneration (the combined production of heat and power) will also spread widely. Many factories will generate their own power with biomass, using the waste heat for industrial processes as well as heating and cooling. Such systems are in wide use in some parts of the world already and can raise total plant efficiency from 50 to 70 percent to as high as 90 percent. Excess power can be transferred to the electric grid and used by other consumers.[31]

Improving energy efficiency will not noticeably change lifestyles or economic systems. A highly efficient refrigerator or light bulb provides the same service as an inefficient one—just more economically. Gains in energy efficiency alone, however, will not reduce fossil fuel carbon emissions by the needed amount. Additional steps to limit the use of fossil fuels are likely to reshape cities, transportation systems, and industrial patterns, fostering a society that is more efficient in all senses.

By the year 2030, a much more diverse set of transportation options will exist. The typical European or Japanese city today has already taken one step toward this future. Highly developed rail and bus systems move people efficiently between home and work. In Tokyo only 15 percent of commuters drive cars to the office. The world of 2030 is apt to rely particularly heavily on light trail—systems built at street level, relatively inexpensively, that allow people to move quickly between neighborhoods.[32]

Automobiles will undoubtedly still be in use four decades from now, but their numbers will be fewer and their role smaller. Within cities, only electric or clean hydrogen-powered vehicles are likely to be permitted, and most of these will be highly efficient "city cars." The energy to run them may well come from solar power plants. Families might rent efficient larger vehicles for vacations.

The bicycle will also play a major role, as it already does in much of Asia as well as in some industrial-country towns and cities. In Amsterdam and many other communities such as Davis, California, bike-path networks have been developed that encourage widespread use of this form of personal transport. Also likely to develop rapidly is the concept of bike-and-ride, using the bicycle to reach rail systems that then move commuters into the center city. There are already twice as many bikes as cars worldwide. In the bicycle-centered transport system of 2030, the ratio could easily be ten to one.[33]

Forty years from now, people will live closer to their jobs, and much socializing and shopping will be done by bike rather than in a one-ton automobile. Computerized delivery services may allow people to shop from home—consuming less time as well as less energy. In addition, a world that allows only 2 billion tons of carbon emissions cannot be trucking vast quantities of food and other items thousands of kilometers.

Telecommunications will substitute for travel as well. Many people may work at home or in special satellite offices, connected to colleagues and supervisors by electronic lines rather than crowded highways. Daily trips to the office could be replaced by occasional visits. The saved time and frustration will raise both worker productivity and the quality of life. The current need of many businesspeople to jet frequently from place to place may be substituted by ever more creative uses of electronic communications. And the current transition from overnight delivery services to computerized facsimile transmissions will be nearly complete.

The automobile-based modern world is now only about forty years old, but it is already apparent to many that, with its damaging air pollution and traffic congestion, it does not represent the pinnacle in human social evolution. Although a world where cars play a minor role may be difficult for some to imagine, it is worth remembering that our grandparents would have had a hard time visualizing today's world of traffic jams and smog-filled cities. Ultimately, a more efficient world is likely to be less congested and less polluted.[34]

Reusing and Recycling Materials

In the sustainable, efficient economy of 2030, waste reduction and recycling industries will have largely replaced the garbage collection and disposal companies of today. The throwaway society that has emerged during the late twentieth century uses so much energy, emits so much carbon, and generates so much air pollution, acid rain, water pollution, toxic waste, and rubbish that it is strangling itself. Rooted in the concept of planned obsolescence and appeals to convenience, it will be seen by historians as an aberration.

Most materials used today are discarded after one use—roughly two-thirds of all aluminum, three-fourths of all steel and paper, and an even higher share of plastic. Society will become dramatically less energy-intensive and less polluting only if the throwaway mentality is replaced by a recycling ethic. Just 5 percent as much energy is needed to recycle aluminum as to produce it from bauxite, the original raw material. For steel produced entirely from scrap, the saving amounts to roughly two-thirds. Newsprint from recycled paper takes 25 to 60 percent less energy to make than that from wood pulp. And recycling glass saves up to a third of the energy embodied in the original product.[35]

Recycling is also a key to getting land, air, and water pollution down to acceptable levels. For example, steel produced from scrap reduces air pollution by 85 percent, cuts water pollution by 76 percent, and eliminates mining wastes altogether. Paper from recycled material reduces pollutants entering the air by 74 percent and the water by 35 percent, as well as reducing pressures on forests in direct proportion to the amount recycled.[36]

A hierarchy of options can guide materials policy: The first priority, of course, is to avoid using any nonessential item. Second is to directly reuse a product—for example, refilling a glass beverage container. The third is to recycle the material to form a new product. Fourth, the material can be burned to extract whatever energy it contains, as long as this can be done safely. And finally, the option of last resort is disposal in a landfill.

The first check on the worldwide movement toward a throwaway society came during the seventies as oil prices and environmental consciousness climbed. Rising energy costs made recycling more attractive, reversing the trend toward tossing out more metal, glass, and paper. The second boost came during the eighties as many urban landfill sites filled, forcing municipal governments to ship their garbage to faraway places for disposal. For many U.S. cities, garbage disposal costs during the last decade increased severalfold, making it cost-effective for them to help establish recycling industries.[37]

During the nineties, this trend will be reinforced by the need to reduce carbon emissions, air pollution, acid rain, and toxic waste. In the early stages, countries will move toward comprehensive, systematic recycling of metal, glass, paper, and other materials, beginning with source separation at the consumer level. Many communities in Europe, Japan, and, more recently, the United States have already taken steps in this direction.

Steady advances in technologies are speeding the transition. The electric arc furnace, as mentioned earlier, produces high-quality steel from scrap metal using far less energy than a traditional open-hearth furnace does. In the United States, a leader in this technology, roughly a third of all steel is already produced from scrap in such furnaces.[38]

Historically, the steel industry has been concentrated near areas with coal and iron ore, such as Wales in the United Kingdom or western Pennsylvania in the United States. By 2030, the industry will be widely dispersed. Electric arc furnaces can operate wherever there is electricity and a supply of scrap metal, and they can be built on a scale adapted to the volume of locally available scrap. The steel mills of the future will feed heavily on worn-out automobiles, household appliances, and industrial equipment. Further, they will provide local jobs and revenue, while eliminating a source of waste.

In the sustainable economy of 2030, the principal source of materials for industry will be recycled goods. Most of the raw material for the aluminum mill will come from the local scrap collection center, not from the bauxite mine. Paper and paper products will be produced at recycling mills, with recycled paper moving through a hierarchy of uses, from high-quality bond to newsprint and, eventually, into cardboard boxes. When, after several rounds of recycling, the fibers are no longer reusable, they can be burned as fuel in a cogenerating plant. In a paper products industry that continually uses recycled materials, wood pulp will play a minor role. Industries will feed largely on what is already within the system, turning to virgin raw materials only to replace any losses in use and recycling.

Although early moves away from the throwaway society are concentrating on recycling, sustainability over the long term depends more on eliminating waste flows. One of the most obvious places to reduce the volume of waste generated is in industry, where a restructuring of manufacturing processes can easily slash wastes by a third or more. The 3M Company halved its hazardous waste flows within a decade of launching a corporation-wide program. A pioneer in waste reduction, 3M also boosted its profits in the process.[39]

Another major potential source of waste reduction lies in the simplification of food packaging. In the United States, consumers spent more on food packaging in 1986 than American farmers earned selling their crops. In the interest of attracting customers, items are sometimes buried in three or four layers of packaging. For the final trip from supermarket to home, yet another set of materials is used in the form of paper or plastic bags, also typically discarded after one use. Forty years from now, government regulation is likely to have eliminated excessive packaging. Throwaway grocery bags will have been replaced by durable, reusable bags of canvas or other material.[40]

Societies in 2030 may also have decided to replace multisized and shaped beverage containers with a set of standardized ones made of durable glass that can be reused many times. These could be used for most, if not all, beverages, such as fruit juices, beer, milk, and soda pop. Bottlers will simply clean the container, steam off the old label, and add a new one. Containers returned to the supermarket or other outlet might become part of an urban or regional computerized inventory, which would permit their efficient movement from supermarkets or other collection centers to local dairies, breweries, and soda bottling plants as needed. Such a system will save an enormous amount of energy and materials.

In addition to recycling and reusing metal, glass, and paper, a sustainable society also recycles nutrients. In nature, one organism's waste is another's sustenance; in urban societies, however, human sewage has become a troublesome source of pollutants in rivers, lakes, and coastal waters. The nutrients in human wastes can be reused safely as long as the process includes measures to prevent the spread of disease.

Fortunately, cities in Japan, South Korea, and China already provide some examples of this kind of nutrient recycling. In these countries, human waste is systematically returned to the land in vegetable-growing greenbelts around cities. Intensively farmed cropland surrounding some cities there produces vegetables year-round using greenhouses or plastic covering during the winter to extend the growing season. Perhaps the best model is Shanghai: after modestly expanding its urban political boundaries to facilitate sewage recycling, the city now produces an exportable surplus of vegetables.[41]

Some cities will probably find it more efficient to use treated human sewage to fertilize aquacultural operations. A steady flow of nutrients from human waste into ponds can supply food for a vigorously growing population of algae that in turn are consumed by fish. In Calcutta, a sewage-fed aquaculture system now provides two thousand kilograms of fresh fish each day for sale in the city. In a society with a scarcity of protein, such an approach, modeled after nature's nutrient recycling, can both eliminate a troublesome waste problem and generate a valuable food resource.[42]

As recycling reaches full potential over the next forty years, households will begin to compost yard wastes rather than put them out for curbside garbage pickup. A lost art in many communities, composting not only reduces garbage flows, it provides a rich source of humus for gardening, lessening the need to buy chemical fertilizers to maintain lawn and garden fertility.

By systematically reducing the flow of waste and reusing or recycling most remaining materials, the basic needs of the planet's growing number of human residents can be satisfied without destroying our very life-support systems. Moving in this direction will not only create a far more livable environment with less air and water pollution, it will also reduce the unsightly litter that blights the landscape in many industrial societies today.

With a Restored Biological Base

Imagine trying to meet the food, fuel, and timber needs of some 8 billion people—nearly 3 billion more than the current population—with 960 billion fewer tons of topsoil (more than twice the amount on all U.S. cropland) and 440 million fewer hectares of trees (an area more than half the size of the continental United States). That, in a nutshell, will be the predicament of society in 2030 if current rates of soil erosion and deforestation continue unaltered for the next forty years.[43]

Fortunately, or unfortunately, that predicament will not arise. If the earth's croplands, forests, and rangelands are not soon restored and stabilized, world population will never grow that large; human numbers will drop because of malnutrition, famine, and rising death rates, as stated earlier. If, on the other hand, the population of 2030 is adequately being supported, it will be because our use of the earth's biological resources was put on a sound footing long before then, and because population growth was slowed before it completely overwhelmed life-support systems.

Of necessity, societies in 2030 will be using the land intensively; the needs of a population more than half again as large as today's cannot be met otherwise. But unlike the present, land use patterns would be abiding by basic principles of biological stability: nutrient retention, carbon balance, soil protection, water conservation, and preservation of species diversity. Rather than the earth's photosynthetic productivity being eaten away, as is the case now, it will be safe-guarded or even enhanced. Harvests will rarely exceed sustainable yields.

Meeting food needs will pose monumental challenges, as some simple numbers illustrate. Currently, 0.28 hectares of cropland is available for every man, woman, and child. By 2030, assuming cropland area expands by 5 percent between now and then and that population grows to 8 billion, cropland per person will have dropped to 0.19 hectares—a third less than we have in today's inadequately fed world. Virtually all of Asia, and especially China, will be struggling to feed its people from a far more meager cropland area per person.[44]

In light of these constraints, the rural landscapes of 2030 are likely to exhibit greater diversity than they do now. Variations in soils, slope, climate, and water availability will require different patterns and strains of crops grown in different ways so as to maximize sustainable output. For example, farmers may adopt numerous forms of agroforestry—the combined production of crops and trees—to provide food, biomass, and fodder, while also adding nutrients to soils and controlling water runoff. Many such systems already are successfully used.[45]

Efforts to arrest desertification, now claiming 6 million hectares each year, may by then have transformed the gullied highlands of Ethiopia, China's Loess Plateau, and other degraded areas into productive, income-generating terrain. A mobilization of villagers, scientists, and development workers will have spread widely the successes in land restoration evident by the late eighties. Much sloping land now losing topsoil rapidly will be terraced, enhanced by shrubs or nitrogen-fixing trees planted along the contour. With improved crop varieties and planting patterns that conserve soil and water, many of these areas are likely to be largely self-sufficient and economically more diverse by 2030.[46]

Halting desertification also depends on eliminating overgrazing. The global livestock herd in 2030 is thus likely to be much smaller than today's 3 billion. Since open grazing is likely to diminish, more farmers will integrate livestock into their diverse farming systems, using for fodder the leaves from trees in their agroforestry systems or the cover crop in their rotational cropping patterns. It seems inevitable that adequately nourishing a world population 60 percent larger than today's will preclude feeding one-third of the global grain harvest to livestock and poultry, as is currently the case. As meat becomes more scarce and expensive, the diets of the affluent will move down the food chain.[47]

It is difficult to foresee whether the vast areas of monoculture wheat, rice, and corn so crucial to the global food supply in the late twentieth century will play as great a role in 2030. In the Corn Belt of the United States, farmers will undoubtedly be rotating crops much more extensively to help curb soil erosion, conserve moisture, and reduce pesticide and fertilizer use, a trend already under way.

Farmers in some parts of the world may opt to grow seed-bearing perennial grasses, creating a cropping pattern that resembles the native prairies that much of modern agriculture replaced. Such "polycultures," like their monoculture counterparts, would yield edible grains, oils, and other commodities. They take advantage of the prairie's natural diversity, drought resistance, and soil-renewing capacity, and thus greatly reduce the need for chemicals, irrigation water, and other intensive inputs. The Land Institute in Salina, Kansas, is pioneering such work, which could result in an altogether different, inherently more enduring form of crop production.[48]

Another option some farmers may choose is that of a mixed enterprise of food and energy production. They might grow a winter grain, such as wheat, followed by sweet sorghum as a summer energy crop, which would be used to make ethanol. Besides increasing the amount of sunlight converted into biochemical energy, this cropping pattern would help check soil erosion since the land would be covered year-round.

Successfully adapting to changed climatic regimes resulting from greenhouse warming, as well as to water scarcity and other resource constraints, may lead scientists to draw on a much broader base of crop varieties. A greater area will be devoted, for example, to crops that are salt-tolerant and drought-resistant, whether they are new varieties of familiar crops such as wheat, or less familiar crops such as amaranth, a grain native to the Andean highlands of South America. The extensive gene pool needed to revamp agricultural systems depends on the collection of wild plants from their native areas and storage of their genetic material in international gene banks. So far this effort has focused on the world's thirty major food crops, but less on unfamiliar plants that could become an important component of diets forty years from now.[49]

Forests and woodlands will be valued more highly and for many more reasons in 2030 than is the case today. The planet's mantle of trees, already a third less than in preagricultural times and shrinking by more than 11 million hectares per year now, will be stable or expanding as a result of serious efforts to slow deforestation and to replant vast areas.[50]

Long before 2030, the clearing of most tropical forests will have ceased. Since the nutrients in these ecosystems are held in the leaves and biomass of the vegetation rather than in the soil, only activities that preserve the forest canopy are sustainable. Those forestlands that can support crop production will already have been identified and converted during the intervening forty years. While it is impossible to say how much virgin tropical forest would remain in 2030 if sustainability is achieved, certainly the rate of deforestation will have had to slow dramatically by the end of this decade and come to a halt soon thereafter.[51]

Efforts to identify and protect unique parcels of forest will probably have led to a widely dispersed network of preserves. But a large portion of tropical forests still standing in 2030 will be exploited in a variety of ways by people living in and around them. Hundreds of "extractive reserves" will exist, areas in which local people harvest rubber, resins, nuts, fruits, medicinal substances, and other nontimber forest products for domestic use or export. Long-term benefits—both economic and ecological—from a tropical forest area managed in this way are greater than those from burning off an equivalent area and planting it in crops or pasture. Although the latter yields greater monetary returns in the initial few years after clearing, income drops to zero when the land's productivity is gone, usually within a decade or so, and virtually all ecological benefits are lost.[52]

By definition, a sustainable society will not be overcutting or degrading its forests for lumber or other wood products. Today's logging operations often damage or destroy large areas, and regulations governing timber practices—including reforestation—routinely are ignored. Needed efforts to understand how to exploit a natural forest for timber without diminishing its productivity, species diversity, and overall health are still in their infancy.[53]

Since societies will be recycling most of their paper products, demand for pulping wood per person may be less in 2030 than today. Still, large areas of partially desertified land, degraded watersheds, railroad and highway borders, and open countryside will need to be in trees. Serious efforts to alleviate the fuel-wood crisis in developing countries, to reduce flooding and landslides in hilly regions, to meet industrial wood needs sustainably, and to slow the buildup of carbon dioxide may have spurred the planting of an additional 200 million hectares or so of trees.[54]

Many of these plantings will be on private farms as part of agroforestry systems. But plantations may also have an expanded role. Cities and villages will turn to managed woodlands on their outskirts to contribute fuel for heating, cooking, and electricity. Wood from these plantations will substitute for some portion of coal and oil use, and, since harvested on a sustained-yield basis, will make no net contribution of carbon dioxide to the atmosphere.

Restoring and stabilizing the biological resource base by 2030 depends on a pattern of land ownership and use far more equitable than today's. Much of the degradation now occurring stems from the heavily skewed distribution of land that, along with population growth, pushes poor people into ever more marginal environments. Good stewardship requires that people have plots large enough to sustain their families without abusing the land, access to the technological means of using their land productively, and the right to pass it on to their children.[55]

This inevitably will require large land-holdings in densely populated agrarian societies to be broken up and redistributed to the poorer majority who lack viable livelihoods. Similarly, much government-owned common land, such as forests and pastures, likely will revert to communities and villages that have a stake in optimizing the productivity of these lands and managing them sustainably.[56]

No matter what technologies come along, including unforeseen advances in biotechnology, the biochemical process of photosynthesis, carried out by green plants, will remain the basis for meeting human needs. Given that humanity already appropriates an estimated 40 percent of the earth's annual photosynthetic product on land, leaving only 60 percent for the millions of other species and for protecting basic ecosystem functions, the urgency of slowing the growth in human numbers and demands is obvious. The sooner societies stabilize their populations, the greater will be their opportunities for achieving equitable and stable patterns of land use that can meet their need indefinitely.[57]

With a New Set of Values

The fundamental changes we have outlined in energy, forestry, agriculture, and other physical systems cannot occur without corresponding shifts in the social, economic, and moral character of human societies. During the transition to sustainability, political leaders and citizens alike will be forced to reevaluate their goals and aspirations, to redefine their measures of success, and to adjust work and leisure to a new set of principles that have at their core the welfare of future generations.

Given the enormity of the tasks involved, many people may assume that moving in this direction will be painful and limiting, and thus something to resist. But given the choice of repairing your house or having it collapse around you, you would not question whether to undertake the project.

Shifts in employment will be among the most visible as the transition gets under way. Moving from fossil fuels to a diverse set of renewable energy sources, extracting fewer materials from the earth and recycling more, and revamping framing and forestry practices will greatly expand opportunities in new areas even as the number of some traditional jobs contracts.

Losses in coal mining, auto production, road construction, and metals prospecting will be offset by gains in the manufacture and sale of photovoltaic solar cells, wind turbines, bicycles, mass transit equipment, and a host of materials recycling technologies. In land-rich countries and those with an abundance of agricultural wastes, alcohol-fuel plants will replace oil refineries. Since planned obsolescence will itself be obsolete in a sustainable society, a far greater share of workers will be employed in repair, maintenance, and recycling activities than in the extraction of virgin materials and production of new goods.

Wind prospectors, energy efficiency auditors, and solar architects will be among the booming professions stemming from the shift to a highly efficient, renewable energy economy. Numbering in the hundreds of thousands today, jobs in these fields may collectively total in the millions worldwide within a few decades. Opportunities in forestry will expand markedly with the need to design and extend highly productive agroforestry systems, to better manage natural forests, and to plant and maintain vast areas of trees. Similarly, as new cropping patterns are devised and toxic chemical use is reduced or eliminated, agronomists will be in far higher demand, as will specialists in biological methods of pest control.

Many people will find their skills valued in new or expanded lines of work. Petroleum geologists may be retrained as geothermal geologists, for example, while traditional midwives continue to broaden their roles to include the spectrum of family planning needs.

Long before 2030, the trend toward ever larger cities and an increasing ration of urban-to rural dwellers is likely to have reversed. Each person who moves from countryside to city requires that a corresponding surplus of food be produced in some rural part of the world. Getting more food from less labor requires the use of more energy, as does processing the food and transporting it to the distant city center. An inexorable trend over the last several decades, the increasing energy intensity of food production and distribution cannot continue indefinitely.

Smaller human settlements will also be favored by the shift to renewable energy sources. In contrast to the large centralized fossil-fuel and nuclear plants dominating energy systems today, power from renewable technologies—whether photovoltaic cells, wood-fired plants, or wind generators—can be developed cost-effectively across a range of scales. They also allow local areas to capitalize on their natural endowments, whether that be strong winds, bright sunshine, abundant woodlands, or proximity to geothermal reservoirs. In so doing, they foster greater local self-reliance.

As the transition to a more environmentally benign economy progresses, sustainability will gradually eclipse growth as the focus of economic policy-making. Over the next few decades, government policies will encourage investments that promote stability and endurance at the expense of those that simply expand short-term production. Companies would thus devote a greater share of their investment capital, for example, to converting to renewable energy sources and to installing recycling technologies—and proportionately less to expanding the output of goods.

As a yardstick of progress, the gross national product (GNP) will be seen as a bankrupt indicator. By measuring flows of goods and services, GNP undervalues qualities a sustainable society strives for, such as durability and resource protection, and overvalues many it does not, such as planned obsolescence and waste.[58]

Shoddy appliances that require repair and fast replacement, for instance, raise the GNP more than a well-crafted product that lasts, even though the latter is really more valuable. Similarly, the pollution caused by a coal-burning power plant raises GNP by requiring expenditures on lung disease treatment and the purchase of a scrubber to control emissions. Yet society would be far better off if power were generated in ways that did not pollute the air in the first place.

In 2030, planners will measure economic and social advances by sustainability criteria rather than simply by growth in short-term output. As economist Herman Daly observes, a new direction of technical progress is needed, "one that squeezes more service per unit of resource, rather than one that just runs more resources through the system." Furthermore, he points out that "as long as the GNP is thought to measure human well-being, the obstacles to change are enormous. . . . The market sees only efficiency—it has no organs for hearing, feeling, or smelling either justice or sustainability."[59]

National military budgets in a sustainable world will be a small fraction of what they are today. Now totaling some $1 trillion per year, global military expenditures will be cut heavily as countries recognize that environmental threats to security have supplanted traditional military ones. Moreover, sustainability cannot be achieved without a massive shift of resources from military endeavors into energy efficiency, soil conservation, tree planting, family planning, and other needed development activities. Rather than maintaining their own large defense establishments, governments may come to rely on a greatly expanded and strengthened U.N. peace-keeping force, one that would have the power and authority to defend any member country against an aggressor. This might allow more countries to follow Costa Rica's example and eliminate their armies altogether.[60]

Nations will undoubtedly be cooperating in numerous other ways as well. Careful tracking of changes in atmospheric chemistry, forest cover, land productivity, and ocean resources will be among the many efforts handled by multinational teams of scientists and government workers. It may be among the ironies of future political development that even as individual nations move to decentralize power and decision-making within their own borders, they simultaneously establish a degree of cooperation and coordination at the international level that goes well beyond anything witnessed to date.

Movement toward a lasting society cannot occur without a transformation of individual priorities and values. Throughout the ages, philosophers and religious leaders have denounced materialism as a viable path to human fulfillment. Yet societies across the ideological spectrum have persisted in equating quality of life with increased consumption. Personal self-worth typically is measured by possessions, just as social progress is judged by GNP growth.

Because of the strain on resources it creates, materialism simply cannot survive the transition to a sustainable world. As public understanding of the need to adopt simpler and less consumptive lifestyles spreads, it will become unfashionable to own fancy new cars and clothes. This shift, however, will be among the hardest to make, since consumerism so deeply permeates societies of all political stripes. Yet the potential benefits of unleashing the tremendous quantities of human energy now devoted to designing, producing, advertising, buying, consuming, and discarding material goods are enormous. Much undoubtedly would be channeled into forming richer human relationships, stronger communities, and greater outlets for cultural diversity, music, and the arts.

As the amassing of personal and national wealth becomes less of a goal, the gap between haves and have-nots will gradually close, eliminating many societal tensions. Ideological differences may fade as well, as nations adopt sustainability as common cause, and as they come to recognize that achieving it requires a shared set of values that includes democratic principles, freedom to innovate, respect for human rights, and acceptance of diversity. With the cooperative tasks involved in repairing the earth so many and so large, the idea of waging war could become an anachronism.

Fortunately, there is as much a pull as a push toward an enduring society. As economist Herman Daly and theologian John Cobb write, "People can be *attracted* by new ways of ordering their lives, as well as *driven* by the recognition of what will happen if they do not change."[61]

The opportunity to build a lasting foundation will pass us by if we do not seize it soon. To get under way, we need only stop resisting the push, and embrace the pull, of building a sustainable society.

---

[1] World Commission on Environment and Development, *Our Common Future* (New York: Oxford University Press, 1987).

[2] U.S. Environmental Protection Agency, *Policy Options for Stabilizing Global Climate* (draft) (Washington, D.C.: 1989); Gregg Marland et al., *Estimates of CO_2 Emissions from Fossil Fuel Burning and Cement Manufacturing, Based on the United Nations Energy Statistics and the U.S. Bureau of Mines Cement Manufacturing Data* (Oak Ridge, Tenn.: Oak Ridge National Laboratory, 1989); United Nations Secretariat, "Long-Range Global Population Projections as Assessed in 1980," *Population Bulletin of the United Nations* (New York: 1983).

[3] Worldwatch Institute estimate based on "World List of Nuclear Power Plants," *Nuclear News*, August 1989; Christopher Flavin, *Reassessing Nuclear Power: The Fallout from Chernobyl*, Worldwatch Paper 75 (Washington, D.C.: Worldwatch Institute, March 1987).

[4] John J. Taylor, "Improved and Safer Nuclear Power," *Science*, April 21, 1989; "Outlook on Advanced Reactors," *Nucleonics Week*, March 30, 1989; Armory B. Lovins and L. Hunter Lovins, *Brittle Power: Energy Strategy for National Security* (Andover, Mass.: Brick House Publishing Co., 1982); R. H. Williams and H. A. Feiveson, "Diversion-Resistance Criteria for Future Nuclear Power," Center for Energy and Environmental Studies, Princeton University, Princeton, N.J., May 22, 1989; Klaus Michael Meyerabich and Bertram Schefold, *Die Grenzen der Atomwitschaft* (Munich: Verlag C. H. Beck, 1986).

[5]Population figure is authors' estimate derived from United Nations (UN), Department of International Economic and Social Affairs (DIESA), *World Population Prospects 1988* (New York: 1989); extrapolating from medium projection for 2025 yields 8.85 billion.

[6]Population Information Program, "Population and Birth Planning in the People's Republic of China," *Population Reports*, January/February 1982; UN, DIESA, *World Population Prospects 1988*; Population Reference Bureau, *1989 World Population Data Sheet* (Washington, D.C.: 1989).

[7]UN, *1987 Energy Statistics Yearbook* (New York: 1989); Meridian Corporation, "Characterization of U.S. Energy Resources and Reserves," prepared for Deputy Assistant Secretary for Renewable Energy, U.S. Department of Energy (DOE), Alexandria, Va., June 1989.

[8]D. Groues and I. Segal, *Solar Energy in Israel* (Jerusalem: Ministry of Energy & Infrastructure, 1984); International Energy Agency (IEA), *Renewable Sources of Energy* (Paris: Organisation for Economic Cooperation and Development, 1987).

[9]Paul Savoldelli, Luz International Ltd., private communication and printout, July 9, 1989; Charles Komanoff, Komanoff Energy Associates, New York, private communication and printout, February 10, 1989.

[10]H. M. Hubbard, "Photovoltaics Today and Tomorrow," *Science*, April 21, 1989; Solar Energy Research Institute (SERI), "Photovoltaics: Electricity from Sunshine," unpublished, Golden, Colo., 1989.

[11]Hubbard, "Photovoltaics"; Christopher Flavin, *Electricity from Sunlight: The Emergence of Photovoltaics* (Washington, D.C.: U.S. Government Printing Office, 1984).

[12]Hubbard, "Photovoltaics"; V. Elaine Glimore, "Solar Shingles," *Popular Science*, June 1989.

[13]Robert R. Lynette, "Wind Energy Systems" (paper presented to the Forum on Renewable Energy and Climate Change, Washington, D.C., June 14–15, 1989); Worldwatch Institute estimates based on Shepard Buchanan, Bonneville Power Administration, Portland, Ore., private communication and printout, July 28, 1989.

[14]Mark Newman, "West Germany to Build 150 MWe of Wind Farms by Mid-1990s," *International Solar Energy Intelligence Report*, November 22, 1988; Department of Non-Conventional Energy Sources, Ministry of Energy, *Annual Report 1987–88* (New Delhi, India: undated).

[15]Christopher Flavin, *Wind Power: A Turning Point*, Worldwatch Paper 45 (Washington, D.C.: Worldwatch Institute, July 1981).

[16]Worldwatch Institute estimate, based on Larry Langemeier, Kansas State University, Manhattan Kans., private communication, November 3, 1989.

[17]UN, *1987 Energy Statistics Yearbook*.

[18] Worldwatch Institute estimate based on D. O. Hall et al., *Biomass for Energy in Developing Countries* (Elmsford, N.Y.: Pergamon Press, 1982); Daniel Deudney and Christopher Flavin, *Renewable Energy: The Power to Choose* (New York: W. W. Norton & Co., 1983); and British Petroleum, *BP Statistical Review of World Energy* (London: 1989).

[19] Lynn Wright, Oak Ridge National Laboratory, Oak Ridge, Tenn., private communication, August 25, 1989; Norman Hinman, SERI, Boulder, Colo., private communication, August 25, 1989.

[20] Worldwatch Institute estimate based on Brad Karmen, U.S. Department of Agriculture (USDA), Washington, D.C., private communication, October 25, 1989, on Energy Information Administration (EIA), *Monthly Energy Review*, March 1989 (Washington, D.C.: DOE, 1989), on Wright, private communication, and on Hinman, private communication.

[21] UN, *1987 Energy Statistics Yearbook*.

[22] Ronald DiPippo, "International Developments in Geothermal Power Development," *Geothermal Resources Council Bulletin*, May 1988.

[23] Meridian Corporation, "Energy System Emissions and Matériel Requirements," prepared for U.S. DOE, Alexandria, Va., February 1989; Savoldelli, private communication.

[24] Worldwatch Institute estimates based on Savoldelli, private communication and printout, and on EIA, *Monthly Energy Review*, March 1989, assuming a solar-only mode and a capacity factor of 26 percent for the solar thermal stations; Paul Gipe, Paul Gipe and Associates, Tehachapi, Calif., private communication and printout, October 22, 1989.

[25] Christopher Flavin and Alan Durning, *Building on Success: The Age of Energy Efficiency*, Worldwatch Paper 82 (Washington, D.C.: Worldwatch Institute, March 1988).

[26] Deborah Bleviss, *The New Oil Crisis and Fuel Economy Technologies: Preparing the Light Transportation Industry for the 1990's* (New York: Quorum Press, 1988).

[27] Flavin and Durning, *Building on Success*; Arthur Rosenfeld and David Hafemeister, "Energy-Efficient Buildings," *Scientific American*, April 1988; Peter Weiss, "Lighting the Way Towards More Efficient Lighting," *Home Energy*, January/February 1989.

[28] José Goldemberg et al., "An End-Use Oriented Global Energy Strategy" in Annual Review, Inc., *Annual Review of Energy*, Vol. 10 (Palo Alto, Calif.: 1985).

[29] Jørgen Norgaard, Technical University of Denmark, Lyngby, Denmark, private communications, October 28–29, 1987; Howard Geller, "Energy-Efficient Residential Appliances: Performance Issues and Policy Options," *IEEE Technology and Society Magazine*, March 1986; David B. Goldstein and Peter Miller, "Developing Cost Curves for Conserved

Energy in New Refrigerators and Freezers," American Council for an Energy-Efficient Economy, Washington, D.C., 1986.

[30]Marc Ross, "Industrial Energy Conservation," *Natural Resource Journal*, August 1984; Marc Ross, "Industrial Energy Conservation and the Steel Industry," *Energy, The International Journal*, October/November 1987.

[31]U.S. Congress, Office of Technology Assessment, *Industrial Energy Use* (Washington, D.C.: U.S. Government Printing Office, 1983).

[32]Bundesministerium für Verkehr, *Verkehr in Zahlen 1987* (Bonn: 1987).

[33]Marcia D. Lowe, *The Bicycle: Vehicle for a Small Planet*, Worldwatch Paper 90 (Washington, D.C.: Worldwatch Institute, September 1989); A. Wilmink, "The Effects of State Subsidizing of Bicycle Facilities," *Velo City '87 Congress: Planning for the Urban Cyclist*, proceedings of the Third International Velo City Congress, Groningen, the Netherlands, September 22–26, 1987; Michael A. Replogle, "Major Bikeway Construction Effort in the Netherlands," *Urban Transportation Abroad*, Winter 1982; David Peltz, Davis Department of Public Works, Davis, Calif., private communication, July 28, 1989; Michael A. Replogle, *Bicycles and Public Transportation: New Links to Suburban Transit Markets*, 2nd ed. (Washington, D.C.: The Bicycle Federation, 1988).

[34]Worldwatch Institute estimate based on International Road Federation, *World Road Statistics 1981-1985* (Washington, D.C.: 1986), and on Motor Vehicle Manufacturers Association, *Facts and Figure '87* (Detroit, Mich.: 1987); "The Motorization of the 3rd World," *National Association of Railroad Passengers News*, July 1987.

[35]Share discarded of various materials and energy savings of aluminum and glass recycling from Cynthia Pollock, *Mining Urban Wastes: The Potential for Recycling*, Worldwatch Paper 76 (Washington, D.C.: Worldwatch Institute, April 1987); energy savings of steel recycling from William U. Chandler, *Materials Recycling: The Virtue of Necessity*, Worldwatch Paper 56 (Washington, D.C.: Worldwatch Institute, October 1983); energy savings of newsprint recycling from Roberta Forsell Stauffer, "Energy Savings from Recycling," *Resource Recycling*, January/February 1989.

[36]Pollock, *Mining Urban Wastes*.

[37]Chandler, *Materials Recycling*; Pollock, *Mining Urban Wastes*.

[38]Donald F. Barnett and Robert W. Crandall, *Up from the Ashes: The Rise of the Steel Minimill in the United States* (Washington, D.C.: Brookings Institution, 1986).

[39]Kirsten U. Oldenburg and Joel S. Hirschhorn, "Waste Reduction: A New Strategy to Avoid Pollution," *Environment*, March 1987.

[40]"Cost of Packaging Food Could Exceed Farm Net," *Journal of Commerce*, August 12, 1986.

⁴¹Lester R. Brown and Jodi L. Jacobson, *The Future of Urbanization: Facing the Ecological and Economic Constraints*, Worldwatch Paper 77 (Washington, D.C.: Worldwatch Institute, May 1987); Shanghai example from Yue-Man Yeung, "Urban Agriculture in Asia," the Food Energy Nexus Program of the United Nations University, Tokyo, September, 1985.

⁴²Peter Edwards, *Aquaculture: A Component of Low Cost Sanitation Technology* (Washington, D.C.: United Nations Development Programme and World Bank, 1985).

⁴³Assumes worldwide soil erosion rate of 24 billion tons per year and forest loss of 11 million hectares per year; see Lester R. Brown and Edward C. Wolf, *Soil Erosion: Quiet Crisis in the World Economy*, Worldwatch Paper 60 (Washington, D.C.: Worldwatch Institute, September 1984); U.N. Food and Agriculture Organization (FAO), *Tropical Forest Resources*, Forestry Paper 30 (Rome: 1982).

⁴⁴Per capita cropland area calculated from FAO, *Production Yearbook 1987* (Rome: 1988), and from Population Reference Bureau, *1989 World Population Data Sheet*; assumed cropland expansion from Francis Urban, "Agricultural Resources Availability," *World Agriculture Situation and Outlook Report*, USDA, Economic Research Service, Washington, D.C., June 1989.

⁴⁵Walter V. C. Reid, "Sustainable Development: Lessons from Success," *Environment*, May 1989; International Council for Research in Agroforestry (ICRAF)-Nitrogen Fixing Tree Association International Workshop, *Perennial Sesbania Species in Agroforestry Systems* (Nairobi: ICRAF, 1989).

⁴⁶Sandra Postel, "Halting Land Degradation," in Lester R. Brown et al., *State of the World 1989* (New York: W. W. Norton & Co., 1989).

⁴⁷Ibid.; grain fed livestock from USDA, Foreign Agricultural Service (FAS), *World Wheat and Coarse Grains Reference Tables* (unpublished printout) (Washington, D.C.: August 1988), and Gerald Ostrowski, USDA, FAS, private communication, September 1989.

⁴⁸For discussion of the work of the Land Institute, see Evan Eisenberg, "Back to Eden," *Atlantic Monthly*, November 1989; Wes Jackson, *Altars of Unhewn Stone: Science and the Earth* (San Francisco: North Point Press, 1987).

⁴⁹Omar Sattaur, "The Shrinking Gene Pool," *New Scientist*, July 29, 1989; National Research Council, *Amaranth: Modern Prospects for an Ancient Crop* (Washington, D.C.: National Academy Press, 1984).

⁵⁰Sandra Postel and Lori Heise, *Reforesting the Earth*, Worldwatch Paper 83 (Washington, D.C.: Worldwatch Institute, April 1988).

⁵¹Philip M. Fearnside, "A Prescription for Slowing Deforestation in Amozonai," *Environment*, May 1989.

[52]Reid, "Sustainable Development"; Charles M. Peters et al., "Valuation of an Amazonian Rainforest," *Nature*, June 29, 1989.

[53]Postel and Heise, *Reforesting the Earth*.

[54]Lester R. Brown et al., "Outlining a Global Action Plan," in Brown et al., *State of the World 1989*.

[55]Postel, "Halting Land Degradation."

[56]William C. Thiesenhusen, ed., *Searching for Agrarian Reform in Latin America* (Boston: Unwin Hyman, 1989); for some interesting examples of village land management, see Anil Agarwal and Sunita Narain, "The Greening of India," *Illustrated Weekly of India*, June 10, 1989.

[57]Peter M. Vitousek et al., "Human Appropriation of the Products of Photosynthesis," *BioScience*, June 1986; Paul R. Ehrlich et al., "Global Change and Carrying Capacity: Implication for Life on Earth," in Ruth S. DeFries and Thomas F. Malone, eds., *Global Change and Our Common Future: Papers from a Forum* (Washington, D.C.: National Academy Press, 1989).

[58]For discussion of the shortcomings of traditional accounting measures, see Robert Repetto, *Wasting Assets: Natural Resources in the National Income Accounts* (Washington, D.C.: World Resources Institute, 1989); Herman E. Daly and John B. Cobb, Jr., *For the Common Good: Redirecting the Economy Toward Community, the Environment, and a Sustainable Future* (Boston: Beacon Press, in press).

[59]Herman E. Daly, "Sustainable Development: From Concept and Theory Towards Operational Principles," *Population and Development Review*, Spring 1990 (in press); Daly and Cobb, *For the Common Good*.

[60]World military expenditures from U.S. Arms Control and Disarmament Agency, *World Military Expenditures and Arms Transfers 1988* (Washington, D.C.: U.S. Government Printing Office, 1989); abolition of Costa Rican army from Muni Figueres de Jimenez, acceptance speech, Better World Society Peace Advocacy and Arms Reduction Medal, New York, November 28, 1988.

[61]Daly and Cobb, *For the Common Good*.

Biographies of
Contributing Authors

Lester Brown

Lester Brown is the founder and president of the Worldwatch Institute, a Washington, D.C., based nonprofit organization devoted to the analysis of global environmental issues. Described by the *Washington Post* as "one of the world's most influential thinkers," Lester Brown received a M.S. in agricultural economics from the University of Maryland and an M.P.A. from Harvard University.

Lester Brown served as an advisor to Secretary of Agriculture Orville Freeman and served as administrator of the Department of Agriculture's International Agricultural Service. In 1969, he assisted James Grant in establishing the Overseas Development Council.

In 1974, with funding from the Rockefeller Brothers Fund, Lester Brown founded the Worldwatch Institute. Widely known for careful analysis of global environmental issues, Lester Brown and the Worldwatch Institute launched the *State of the World* series in 1984. These annual assessments of environmental issues with accompanying recommendations for sustainable policies and actions have been translated into every major language.

In his distinguished career, Brown has received multiple honorary degrees and awards, including (most recently) Environmentalist of the

Year by the Tokyo Jaycees (1992), Humanist of the Year by the American Humanist Association (1991), the United Nations Environment Prize (1987). Brown was also awarded the highly coveted MacArthur Fellowship from the John D. and Catherine T. MacArthur Foundation (1986–1991).

Lester Brown is a much sought-after speaker and a prolific writer who has authored and coauthored thirteen books including *Man, Land, and Food, Building a Sustainable Society, Saving the Planet* (with Christopher Flavin and Sandra Postel), and *Full House: Reassessing the Earth's Population Carrying Capacity* (with Hale Kane). Brown serves as project director on the three book series: *State of the World, Vital Signs: The Trends That Are Shaping Our Future*, and Worldwatch's Environmental Alert Series.

Daniel D. Chiras

Dan Chiras is a nationally renowned author, educator, and consultant. In 1976, he received a Ph.D. in reproductive physiology from the University of Kansas Medical Center. His studies of reproduction led him to population issues and then to many environmental issues. Over the past twenty years, he has taught a variety of courses at the University of Colorado at Denver, the University of Washington, and the University of Denver.

Dan Chiras has published over one hundred articles and nine books. He is perhaps best known for his popular college texts, *Environmental Science: Actions for a Sustainable Future, Natural Resource Conservation* (with Oliver Owen), *Human Biology: Health, Homeostasis and the Environment*, and *Biology: The Web of Life*. In 1992, his high school textbook *Environmental Science: Framework for Decision Making* was nominated as the official book of the 1992 U.S. Academic Decathlon competition, a nationwide competition of high school students.

Dan Chiras has also written two books for the general public, *Beyond the Fray: Reshaping America's Environmental Response* and *Lessons From Nature: Learning to Live Sustainably on the Earth*, featured in this anthology. Dr. Chiras also writes the environment section for World Book Encyclopedia's annual publication, *Science Year*, and is author of the environmental issues section in *Encyclopedia Americana* (both CD-ROM (1995) and hardback (1996).

A leading advocate of personal action and responsibility, Chiras cofounded Friends of Curbside Recycling, a small but influential volunteer organization that helped convince the city of Denver to start a curbside recycling program. He also served two terms as president of the Colorado Environmental Coalition. In 1993, Dan Chiras cofounded the Sustainable Futures Society.

Dan has received numerous awards, including the Latimer Award for Research (1976), the Colorado Energy Research Institute Award (1980), and the Governor's Award for Service (1985).

Dr. Chiras lives with his two children in a passive solar off grid home in Evergreen, Colorado, where he practices what he preaches. He is an avid gardener, bicyclist, and kayaker.

Christopher Flavin

Christopher Flavin is vice president for Research at the Worldwatch Institute. His management responsibilities include planning and supervision of the research program as well as personnel and funding matters. He is a regular contributor to the annual *State of the World* report, which was nominated for inclusion in this book. He was coauthor of *The Blueprint for the Environment* presented to President-elect George Bush in 1989.

Mr. Flavin's research focuses on energy, technology, and policy issues. He is active in U.S. energy debates and in international discussions about climate change, nuclear power, and the development of new energy sources. He has also written on national and international economic issues.

Mr. Flavin has lectured at conferences and universities around the world and has testified before U.S. House and Senate committees and has appeared at parliamentary hearings in Canada, Italy, and the United Kingdom. His advice has also been sought by major corporations, including Royal Dutch Shell, Enron Corporation, and General Motors. Mr. Flavin makes regular radio and television appearances on the *BBC World Service*, the *Today Show*, the *McNeil-Lehrer Newshour*, and *Nightline*. He has published articles in over fifty popular and scholarly periodicals. In 1992, he helped draft energy position papers for the Clinton-Gore campaign and helped found the board of the Washington-based Business Council for a Sustainable Energy Future.

Mr. Flavin is a graduate of Williams College with a B.A. in economics, biology, and environmental studies.

Dave Foreman

Dave Foreman has spent the last twenty years as a full-time conservationist. During the 1970s, he worked for the Wilderness Society as its southwestern regional representative and later as its lobbying coordinator in Washington, D.C. After leaving the Wilderness Society, Foreman cofounded Earth First! and served as editor of the *Earth First! Journal* from 1982 to 1988. Since leaving Earth First!, Foreman has launched a new conservation magazine, *Wild Earth*, which promotes the establishment of large wilderness preserves to protect biodiversity. He also works with a variety of groups to develop a comprehensive North American Wilderness Recovery Strategy and is director and Chairman of the Wildlands Project, which was created to implement the strategy. Foreman owns a conservation mail-order bookstore and speaks frequently at college campuses and conservation conventions. Foreman is author of *Confessions of an Eco-Warrior* (Harmony, 1991), co-author of *The Big Outside* (Harmony, 1989), and co-editor of *Ecodefense* (Nedd Ludd Books, 1985).

Garrett Hardin

Garrett Hardin is a professor emeritus of human ecology at the University of California in Santa Barbara and is best known for his 1968 essay, "The Tragedy of the Commons," and his 1974 essay, "Living on a Lifeboat." Dr. Hardin was trained as an ecologist and microbiologist at the University of Chicago and Stanford University. Hardin speaks widely on environmental issues, traveling fifty thousand miles a year. He also plays first violin in the Salsipudes Quartet (a string group he formed over twenty years ago).

His books include *Exploring New Ethics for Survival: The Voyage of the Spaceship Beagel, Filters Against Folly,* and *Living Within Limits: Ecology, Economics and Population Taboos,* which received the 1993 Award in Science by the honor fraternity Phi Beta Kappa.

Daniel Kemmis

Daniel Kemmis is the Mayor of Missoula, Montana, and is a former speaker of the Montana House of Representatives. He served in the Montana legislator for eight years and was chair of the National League of Cities Leadership Training Council. Mayor Kemmis is also a member of the Board of Directors of the Kettering Foundation and the Pew Partnership for Civic Change.

He is the author of the book *Community and the Politics of Place*, featured in this work, and is now at work on a second book, *The Good City and the Good Life*, to be published in 1995 by Houghton Mifflin Company.

Mayor Kemmis has had numerous articles published in national publications on such topics as the city center, community and community building, and the economy of the West. He is a graduate of Harvard University and the University of Montana Law School.

Anne LaBastille

Anne LaBastille is an ecologist and author of international repute. Living much of the year in a cabin she built in the Adirondack Mountains of New York, she has become a leading advocate of wildlife and wildland conservation. Dr. LaBastille is a licensed Adirondack guide and certified scuba diver. She also serves as a scientific advisor to many conservation organizations and lectures widely to university students and adult groups on natural history, environmental protection, and wilderness literature.

Anne earned a Ph.D. from Cornell University and has received three honorary doctorates and numerous awards, including the Chevron Conservation Award (1989) and the Conservationist of the Year Gold Medal from the World Wildlife Fund (1974). In 1994, Anne received the National Nature Educator award from Roger Tory Peterson.

Anne served as a commissioner of New York State's Adirondack Park Agency for seventeen years. Her books include *Woodswoman, Beyond Black Bear Lake, Women and Wilderness, Assignment: Wildlife, Mama Poc, The Wilderness World of Anne LaBastille*, and *Birds of the Mayas*. Anne has also published numerous articles in *National Geographic, Audubon, Natural History*, and *International Wildlife*.

Dennis L. Meadows

Dennis Meadows is director of the Institute for Policy and Social Science Research and is a professor of systems management at the University of New Hampshire. He holds a Ph.D. in management from MIT and honorary doctorates from two European universities in acknowledgement of his contributions to international environmental policy analysis and computer-aided education. Dr. Meadows is co-author of the best-selling books, *Limits to Growth* and *Beyond the Limits*, featured in this anthology.

Donella Meadows

Few people have contributed more significantly to environmental thinking and the advancement of our knowledge on sustainability than Donella H. Meadows. A systems analyst, journalist, college professor, and farmer, Donella Meadows received her Ph.D. in biophysics from Harvard University in 1968.

In the early seventies, Donella Meadows was on a team at MIT that produced the global computer model World3 for the Club of Rome. That work, in turn, led to the publication of the highly acclaimed book *The Limits to Growth*, which has sold millions of copies and has been translated into twenty-eight languages.

In 1985, Donella Meadows launched a weekly newspaper column, "The Global Citizen," which provides a forum for commentary on global issues, especially environmental concerns, from a systems point of view. Donella received the Walter C. Paine Science Education Award in 1990 for the column and was nominated for a Pulitzer Prize in 1991.

During 1988 to 1990, she worked with producers at WGBH-TV in Boston on a ten-part series, "Race to Save the Planet." Donella Meadows has served on the boards of several nonprofit organizations, including the Hunger Project, and has served as a consultant to the Office of Technology Assessment.

In 1991, she was selected as one of ten Pew Scholars in Conservation and the Environment. This three-year award supported her international work in resource management from a systems point of view.

In 1992, Dr. Meadows coauthored *Beyond the Limits* (also featured in this collection). A much-needed sequel to *The Limits to Growth*, this book has already been translated into fourteen languages. Donella lives on a small, communal organic farm in New Hampshire where she applies her knowledge to the care and nurturance of the land.

Helena Norberg-Hodge

Like many other authors whose work graces the pages of this book, Helena Norberg-Hodge is something of a phenomenon. A highly accomplished linguist who speaks seven languages fluently, she is the first outsider to have mastered the language of the country of Ladakh or Little Tibet, where she has worked since 1975. In fact, Helena Norberg-Hodge helped write down the language for the first time to create a Ladakhi dictionary.

In her stellar career, Helena Norberg-Hodge has had the rare opportunity to become intimately acquainted with an ecologically stable culture. She arrived at the time of its first exposure to Western-style development. Since that time, she has observed the profound social, economic, and environmental changes that this development has wrought. Her observations have led to many of her insights on sustainable development.

Ms. Norberg-Hodge is founder and director of the Ladakh Project, a project of the International Society for Ecology and Culture, a small international organization concerned with the search for sustainable ways of living. Her work has not been simply aimed at maintaining the status quo, but rather at assisting in the introduction of appropriate technologies in Ladakh. Helena Norberg-Hodge helped form the Ladakh Ecological Development Group, an organization composed entirely of Ladakhis. It now carries on the work, teaching and demonstrating the benefits of appropriate technology and agriculture to raise the standard of living without disrupting the culture's traditional harmony with natural systems. Ms. Norberg-Hodge also works on ways to help forge a sustainable future in the West.

Recipient of the Right Livelihood Award (the alternative Nobel Prize) in 1986, Ms. Norberg-Hodge has helped the people of Ladakh improve their standard of living without sacrificing their cultural values or the environment. Her organization has lobbied the local government to adopt policies that do not undermine the culture or environment and have sponsored numerous educational programs for

Ladakhis. Helena Norberg-Hodge speaks widely to university audiences, government agencies, and private institutions throughout Europe and North America. Her book, *Ancient Futures*, has been published in the United States, England, India, Sweden, Denmark, Germany, and Italy.

David W. Orr

David Orr holds a Ph.D. from the University of Pennsylvania and is currently a professor of environmental studies and politics and chair of the Environmental Studies Program at Oberlin College. In 1979, he cofounded the Meadowcreek Project, an environmental education center in Fox, Arkansas. From 1979 to 1990, he was also a professor of political science at Agnes Scott College. From 1971 to 1979, he was a professor at the University of North Carolina-Chapel Hill.

He is author of *Earth in Mind: Essays on Education, Environment. and the Human Prospect; Ecological Literacy: Education and the Transition to a Post-Modern World* (featured in this anthology); and over seventy articles. David Orr was co-editor of *The Campus and Environmental Responsibility* (with David Eaganand) and co-editor of *The Global Predicament* (with Marvin Soroos).

David Orr is a trustee of the Jessie Smith Noyes Foundation and of the Educational Foundation of America. He currently serves as the education editor of *Conservation Biology* and is an editor of the State University of New York series on environmental and public policy.

For his work he has received an honorary degree from Arkansas College. In 1992, he was awarded the Lyndhurst Prize and, in 1993, he was given the National Achievement Award from the National Wildlife Federation.

Sandra Postel

Sandra Postel is vice president for research at the Worldwatch Institute. During her many years with the institute, she has written seven Worldwatch papers, served as associate project director for four of the institute's annual *State of the World* reports, which are featured in this volume. She is also co-author of *Saving the Planet: How to Shape an Environmentally Sustainable Global Economy*.

Prior to joining Worldwatch, Ms. Postel was a consultant with a private firm in California, where she worked primarily on water conservation and groundwater issues. She studied geology and political science at Wittenberg University and resource economics and policy at Duke University.

Ms. Postel has lectured at several leading universities, including Stanford and Duke, from which she received the School of Forestry and Environmental Studies' Distinguished Alumni Award in 1991.

Thomas Michael Power

Thomas Michael Power is professor and chairman of the economics department at the University of Montana. He received a Ph.D. in economics from Princeton University.

His books include *The Economic Value of the Quality of Life* and *The Economic Pursuit of Quality*, which is featured in this anthology. He is currently working on a book entitled *Extraction and the Environment: The Economic Battle for Control of Our Natural Landscapes*.

In addition to his books, Dr. Power has published over a hundred papers, reports, and monographs on resource economics and regional economic development. Dr. Power lives in Missoula, Montana, with his wife and two teenage children. He is an avid mountaineer, skier, and runner and has been actively involved in most of the major environmental issues in the West during the past twenty-five years.

Jørgen Randers

Jørgen Randers is a policy analyst and president emeritus of the Norwegian School of Management. He is chairman of the Norwegian Bank for Industry and the Norwegian Institute for Market Research. He holds a graduate degree in solid state physics and a Ph.D. in management from MIT and lives in Oslo, Norway.

Stephan Schmidheiny

Stephan Schmidheiny is a Swiss industrialist involved in manufacturing a variety of products, including electrical equipment, scientific instruments, water supply systems, and construction materials. Trained in law in Zurich and Rome, he took over a family-owned multinational industrial group in 1976.

He is currently a member of the boards of several major corporations and is chair of the FUNDES Foundation, which promotes small business enterprises in Latin America. Dr. Schmidheiny is also the chair of the board of the Max Schmidheiny Foundation at the St. Gallen Graduate School of Economics, Law, Business, and Public Administration.

In 1990, Dr. Schmidheiny was asked to be a principal advisor for business and industry to the secretary general of the 1992 United Nations Conference on Environment and Development. He also founded and chaired the Business Council for Sustainable Development and is best known for his crusade to encourage businesses to "think green." In 1992, he and the council published the book *Changing Course: A Global Business Perspective on Development and the Environment*, featured in this anthology. *Changing Course* has sold more than 100,000 copies and has been translated into ten languages.

James Swan

James Swan is a writer, entertainer, media and events producer, consultant, and counselor. One of the founders of the field of environmental psychology (the study of the interaction between people and the world around them), Dr. Swan received a Ph.D. from the University of Michigan in natural resources and psychology.

Dr. Swan has published over one hundred articles in popular magazines, such as *Audubon* and *New Age*. His books include *Sacred Places, The Power of Place, Nature As Teacher and Healer* (featured in this anthology), and *Bound to the Earth* (with his wife, Roberta).

Dr. Swan has appeared as a guest on "Donahue," "Good Morning America," and numerous other radio and TV programs. He has also recently appeared in a number of feature films, including "Murder in the First," "Angels in the Outfield," and "Tucker."

Dr. Swan produces symposia, concerts, and expositions. He has also produced a number of films and videos, including "Buffalo Restoration on Indian Lands" and "Wopila Tatanka."

For this rich and diverse contribution to society, James Swan has received a number of awards, including the California State Assembly

Certificate of Recognition (1992) and the Certificate of Recognition from the National Psychology Honorary Psi Chi.

Steve Van Matre

Steve Van Matre's popularity in nature education began with the publication of the Acclimatization books nearly twenty years ago. These books are now viewed as pioneering classics in their field. In 1974, *National Geographic* ran a story on his program. Today, Steve Van Matre enjoys a worldwide reputation as an author, designer, educator, and as an organizer, speaker, and "provocateur."

As chairman and founder of the Institute for Earth Education, a nonprofit volunteer organization consisting of an international network of individuals and member organizations, Steve has presented over eight hundred sessions on the institute's work in over forty states and provinces and numerous countries during his ten world speaking tours.

Earth Education is the process of helping people build an understanding of, appreciation for, and harmony with the Earth and its life. Steve Van Matre is a former classroom teacher, camp director, youth leader, educational consultant, and university professor.

He currently lives in Greenville, West Virginia, at Cedar Cove, the first international living and learning center dedicated exclusively to training educators in building comprehensive instructional programs that address the root causes of our environmental problems.

His books include *Acclimatization, Acclimatizing, Sunship Earth, Earthkeepers,* and *Earth Education . . . A New Beginning* (featured in this anthology).

Books of related interest also available from Johnson Books:

Biologic: Designing with Nature to Protect the Environment by David Wann

Echo Park: Struggle for Preservation by Jon M. Cosco

Saving Our Soil by James Glanz

Winter: An Ecological Handbook by James Halfpenny and Roy Ozanne

The Xeriscape Flower Gardener: A Waterwise Guide for the Rocky Mountain Region by Jim Knopf